Please return/renew this item by the last date shown to avoid a charge. Books may also be renewed by phone and Internet. May not be renewed if required by another reader.

www.libraries.barnet.gov.uk

BARNET
LONDON BOROUGH

with *tête-à-tête* interviews ... lucidly written and well-plotted

The Economist

'Quick-paced, witty and elegantly written ... Pedder's book is a breath of fresh air for the calmness and intelligence with which ... dissects the man and the politician.'

The Times

REVOLUTION FRANÇAISE

*Emmanuel Macron and the
Quest to Reinvent a Nation*

SOPHIE PEDDER

BLOOMSBURY CONTINUUM
LONDON · NEW YORK · OXFORD · NEW DELHI · SYDNEY

BLOOMSBURY CONTINUUM
Bloomsbury Publishing Plc
50 Bedford Square, London, WC1B 3DP, UK

BLOOMSBURY, BLOOMSBURY CONTINUUM and the Diana logo
are trademarks of Bloomsbury Publishing Plc

First published in Great Britain 2018
Paperback 2019

A catalogue record for this book is available from the British Library

Library of Congress Cataloguing-in-Publication data has been applied for

ISBN: TPB: 9781472966308; ePDF: 9781472948625; ePUB: 9781472948618

2 4 6 8 10 9 7 5 3 1

Typeset by Newgen KnowledgeWorks Pvt. Ltd., Chennai, India
Printed and bound in Great Britain by CPI Group (UK) Ltd, Croydon CR0 4YY

To find out more about our authors and books visit
www.bloomsbury.com and sign up for our newsletters

For Bertrand, Chloé and Luc
And in memory of my mother, Sue Pedder

CONTENTS

LIST OF ILLUSTRATIONS

FOREWORD

MACRON IN THE GLARE OF THE *GILETS JAUNES*

Little did I realize when this book was first published how apt the title would feel six months later. On successive Saturdays from 17 November 2018, protesters wearing *gilets jaunes* (yellow jackets) invaded the chic, cobbled boulevards of Paris. What began as a demonstration against a rise in eco-taxes on diesel and petrol turned over consecutive weekends into outright mob rioting, in the capital and beyond. Cobblestones dug up from the road were hurled into the streets and at riot police. Shop windows were smashed, cars torched, and barricades set alight. Plumes of tear gas filled the air. On the first Saturday, a group surged towards the Elysée Palace, vowing to invade the seat of the presidency. On another, protesters rammed a stolen forklift truck through the gates of a ministry, prompting bodyguards to evacuate the minister. Revolution Française, it seemed, was underway, just not quite in the way my book's title had intended.

Street theatre and violent protest are no novelty for France. Emmanuel Macron faced down months of strikes and demonstrations earlier in 2018. Yet those protests by and large obeyed codified rules. They were organized, authorized by the police, and produced coherent demands. The scenes of urban warfare that broke out in late 2018, as *gilets jaunes* were joined by ultra-left anarchists and far-right agitators, were quite different. They were leaderless, structureless and highly volatile. In a matter of weeks an anti-fuel tax complaint mutated into a revolt against Macron. An effigy of the president was decapitated. 'People want to see your head on the end of a pike,' a local official told the dumbfounded president.[1] The leader who 18 months previously had led an insurgency against the country's established parties, and their grip on French power, was facing another popular insurrection. This time, he was the target.

Just as En Marche became a case study in how to forge a non-partisan grass-roots movement from nothing via unmediated social media, so the *gilets jaunes* emerged both on roundabouts and in cyberspace. Protesters found each other through disparate internet initiatives: an online petition demanding a reduction in petrol prices; a call by a lorry driver on Facebook for a day of action against the rising cost of fuel; a home-made YouTube video lambasting Macron for persecuting motorists, which went viral. The movement's mobilizing strength was Facebook. Its unifying force was not ideology but rage. And its potent symbol was the high-visibility fluorescent jacket, which French law requires all motorists to carry in case of breakdown. Protesters found themselves a colour, instant visibility and a defiant identity for a different sort of emergency. It was, said one French newspaper, 'the revenge of the invisible'.[2]

Within weeks the *gilets jaunes* succeeded in articulating a howl of anger that no organized union or political party had come close to achieving on Macron's watch. The absolute numbers of protesters who took part in countrywide demonstrations – an estimated 280,000 on 17 November, 136,000 on 1 December, and 41,500 by 16 February 2019 – were not massive. But the symbolism, insurrectional nature, and the backing of over two-thirds of the public combined to lend the movement a force that far outweighed its numerical strength. This was not just a polit-ical crisis, and the first real one of Macron's tenure. It was also a test of France's institutions, and their resilience in the face of a crisis of legitimacy.

It is always a perilous exercise to write about a sitting political leader, and all the more so in as volatile a country as France, at once idealistic and rebellious, prone to dissatisfaction and revolt. I certainly can't claim in this book to have foreseen the emergence of the *gilets jaunes*. But I did warn in the conclusion: 'There is a perfectly plausible scenario in which promise leads to disappoint-ment. High hopes vested in young leaders often do. Revolutions are usually followed by counter-revolutions, and France is no stranger to either.' Deep down, Macron knew this. 'I am not the natural child of calm political times,' he said, not long after taking office. 'I am the fruit of a form of historical brutality, an infrac-tion, because France was unhappy and fearful.'[3] What exactly happened during the course of 2018, to turn a year of renewed promise and pride in France into one that ended in rage, loathing and violence? How far do these events alter my assessment of Macron and of France in this book? Most importantly, what does the *gilets jaunes* crisis mean for the rest of his presidency, and its potential legacy?

As scenes of civil unrest were beamed around the world in late 2018, commentators almost unanimously wrote Macron off. He was a 'sickly lame duck', a 'diminished figure', whose presidency was a 'broken dream', if not a 'failure'.[4] 'Many people rested their hopes for western leadership on Mr Macron's slim shoulders. Those now look sorely misplaced,' wrote one observer.[5] 'Can Emmanuel Macron survive France's civil war?' asked another.[6] At the end of 2018 that question did not feel absurd. Yet, for much of the year, the French president had in fact kept a steady hand, defied the sceptics, and nudged France on to a more promising course.

For its first 18 months, Macron's reform programme went broadly according to plan. He cleaned up rules on parliamentary expenses, and banned deputies from hiring close family members. French labour laws were loosened, and employers began to create more permanent new jobs as the risk of doing so receded. In edu-cation, primary class sizes for younger pupils in disadvantaged areas were halved. I visited some of these in Calais; a year on, reading levels had improved, and the programme was expanded. The *baccalauréat* was redesigned, a form of selection introduced for undergraduates, apprenticeships were increased, and more control of vocational-training credits transferred to individuals. After this book was published, and in line with Macron's focus on education, nursery schooling was made compulsory from the age of three, and free breakfasts were introduced for pupils in poorer areas. The anger of the *gilets jaunes* was directed at what they felt was his unfair tax policy and at the symbols of the state – the *préfecture*, the police – but most protesters on the roundabouts did not contest Macron's other reforms.

Indeed, one paradox was that Macron's popularity tumbled even as – or perhaps because – he built up a solid track record. Each time an upcoming reform looked tough, it was heralded as Macron's decisive challenge, if not his 'Thatcher moment'. Strikes set in. Demonstrations and marches, flares and banners, filled the streets. Yet resistance repeatedly failed to secure the backing of public opinion, and Macron kept his nerve. In the spring of 2018, as France approached the 50th anniversary of the May 1968 uprising, students set up barricades and occupied university campuses to protest against selection. Railway workers staged a rolling strike, on two days out of every five, against the end of recruitment to the SNCF on the basis of jobs for life. Talk shows evoked a replay of *les événements*. By taking on the SNCF, wrote *Le Figaro*, Macron was 'attacking the Everest of French conservatism and the last regiments of the most radical trade unionism'.[7] By the end of June, however, the railwaymen had gone back to work and students had deserted the campuses. 'France is undergoing a profound transformation,' wrote Charles Wyplosz, an economist and France-watcher, noting that strangely 'each reform erases the memory of the previous one'.[8] As he had argued he would, Macron used the legitimacy of his electoral mandate to keep public opinion on his side, withstood the pressure from the street, and did not cave in.

The French president also showed that on the bigger principles he has the right instincts. His speech to mark the centenary of the end of the First World War, before world leaders assembled at the Arc de Triomphe, was a powerful call to reclaim patriotism from the nationalists. His acknowledgement of France's systematic use of torture during the Algerian War, and responsibility for the killing in 1957 of Maurice Audin, a young pro-independence communist, was a courageous attempt to reckon with France's darker past. The president's solemn set-piece speeches, such as that to mark the burial of Simone Veil in the Panthéon, or in defence of multilateralism and the rules-based order before the US Congress, which gave him a three-minute standing ovation, were compelling moments.

The French president did not always get it right. A decision not to offer a French harbour to the *Aquarius*, a refugee rescue ship that was refused a berth in Italy, was a missed opportunity to occupy the moral high ground. But for much of the time Macron said the things that needed saying, even if, as over Brexit and 'the liars' of the Leave campaign, they were uncomfortable for some to hear. And if progress in translating some of his words into action was disappointing, notably over Europe, not only he was to blame. Macron's speech in the amphitheatre of the Sorbonne in September 2017, packed with ideas to reform Europe and aching with ambition, was followed by months of stasis, as Angela Merkel struggled to form a coalition government in Germany, populists took power in Italy, and Brexit dragged on.

In reality, Macron's year took a turn for the worse over three days in the summer of 2018. On 15 July, France had beaten Croatia to win the football World Cup. The French president leapt to his feet in the Moscow stadium, punching the air with delight. The triumphant atmosphere in Paris that night was electric. 'Emmanuel Macron is a lucky leader,' wrote one commentator. 'You feel that if François Hollande were still in the Elysée, France wouldn't have won the World Cup.'[9]

Three days later, triumph in Moscow turned to consternation in Paris when the Benalla affair broke. A close aide and former bodyguard, Alexandre Benalla had worked for Macron during the election campaign and joined his staff at the Elysée Palace. He earned the president's trust, and enjoyed a position within his inner circle coordinating his protection at public and private events. On 18 July, *Le Monde* revealed that the presidential staffer had been caught on camera, wearing police gear, beating a protester at a May Day demonstration.[10] Worse, he had kept his job. At first, the presidency insisted that it had sanctioned him adequately with a two-week suspension. It was not until 20 July, and after the opening of a preliminary judicial investigation, that the Elysée realized he had to go. *Le Monde* called it a 'state scandal'. Jean-Luc Mélenchon, leader of the far-left Unsubmissive France, compared it to Watergate. Macron insisted that all this was media hysteria, and invited those seeking a figure to blame 'to come and get' him instead. But the crassly handled affair left the distinct impression that there was a self-protecting inner circle at the Elysée, which failed to grasp how troubling things looked to everybody else.

The mood in the country soured. By the end of August, Macron began to bleed ministers. Nicolas Hulot, his iconic environment minister, resigned, followed by Gérard Collomb, the interior minister, who had spoken out about a 'lack of humility' and 'hubris'.[11] As disenchantment set in, the strain began to show. Macron cleared his diary to take a few days off with Brigitte in the Normandy harbour town of Honfleur. Rumours swirled around Paris that he was exhausted, even suffering from burnout. His aides dismissed such talk as nonsense. But, when I spoke to Macron at the Elysée in mid-November, he had visibly aged. His face was paler, and more lined. The first few grey hairs had appeared. And then the *gilets jaunes* protest erupted. By the end of the year, said friends, the president's morale was at a low ebb. His poll numbers tumbled to 23 per cent, down from 52 per cent in December 2017. The leader I had described as unflappable looked genuinely shaken. 'It's the first time in two years that I've seen him worried,' said a regular visitor to the Elysée Palace. The presidential team, including Brigitte, was shown how to reach the Elysée's nuclear bunker.[12] Dazed, Macron first cancelled the eco-tax rise he had so vigorously defended, and then unveiled a massive €10 billion of income-support measures. In under a month the *gilets jaunes* succeeded where all others had failed: Macron gave in to the street.

Looking back, it should not have been a surprise that Macronism had its discontents. The candidate broadened his score at the 2017 presidential election, from 24 per cent in the first round to 66 per cent in the second, partly thanks to a protest vote against his far-right opponent, Marine Le Pen. The first choice of 48 per cent of French voters was an extremist or anti-European candidate. The reason I devoted a long chapter to 'Fractured France' in this book was that these disillusioned voters fell quiet, but never went away: 'This fracture running through the country, between prosperous and confident metropolitan centres and the fragile towns and deserted rural areas, will be one of the greatest challenges to the Macron presidency in the coming years.' Moreover, such long-simmering grievances were not exclusive to France. The *gilets jaunes* have more in common with parts of Trumpland, or Brexit-voting Britain, than they do with the yoga-practising classes of Paris, Lyon or Bordeaux. In the face of technological change, globalization and the hollowing out of work, they are the squeezed middle in every Western democracy: those with jobs or pensions, modest incomes that have risen little, living on tight budgets, unable to see any prospect of things improving for themselves or the next generation, and angry at the elite's indifference.

On an overcast weekday in late November, I drove out to Evreux, in rural southern Normandy, to learn more about the *gilets jaunes*. They weren't hard to find. Roundabouts were their preferred site of occupation, places that reflect lives spent in the car between jobs, homes and out-of-town discount stores, far from the Uber-hailing, bike-sharing lifestyles of metropolitan France. Sure enough, on a roundabout on the outskirts of town, between a cement silo and a garden centre, I came across protesters who had blocked off a lane of traffic with rubber tyres. On the muddy ground beside them, a fire of wooden crates was blazing. Bags of croissants were piled up on a camping table. 'We're not blocking the traffic, just filtering it,' said Loup, a 64-year-old retired education assistant, who had a hand in each pocket and a silver ring in each ear. When motorists crawled past, drivers hooted their horns – not in protest, but in support.

Over time, the movement mutated, radicalized and split. But the *gilets jaunes* I spoke to on the Evreux roundabout, sharing hot drinks in plastic cups in spirited solidarity, were not activists whipped up by populist parties or unions. Nor were they the 'hateful mob' that Macron later described, nor the *anarcho-nihilistes* who urged ongoing insurrection, nor part of the movement's xenophobic or anti-Semitic fringe. They were closer to the 'downtrodden, the trashed, the ripped off, the humiliated' rallied by Pierre Poujade in the 1950s. These were locals struggling to make ends meet, who saw the rise in the eco-tax as a form of punishment of working people by an out-of-touch Paris-based elite that had already curbed the speed limit on rural roads, and a president who seemed contemptuous of their objections and indifferent to their plight. 'We're not rich, but we're not poor,' said Sandra, a single mother of two small children, employed at an optician's and who drove 20 kilometres each way to her job. 'It's an attack on the middle classes who work.'

What I did not anticipate in this book, however, was that the backlash against Macron would emerge outside the structures of France's own populist parties, whose legitimacy was challenged by a movement that claimed to be the leaderless expression of 'the people'. Mélenchon and Le Pen furiously courted the *gilets jaunes*, whose weekly protests reached from Rennes to Marseille. But such leaders, with their comfortable salaries and seats in the National Assembly, were themselves seen as part of the system. To their consternation, France's established populists discovered that they had no monopoly on anger.

Nor did I foresee the stupefying degree of loathing for the president, and the violence that this unleashed. Those I spoke to on the Evreux roundabout did not agree with each other about the protest's ultimate objective, but they did share a visceral dislike of the president, and the elite he was seen to represent. 'Monsieur Macron is arrogant and has little respect for the people,' Loup told me. Later in the day, I came across another group of *gilets jaunes*, who had gathered outside the *préfecture*. Three police officers stood warily guarding the door. 'France has a social pyramid, and Macron sits on the top,' one *gilet jaune*, who worked at a fairground, said. 'We want him to smell what it's like down here at the bottom.'

With hindsight, it is all too easy to see how a series of decisions combined to give the impression that Macron was ruling only for the benefit of the metropolitan elite. A one-time investment banker, he was always going to be vulnerable to the charge, even though, as I recount in the book, his personal wealth was earned and his provincial roots were far from the established, moneyed Parisian classes. Sure enough, Macron's early decision to get rid of the country's wealth tax (ISF), in line with a manifesto promise, entrenched the perception that he was a *'président des riches'*. His fiscal policy was designed to show that France was no longer hostile to wealth creation. Macron partially offset it with a new mansion tax, and the abolition of a local tax for all but the richest 20 per cent. And this still left France with one of the most powerful redistribution systems in Europe. Yet the end of the ISF did boost disposable income for the top 1 per cent at a time when Macron had increased social charges for most pensioners, staggered a rise in income-support measures for those on modest incomes, and raised the carbon tax on fuel. The sequencing left him wide open to the charge of helping the rich first.

I would argue nonetheless that most of the analysis I lay out in chapter six on Macronism, and the social-democratic roots of the president's thinking, holds up. Macron is not an advocate of unbridled capitalism, nor a closet conservative, let alone an agent of global finance. He understands the need for wealth creation, but he is also exercised by unregulated globalization (he introduced a new tax on tech giants) and free-market excess (he brought in new incentives for fairer profit-sharing). This was the basis of Macron's carefully crafted vision *en même temps*, as I described it in chapter six: based on 'liberating' as well as 'protecting', and on 'unblocking' French society to create opportunities for all.

If Macron's diagnosis was broadly right, though, he underestimated the change in mindset this implied for France, and the political need for tax policy to be seen to be fair. 'He lost his battle on the fairness of tax reform, and didn't make a strong enough case for his social-empowerment agenda,' Jean Pisani-Ferry, an economist and formerly the director of Macron's election manifesto, told me.[13] The globe-trotting president seemed more absorbed by making speeches at international conferences on how to remake capitalism than ensuring that the French understood his social-mobility strategy. As I wrote in the conclusion: 'Macron may not yet face any credible political opposition. But neither has he found a way to speak to those who did not vote for him, in places where his rootless internationalism and hobnobbing at Davos is an affront.' A core ambition of his campaign somehow disappeared from the public debate. 'He wanted to prove to outsiders that the system could still help them,' Guillaume Liegey, one of the tech consultants who had helped Macron organize the Grande Marche during the summer of 2016, told me: 'But the fact that people still talk about him as an investment banker reflects his failure to establish that other narrative.'[14]

In this respect, the best that might be said is that Macron did not help himself. The candidate may have been right that the French wanted dignity and solemnity restored to the presidency. But dignified did not mean aloof. And this was how Macron increasingly came across. In an age of ruthless and opportunistic populism, and a world powered by social media, a leader who cannot persuade people that he can relate to them is vulnerable to rejection. Anybody who has met Macron is struck by the empathy, openness and sincerity he projects. Yet, with his well-cut suits and polished leather shoes, he also has a tendency to lecture people. There he was on one occasion telling pensioners that they 'shouldn't complain', or, on another, informing a visiting unemployed gardener that he could just 'cross the road' and find himself a job in a restaurant, or, ahead of a town-hall debate, deploring those who 'arse about'. Each comment, individually, might have been shrugged off. But the cumulative effect was damaging. Macron came across as smug, haughty, tone deaf to criticism and intolerant of failure, especially that of others. He seemed to chide the less fortunate, and govern for the successful. To my surprise, Macron had told me, as I recount in the conclusion, that he was 'often' wrong, and cited as an example his controversial comment about railway stations being places where 'people who succeed' pass by 'those who are nothing'. By 10 December, sitting behind an ornate golden desk, his hands immobile as if rigid with fear, a pale-faced waxwork-like president sounded more contrite, declaring that 'I know I have hurt some of you with my words.' Yet he continued to do it. His aides became resigned to the habit. Provocative by nature, and convinced of his own powers of persuasion, Macron seems to regard such controversies as part of the risk you take if you speak your mind in the transparent digital age: 'I'm just like that, I won't change.'[15]

The *gilets jaunes* crisis also exposed the limits of Macron's reliance on smart millennial technocrats, rather than seasoned politicians. At first, an exasperated president tried to justify his environmental tax on the grounds that it was the right thing to do. 'I'd prefer to tax fuel than work,' he explained. 'Those who complain about higher fuel prices also demand action against air pollution because their children get sick.' If protesters were up in arms, it was because they didn't understand. As popular hostility to the president intensified, his entourage closed ranks. His wife, Brigitte, had already worried about a 'sect effect'.[16] En Marche, which had become an empty shell, offered no wise counsel. As I describe in what follows, Macron likes to take decisions alone, and thinks he knows best. As the months went on, some of those once close to him complained of being frozen out. 'The problem is that he doesn't listen to those who tell him it isn't going well,' one of them told me. Surrounded by technocrats, dismissive of the need to listen to mayors or union leaders, or even his own backbenchers, lacking a strong counter-balancing party, and contemptuous of media criticism, Macron seemed almost to thrive on the defiant idea that he was once again *seul contre tous* (alone against everybody). As the president was fond of telling his visitors: 'If I had listened to other people's advice, I wouldn't be where I am now.'

This reluctance to listen had broader consequences. Macron had thought hard about the need to secure legitimacy for policy choices, as I describe in the book, and had built En Marche on the basis of popular consultation. 'If you want to take a country somewhere,' he argued, 'you have to be willing to listen.'[17] Yet he seemed to assume that his electoral mandate would absolve him from the need to renew that consent, and sustain the consensus behind him, as his term in office unfolded. In retrospect, this proved complacent. It was all the more so at a time when society has grown used to instant online judgement – in ratings, or 'likes' – and when rage becomes cyber-charged by social media. This contributed to the erosion of trust in democratic institutions and national political leaders, and in particular representative democracy. En Marche had in fact brought about a wholesale cleansing of the old, entitlement-driven political class, and given the National Assembly a younger, more female, multi-ethnic face. Yet the *gilets jaunes* I spoke to believed that parliament still did not represent 'people like us', and demanded a more direct say. In retrospect, Gilles Le Gendre, the head of En Marche's parliamentary group, told me: 'We were probably wrong to think that our election had calmed the rise in anger.'[18] The president became a lightning rod for deeper frustrations about representative democracy, which were shared far beyond France.[19]

Macron's jet-setting diary choices during the first 18 months suggest a final oversight: the need to supervise the implementation of his domestic policy. When I spoke to him just two months after his election, the president was already worrying about sorting out the world's problems – fighting climate change, finding a way to influence Trump and Putin, reshaping global multilateral institutions – and breezily confident that it would not take too much time to sort out those in France. That impression sunk in on the roundabouts too. 'He spends too much time looking after Europe, and not enough looking after us,' one *gilet jaune* told me. With his hefty majority, Macron had no trouble passing legislation. Yet the commando squad that followed him from En Marche seemed surprised by the difficulty of managing the mighty French state machinery. 'Once a reform is voted in France, we tend to think that the objective has been met,' Ismaël Emelien, then Macron's secretive political strategist, told me. 'We don't then look at whether a measure is efficient, or is producing the right results. I think it's taken us a while to understand this. We didn't realize that things would be this rusty or seized-up. We underestimated the political capital necessary to make things change.'[20] Advisers had run the campaign like a small, agile start-up, with a short command chain, and instant execution of decisions. Managing the colossus of government was altogether different. Bruno Bonnell, a former tech entrepreneur and deputy from Lyon, whom I had first met campaigning behind the wheel of a minivan, had lost none of his upbeat enthusiasm when I went to see him in late 2018, but was candid about the learning curve. 'It's much more complicated than running a business, much more. When you run a company, you give orders, and the company executes. Government is a completely different art.'[21]

So mistakes were made, for sure. Yet, in a way that I did not anticipate in the book, Macron also became a victim of his own party-political success. By crushing the mainstream Republicans and Socialists in 2017, his triumph left a political vacuum, into which the *gilets jaunes* ultimately spread. One consequence was that, instead of robust ideological political discussion, Macron found himself up against the theatrical politics of the extremes. During one debate in the National Assembly, Mélenchon began to unpack groceries – a packet of rice, a bag of sliced bread – in order to make a point about cuts to housing benefit. Once the *gilets jaunes* crisis broke out, François Ruffin, an elected far-left deputy, stood on the street near the Elysée Palace draped in his official *tricolore* sash, and declared coolly that Macron was seen as a 'machine of hate' who would 'end up like Kennedy'. Policy debate became eclipsed by performance politics, and a social-media war of claim and counter-claim. At one point, ahead of the signing of a new Franco-German treaty enshrining closer cooperation, the Elysée Palace felt the need to issue a formal communiqué to deny that France was ceding Alsace and Lorraine to

Germany. 'Sometimes we'd actually like to have a real opposition,' Sylvain Fort, Macron's speechwriter until January 2019, told me. 'If you don't have a debate of ideas, people don't notice the things you are doing.'[22]

The other unforeseen consequence was Macron's political isolation. His electoral triumph forged an unusual post-partisan government, and a new form of consensus centrist politics. But it also left in its wake scores of jobless Socialist and Republican politicians who were in no mood to help a president in trouble. Laurent Wauquiez, the Republican leader, was photographed early on even sporting a *gilet jaune*. The Socialist former president François Hollande told a group of *gilets jaunes*: 'You should continue to speak out.' As the violence intensified, so did the silence of the opposition. When Eric Drouet, the lorry driver who had first called for a day of action against the rising fuel tax, declared on television that if protesters reach the Elysée 'we're going in', few politicians denounced his appeal; Mélenchon later posted a glowing tribute to him online. 'When one talks about the isolation and solitude of Emmanuel Macron, it's true, but not in the sense that people mean. He's not alone by himself with nobody to talk to,' Fort told me. 'It's a political solitude . . . We didn't necessarily anticipate 18 months ago the point to which Macron would become the central figure, partly because he wanted it and has the energy, but also because of the desert that emerged around him.' Macron the Jupiterian had climbed to lofty heights, but once there he found it to be a solitary place. The occupant of one of the most powerful executive electoral offices in the Western world, Macron often appeared both all-powerful and alone.

* * *

Where does this leave the French president? Can Macron recover his authority, continue with his project to transform France, revive Europe, and keep the forces of nationalism and populism at bay? Or have such ambitions been sunk by the weight of popular disapproval, civil unrest and an imperious presidency?

The worst-case scenario for Macron is that the *gilets jaunes* movement spells an abrupt end to his ambitions to reinvent post-partisan politics and remake France. Rather than marking the defeat of populism, his presidency could herald its revival. Rather than a moment of restored faith in centrist politics and democratic institutions, it could entrench the crisis of confidence in them. 'The really scary scenario is that Macron was a one-shot pistol,' one of his former advisers told me. 'He destroyed the entire party-political system. But if he now fails, we're left with only the crazies.' By depicting himself as the last bastion against populism, in France and in Europe, Macron is dividing his friends, legitimizing his adversaries, and providing them with an ideal enemy. 'If they see me as their main opponent, they are right,' the French president warned Italy's Matteo Salvini and Hungary's Viktor Orbán. Macron's political tools of choice – reasoned argument and fact-based evidence – are poor weapons against the forces of fabrication and conspiracy. Far-right groups, and militants seeking to overthrow democratic institutions, will continue to manipulate the French debate, with the help of Russia-linked bots and social-media accounts. Marine Le Pen no longer looks the damaged leader she did in 2017. She has renamed her party the National Rally, rejuvenated its line-up, and ditched a confused and unpopular promise to leave the euro and bring about Frexit, arguing that her friends in Italy, Hungary and elsewhere are now transforming Europe from within. Her single-minded niece, Marion Maréchal, is patiently building options for her own future. By 2022, when France holds its next presidential election, the unthinkable may have become less implausible.

In the short run, the crystallization of a faction or two of the *gilets jaunes* into an electoral force, just as the Five Star Movement achieved in Italy, might be useful to Macron by fragmenting the populist vote and splintering the movement. But it could also radicalize those who reject representative democracy, and entrench semi-permanent unrest. Hard-core *gilets jaunes* have vowed to keep up the pressure on the streets until the day the president is driven out of the Elysée. Violence, both verbal and physical, has been unleashed on a level unseen in France for decades, and has been met by hard-line policing, resulted in serious casualties, and pushed Macron to the right on law and order. The president may have shown that he can seduce participants in a town-hall meeting with the force of words and knowledge. But the mob has also shown that it can push around a sitting president. The French have not forgotten that Charles de Gaulle dissolved parliament after the May '68 uprising – and resigned the following year, having lost a referendum on constitutional change.

French Fifth-Republic institutions remain strong. But Macron has begun to lose trusted members of his former campaign team, who followed him to the Elysée. Policy-making could be fatally compromised, and he might end up, like so many of his predecessors, borrowing and spending his way out of trouble. This would further damage his credibility in Europe, and could herald the end of Macron's reformist ambitions. Already, the sense of possibility ushered in during his early months has faded. The signing of the new Franco-German treaty, in Aachen in January 2019, prompted by a fresh desire to bring the two countries together at a time of Brexit and American geo-strategic retreat, was more about symbols and aspiration than a step towards building strategic autonomy in Europe. Macron's hopes for a massive euro-zone budget have been scaled back, and France's overspend on the *gilets jaunes* has revived German scepticism about French fiscal rigour. For all his powers of persuasion, Macron has had trouble convincing Germany of a sense of urgency, whether over the fragility of the currency area in the face of future shocks, the threat of an increasingly assertive China, the risk of American military disengagement from Europe, or the need to tax tech giants. A jet-setting, relationship-building president, who clocked up trips to 19 EU countries in his first 20 months in office, including Central and Eastern European nations long neglected by France, has found himself on an increasingly fractured continent.

The reality is that Europe is becoming a lonelier place for a liberal democrat seeking to hold the centre ground. Populists have entered government in Italy, robbing France of a natural partner. The erosion of the old established parties of government, and the rise of the extremes, have enfeebled Angela Merkel's leadership. Macron's hopes of taming Trump have sunk. Having brushed invisible dandruff off the French presidential lapels in an alpha-male display of power politics at the White House during Macron's state visit, the American president walked away from the commitments (Iran, Syria) most valued by his French counterpart. A backlash against the liberal multilateral orthodoxy is well underway. Macron cuts an increasingly isolated figure, the champion of pragmatic reasonable politics in turbulent times. 'Donald Trump Embodies the Spirit of our Age' was the title of a chilling piece by the *Financial Times*'s foreign-affairs commentator Gideon Rachman, who went on to argue: 'I fear that Mr Macron, learned though he is, currently looks more like the embodiment of a dying order.'[23] It is alarmingly easy to construct such a dark scenario, all the more so given the backdrop of a worsening global economic outlook, trade wars between America and China, and Russian covert influence.

What if, however, the *gilets jaunes* crisis acted instead as a wake-up call for Macron, one which ushered in a second phase of his presidency? How might such a turn of events play out?

It would have to start with a tempered presidential tone and a fresh readiness to listen: a return, in short, to the founding spirit of En Marche. Overwhelmingly confident in his judgement Macron may be. But the leader I portray in this book is also pragmatic, decisive when he realizes the urgency, and ready to make adjustments when he recognizes the need. True to form, in January 2019, the president began to reinvent his approach. Out went the golden desk and static address. In came a high-risk exercise known as the 'great national debate', designed to solicit ideas from French citizens on how to improve democracy and the tax-and-spend balance. Dismissed at first by a sceptical Paris commentariat, it turned into a form of national group therapy, drawing over a million online contributions and thousands of local debates. It was kicked off by a dynamic president in shirt sleeves, who held a town-hall meeting for nearly seven hours non-stop with 600 initially sceptical local mayors, sitting on plastic chairs in a municipal gym in Normandy. By the end of his marathon, Macron received a standing ovation.

Moreover, as somebody close to him put it to me, 'Macron is an adventurer'. This is the spirit that I try to capture in the conclusion. The president relishes defying the impossible, and the incredulous. 'He is much better when his back is against the wall,' says another friend. In this sense, the need for democratic renewal, to meet the aspiration for more devolved decision-making or direct democracy, without compromising the underlying vision, could be an opportunity. Macron is a leader with unusual stamina, big-picture vision, small-detail knowledge, and a sense of history and purpose. If he gets it right, this might just be a chance to harness these skills to the crisis of representative democracy, and the forging of a new national consensus.

Were Macron able to recover control of the agenda, my best guess is that he would try to stick to his core reform project. Driven by ideas and conviction, not raw power, he has a willingness to sacrifice short-term popularity for long-term vision, and an astonishingly robust capacity to endure reproach. Macron is also a risk-taker, not fixated by re-election, who I think would regard presidential inertia for the rest of his term as a personal failure. He still genuinely believes that he can change France. To improve his chances, the president would nonetheless need a fresh emphasis on his social-empowerment agenda, a close attention to fairness, an effort not to hector the less fortunate – and a good bit of mud on those shiny leather shoes. If he can manage a fair part of this, and improve democratic process, the *gilets jaunes* protest could, perhaps, turn out to have been a salutary shock.

Nor is Macron likely to abandon his efforts to rebuild Europe, defy populism, and bring about what he calls a 'European renaissance'. The French president may irritate *les anglo-saxons* with his talk of a 'European army', which remains a slogan more than a strategic plan, but his European Intervention Initiative has at least bound post-Brexit Britain, the continent's other real military power, into a European security arrangement. Brexit will in reality continue to push France and Germany into each other's arms, including on defence development and procurement, if only because each has nowhere else to go. Despite the humiliation and mockery he receives from Trump, Macron will not give up trying to act as a restraining force on the American president, and still speaks fairly regularly to him on the phone. On his watch, France will stick to its military commitment in Syria, and counter-terrorism operations in the African Sahel, as well as the fight against climate change and for the rules-based multilateral order. Macron's presidency may be more fragile, but his core support remains intact; he still commands a robust parliamentary majority, and runs one of the few single-party governments in Europe. He faces, for now, no convincing mainstream opposition. And, whatever reservations the French have about Macron, it is very hard to identify a better, credible alternative leader.

This is a decisive moment, which matters well beyond France's borders. Macron's presidency is finely poised, and his legacy is in the balance. At stake is not just France's ability to defend its institutions and fend off nationalist forces. It is the capacity of liberal democracy in Europe to deal with the anger and cynicism that thrives on hyper-connectivity, feeds populism and challenges representative democracy. Although it has become unfashionable to say so, Macron remains in so many respects the most promising candidate to take on that task. But his own country needs his attention. Such wider aspirations will amount to little if the French president cannot first turn things around in France.

Paris, February 2019

Introduction

PALACE OF VERSAILLES, 29 MAY 2017

At the end of a long crimson carpet, rolled out across a marble floor, a lone figure stands motionless awaiting his guest. Ramrod straight, arms by his side, his brow is creased, his gaze fixed firmly ahead. Across the cobbled courtyard before him, Louis XIV's royal gates, a riot of gold leaf and imperial motifs, have been flung open wide, allowing the Russian presidential limousine to deliver Vladimir Putin to the palace steps.

For nearly two minutes, solitary and still, Emmanuel Macron stands there, waiting. He does not twitch. He looks neither left nor right. What is he thinking, this young man without a fleck of grey hair who has just been elected president of the French Republic at the age of 39? Is he rehearsing the public dressing-down he is to give Putin later that day, over the use of Russian propaganda during the French presidential campaign? Perhaps he is mulling over what sort of handshake he will offer the Russian leader when he steps from his car, after the success of the knuckle-buster he exchanged with Donald Trump at the NATO summit in Brussels four days previously? Is he focusing on just looking the part, studiously conscious of the need to add gravity and pomp to his visible youth? Or maybe the philosophy graduate's thoughts are roaming higher, to the course of history, and how he hopes to join Germany's Angela Merkel in shaping Europe against the dark forces of illiberalism?

If this is presidency as theatre, the young leader in the well-cut navy suit waiting for Putin on those steps, framed by two plume-helmeted Republican guards, looks as if he has rehearsed the role.

1

With a preternatural self-confidence, and disconcerting taste for the imperial frills of power, Macron seems in a few short weeks to have slipped seamlessly into the part. Equally effortlessly he appears to be crafting a return to a far grander version of the French presidency, complete with pomp and ceremonial diplomacy, which has already earned him the title Jupiter, the Roman king of the gods. The besuited political novice who has that day borrowed the Palace of Versailles, where his silk-stockinged forerunners stepped from their carriages, betrays no trace of apprehension. He exudes the self-assurance of a veteran who has greeted world leaders in palaces many times before. Yet, just over a year earlier, almost nobody outside France had even heard of Emmanuel Macron.

AMIENS, 6 APRIL 2016

On a Wednesday evening on the outskirts of Amiens in northern France, a young government minister climbed tentatively onto a platform clutching a microphone. The room was small, stuffy and municipal. There was no bass beat to pump up the audience, no lighting effects or flags. Alone before a blank backdrop, and dressed in a suit and open-necked shirt, Emmanuel Macron looked as if he was about to do a product launch, or give a power-point presentation on local urban planning. Earnest, verging on coy, he announced that he was launching a new political movement, to be called En Marche ('On the Move'). He wanted to put an end to the stale political divide between left and right, he said, repair national confidence, and unblock stagnant France. The idea was 'a bit mad', he admitted: 'I don't know if it will succeed.' Nobody in the audience that evening, including Macron's petite wife Brigitte, with her signature honey-peroxide bob, and assorted members of her extended family, could possibly have known with any confidence where this project would lead. The intimate event, one of the participants said later, felt more like a wedding. Not a high-society event, but a provincial small-town gathering. Macron had never run for any elected office. No poll then bothered to test the one-time banker's presidential chances. His hopes of building a political movement capable of taking on the existing party machines on the left and the right, which had rotated power between them, under various names, for over half a century, looked like a far-fetched fantasy.

Political barons in Paris dismissed the provincial launch as a quaint distraction by an upstart ingénu. Nothing in modern French history suggested that it was possible to launch a party from scratch a year before a presidential election – and win. Convention stated that presidents had to bear the serial scars of past defeat, or at least of years of political combat. François Mitterrand, in 1981, and Jacques Chirac, in 1995, were each elected at their third attempt. François Hollande first stood for elected office in 1981, 31 years before he ran for the presidency. His predecessor, Nicolas Sarkozy, who was elected president in 2007, first won an election three decades earlier, in 1977 – the year that Macron was born.

Moreover, in those dark days of 2016, when France had been battered by repeated terrorist attacks, Mr Macron's breezy optimism, liberal internationalism and pro-European politics seemed woefully out of touch with the sullen times. A wave of angry populism and political nationalism appeared to be sweeping through Western democracies. Britain turned inward and voted for Brexit on 23 June. Five months later, Americans elected Donald Trump as their president. The only near-certainty about the French presidential election the following year was that one of the two candidates in the final run-off would be Marine Le Pen, of the far-right National Front (FN), a prospect that shrouded the election in dread. That summer, Hollande, the sitting Socialist president, dismissed Macron's project with En Marche as 'an adventure with no future'.

Thirteen months after the launch of En Marche, on 7 May 2017, the French elected the 39-year-old president.

What took place in France in the spring of 2017 marks the greatest wholesale political clear-out that the country has seen in over half a century. It was, in many ways, a form of bloodless revolution. Not in the sense that the structures of power were overturned – in the end, Macron reinforced the very institutions

of the Fifth Republic that he used to secure the highest office –
but because it brought about the eviction of a political caste and
a party duopoly. Macron not only defeated pessimism, defeatism
and anti-European populism in the shape of Marine Le Pen, whom
he beat in the second-round run-off with 66 per cent of the vote.
He also upended an existing political order, and turned the party
system inside out. For the first time since the Fifth Republic was
established by Charles de Gaulle in 1958, the two broad political groups that had run modern France were eliminated from the
second-round presidential run-off. A month later, Macron's cha-
otic fledgling movement was swept into the National Assembly,
bagging 60 per cent of the seats, decimating the Socialist Party, and
reducing the centre-right Republicans to a nationalist rump. In a
country famed for its resistance to change, Mr Macron cast aside
the *ancien régime*, overturned the left-right divide and crushed the
two biggest political parties. Out went a generation of grey-haired
men in suits. Fully 75 per cent of incoming deputies in the National
Assembly had not held seats in the previous parliament. Nearly
half the new legislators were women. 'Everybody told us it was
impossible,' Macron declared on victory night. 'But they didn't
know France.'

* * *

I first met Emmanuel Macron in 2012, shortly after he became
economic adviser to President Hollande. Fresh from Rothschild's
bank, at the age of 34 he already boasted the title of *secrétaire-
général adjoint*, or deputy chief of staff, and occupied a top-floor
corner office under the mansard roof at the Elysée Palace, with
a view through gabled dormer windows over the sweeping back
gardens. A gendarme collected the visitor at the entrance lodge, on
the chic rue du Faubourg Saint-Honoré, and led the way around
the edge of the gravelled palace courtyard to a discreet corner
entrance. There was no lift, and the back staircase, covered in a
faded blue patterned carpet, creaked as you climbed up. During
that meeting, two things about Macron struck me. One was the
length of his sideburns, which he wore just a little too long, and
gave his remarkably boyish face an oddly mod-like look. The

other was his unstuffy and approachable manner. He had none of the airs that you might expect from somebody who had been propelled into a big job at a young age. In a suit and tie, a uniform he seems to have trouble discarding, Macron emerged into the narrow corridor to say hello, his hand outstretched, and we sat down to talk around a small oval table in his office. Neither arrogant know-it-all high-flyer, nor gratingly chummy, his tone was professional, warm, earnest and engaging. 'Keep in touch; come back whenever you like,' he said breezily, in that slightly nasal voice of his, when we were done. Most arresting, this young adviser had a way of focusing on the conversation, of offering his undivided attention, that left you with the uncanny impression, however untrue, that just for that stretch of time he had nowhere else more important to be. It was a precious skill, and one that he went on to use to ruthless effect, both on the campaign trail and later when in office. Macron, as one of his aides put it to me during the election campaign, is a 'networking machine'.

Although a shrewd analyst and clearly heading places, Macron was then a decidedly strange sort of revolutionary-in-the-making. He was an obscure member of the invisible French technocracy: that high-flying sect of ambitious individuals unknown to the general public, who tend to rotate into top jobs in business or the administration. For a journalist from *The Economist*, his office was a natural port of call, and I had regular exchanges with him over the period he spent as a presidential adviser. Anybody hoping for gossip was disappointed. But, if you wanted a thoughtful discussion about the state of France, conversations were always worthwhile. Looking back at my notes from that very first encounter at the Elysée Palace, it was an almost comically technical discussion, all about stabilization of debt, French competitiveness and the rigidities of the labour market. Did I think to ask him then whether he had political ambitions of his own? Not for an instant. He had arrived at the administration from Rothschild's investment bank, and had transferred there from the civil service. The only political comment of his that I noted down was a wry reflection on the nature of Hollande's 2012 election campaign. At the time, the candidate had promised to introduce a crushing top income-tax rate of 75 per cent, and denounced the world of finance as his 'enemy' in a famous speech at Le Bourget. In private, Macron greeted Hollande's income-tax proposal with the line: 'It's Cuba without the sun!' The 2012 campaign, he said, had been 'conducted on the sidelines of reality'.

If anything, as the months went by, Macron was growing restless, frustrated both with the mechanics of government and the Hollande presidency. In April 2014 he was passed over for a job in the new, reformist government of Manuel Valls, the up-and-coming centre-left Socialist prime minister. Macron turned his eyes to a different horizon. By June 2014, when I again climbed up those creaking stairs to see him in his corner office, he had given in his notice. He was quitting public service, would give some lectures at the London School of Economics, he said, perhaps write a book on philosophy. Macron had lined up a couple of his advisers to join him in launching a start-up, and was heading to California with Brigitte, to take a break and meet some tech contacts there. At the time, his departure didn't quite make sense. Why would he bail out of one of the best jobs in the administration? Who was this over-achieving technocrat who wanted to leave public service to write about philosophy? But if anybody had suggested then that he would be running for president three years later, it would have seemed preposterous. At the end of that summer, in the dying days of August, Macron was cycling in Le Touquet, the seaside resort on the Channel coast favoured by the *bourgeoisie* of northern France and where his wife has a house, when his mobile phone rang. It was President Hollande. He was offering him the job of economy minister. The next day, Macron returned to Paris to prepare for government, public life and a wholly different future. 'If Mr Valls wanted to send a message with his new government, Mr Macron is it,' I wrote for *The Economist* when the announcement was made the next day.

From that moment, the young man with the wide gap-toothed smile who went on to become president three years later burst into the public eye. 'Who is Emmanuel Macron, the new economy minister?' asked a puzzled *Sud-Ouest* newspaper, after his nomination to government. Nobody seemed to know. His propulsion into public life was abrupt, and his landing in the unforgiving world of politics uneven. He was, said one observer of French political life, 'accident-prone'. The left wing of the Socialist Party found him insufferably liberal. The right did not know what to make of him. Macron was critical of his own government, tireless in his efforts to get legislation through parliament, and wilfully disruptive in his approach to policymaking. A maverick, or political *'métèque'*, as he described himself later: a foreigner without full citizenship rights, as in the city-states of ancient Greece. Macron slept little, read a lot, and thought hard about the changing nature of France. And he listened. To everybody. Each visitor to his office at the Ministry of Finance at Bercy, an oblong monolith built in 1984 that protrudes like an unfinished viaduct into the river Seine, came away with the disconcerting sense that he might genuinely have been interested in what they had to say. Hard-nosed businessmen with little time for politicians, and older ones in particular, stepped out of his office charmed. Bill Clinton, Barack Obama, or even Tony Blair seemed to have the same effect in their time. There was something of a Macron spell, and his advisers were as prone as anybody. 'When he fixes you with his steel-blue look, you have the impression that you are the only one who counts in the world,' one of them gushed to me. 'For those ten to twenty seconds, you are the only one who counts. The rest of the world could crumble, but he listens, he's all yours.'

Three years later the French made him theirs. On election night, in his first appearance as president-elect, Macron stepped out from the shadows into the Cour Napoléon of the Louvre, a royal palace from the time of Charles V, and made his way towards the modernist glass pyramid. His pace measured, his expression grave, the young leader, dressed in a formal dark overcoat, crossed the courtyard, his figure casting a long shadow across the historic walls, accompanied by Beethoven's 'Ode to Joy', the European Union anthem. The three-minute walk spoke of the country's monarchical past and republican present, of history and modernity, of collective expression and solitary burden. It was a moment that, as often with Macron, prompted mixed feelings. Was this the long-overdue return of presidential dignity? Or an early warning of regal self-regard? The French had voted in a technocratic former banker, and seemed to have ended up with a would-be monarch. They did not know what had hit them, or, really, who it was that they had elected.

'I'm not complicated,' Macron told me when I went to interview him at the Elysée Palace two months later, in late July 2017. I was taken up to meet the president in his high-ceilinged first-floor corner office, which overlooks the landscaped palace gardens, and interconnects with the ornate official bureau next door. It was a sultry 30 degrees in the capital, and a fan was whirring in the corner. The office was awash with sunlight, and the French windows had been thrown open to the lawn below. I knew from photos that real presidential splendour belonged to the far grander neighbouring office, known as the *salon doré*, preserved as it was for the Empress Eugénie in 1861. Furnished with the eighteenth-century Louis XV-style desk used by Charles de Gaulle, Macron receives his formal diplomatic guests there. For everyday work, he has taken over the less imposing corner bureau, more commonly occupied by presidential special advisers, fitting it out with the clean-lined designer furniture he prefers, and modern art. On one wall, behind the table, he has hung a work of modern street art featuring Marianne, a national symbol of the French Republic, and the French motto, *liberté, égalité, fraternité*. Previously in his office at En Marche headquarters, it is a replica of a piece of street art created shortly after one of the Paris terrorist attacks, by Obey (Shepard Fairey), the artist behind the portrait of Obama entitled 'Hope'.

We sat down around the marble-topped table to talk just days after France's top general had resigned following an explosive public row between him and the president. Would there be traces of the stress or burden of power, I wondered? Would Macron assert the formality of office, and default into political question-dodging mode? Would I be meeting the republican monarch? Or the chatty, good-humoured adviser from the top floor? The president, in shirt sleeves, seemed singularly relaxed. The intervening five years since I had first met him had left little physical mark. The hair had receded a little, but the boyish grin was the same. Some of his mannerisms had passed me by during previous meetings: the fiddling with his wedding ring, or the funny way he has of occasionally flicking his nose while he speaks. Or his inclination to switch abruptly from the linguistically elegant to the earthy, from lofty abstractions to quotidian words such as *machin* (whatsit) and *truc* (thingummy). But the disarmingly earnest engagement, and the professional focus, was just as it had been five years earlier. He does not avoid questions, but takes them on. '*Non, mais*' is his interjection of choice. Macron's is a version of power through listening.

'I'm not complicated', the line he used that day, was an intriguing phrase. In one sense, it is true. In his first year in office, Macron turned out to have the uncommon political habit of doing pretty much exactly what he had said he would. He was predictable. 'It's in the manifesto', became the answer to almost any query you might put to a deputy or adviser about a new policy, and sure enough, most of the time it was. This sort of straightforward conduct was in itself a novelty for France, whose presidents had a tendency of discarding promises upon election. To be sure, there were misunderstandings, disappointments and unexpected turns. But there was little policy improvisation, and very few genuine surprises. Macron is indeed, in this sense, not complicated.

Yet the more the French get to know their president, the more impenetrable he seems to be. As he retreated into the Elysée Palace, like Jupiter to Mount Olympus, Macron cultivated a studied distance, including with the press, which aggravated this perception. The word that comes to mind is the untranslatable *insaisissable*, meaning something between inscrutable and elusive. This is a man who is so outwardly charming in private, so breathtakingly confident, that it is hard to grasp what exactly are his gut instincts, what really lurks behind the finely polished exterior. Michel Houellebecq, the French novelist and *enfant terrible* of the Paris literary scene, once tried to interview Macron, and spoke in his inimitable way about the frustration of the experience. 'He's bizarre, you don't know where he comes from, he's a bit of a mutant,' he murmured. Macron speaks 'very well', Houellebecq went on, but like all great politicians, 'I realized the difficulty of making [him] say any sort of truth.' Lots of people say they know him. Very few claim to know Macron really well.

The contradictions that Macron embodies seemed to reflect this unknowable quality. A man of charm and a phenomenal networker, he has few truly close friends. A literary mind, he ended up a civil-service technocrat in the faceless corridors of the Finance Ministry. A graduate of philosophy, who talked of 'moments of philosophical emotion' when first reading Kant, he chose to become an investment banker. A private individual, who struggled to reveal anything intimate in his autobiographical book, he sought the most publicly scrutinized office of state. An unworldly teenager, he won over a drama teacher (now his wife) 24 years his elder. A provincial outsider, he is the embodiment of the French metropolitan elite. A personality with unusual private empathy, he has trouble persuading the French that he likes them. A disruptive innovator, he has ended up strengthening the institutions he used to stage his insolent revolt.

This book is an attempt, after his first year in office, to make sense of Emmanuel Macron, his contradictions, and his ambition to remake France. How did a political novice manage to defy the unwritten rules of the Fifth Republic, and secure the presidency at his first attempt? What had happened to France over the previous 20 years that laid the ground for this improbable feat? What are the ideas and inspirations behind Macronism? What is the nature of the progressivism that he is trying to fashion as a response to the failings of contemporary capitalism? Can it offer a model for liberal moderates on the left and the right in other countries who dream of campaigning for power on the centre ground? Can Macron really hope to restore faith in Europe, and the Western democratic order, against the threat of illiberal nationalism at the continent's door?

Ultimately, the ballot box in 2022 will be the judge. The circumstances that led to his election are also the challenges that Macron inherited. The most elegant of countries, the nation that brought the world *joie de vivre* and Christian Dior's jaunty New Look, France has in recent decades been through an unusually unsettled and morose time. It has lost ground economically, overtaken by Britain in the late 1990s, and then by its continental neighbour, Germany. In 2002 France and Germany shared comparable levels of GDP per head and unemployment. Fifteen years later, Germans were 17 per cent richer on average and their jobless rate was less than half that in France. The last time a French government balanced its budget was in 1974. The last time unemployment dipped below 7 per cent was in 1980. Most startling of all, France began to lose its way in Europe. Invaded three times by Germany since 1870, and on its fifth republic, France has a long disrupted history, insecure even in peace. After the Second World War it responded by helping to build the European Union – a project designed to bind in Germany, and amplify France's own power. Somewhere along the line, however, the passion it once evoked cooled. The share of French people who looked favourably upon Europe shrank from 69 per cent in 2004 to 38 per cent in 2016. A broader malaise set in. A global 'barometer of hope and happiness' put the French second to bottom of a 54-country world ranking in 2013, ahead only of Portugal.

The signs of a festering popular discontent that reached back over 20 years were there for those who cared to read them. In 1992 the French approved the launch of the single currency, Europe's pioneering project of integration, by the slimmest of margins, in a referendum result that hinted at hardening reservations. In 2002 voters put Jean-Marie Le Pen into the second round of the presidential election, in a shock result that spoke of anti-establishment grievance and a deep vein of xenophobia. In 2005 the French rejected a draft European Union constitution, which had been devised under the guiding hand of Valéry Giscard d'Estaing, their own former president.

This unease was compounded by political *immobilisme*. After the paralyzing strikes that greeted an attempt by Jacques Chirac's prime minister, Alain Juppé, to reform welfare in 1995, fear of the street diminished the ambition and resolve of subsequent governments. The election of the hyperkinetic Nicolas Sarkozy in 2007 brought a brief promise of 'rupture' and restored competitiveness. Sarkozy had some successes, but was enfeebled from the start, not least by the financial crisis. Between 2012 and 2017 François Hollande's attempt to embody a 'normal' presidency only served as a reminder to the French how much they valued presidential exception.

The upshot over this period was that reform came to inspire fear and retrenchment, was seldom discussed ahead of elections, and was put into place by stealth, if at all. When all else failed, it could be blamed on Brussels. Successive governments of the left and right defaulted into a form of passivity, putting off difficult choices, confusing and disappointing voters in equal measure. No president managed to find an overarching narrative of hope or progress to combat genuine worries about globalization, technological change and global warming. By the time of the bloody terrorist attacks of 2015 and 2016, the sense of malaise was acute. France, a great country, the cradle of human rights and the Enlightenment, had somehow lost its self-confidence. A highly centralized rule-bound system that once served the country well, bringing fast trains to every region and three-course meals to every nursery school, was generating taxes and debt, little growth and not enough jobs. Many young French people, fed up with the staid conservatism of Paris, had packed up and left to join banks, pull beers and launch start-ups in London. Perhaps most painful of all was a realization that France was no longer a match for Germany, its closest ally. The *décrochage*, or decoupling, between the eurozone's two big economies was felt in France as a loss of stature and national pride.

In the first months after the election, the French did not know quite what to make of the president who took on the leadership of this uneasy country. He seemed to oscillate between the magnificent and the absurd. Sometimes he looked the part, neither awestruck nor ill-prepared. Macron knew his way around the Elysée Palace, the pitfalls of isolation in it, and the perils of presidential mistakes. Under Hollande, he had seen up close how to make them. Once in the job himself, he was decisive, inventive and disciplined, and made the French feel good about themselves again. At other moments, Macron seemed to pick up the tattered presidential mantle with the air of entitlement befitting that of a Bourbon king. There he was with his make-up artist and powdered brow, talking about 'my people'. He developed a look that verged on the haughty and, as if one palace would not do, seemed to be disturbingly fond of operating out of Versailles. To a British or an American ear, his theoretical abstractions and grandiosity came across as pompous. His speeches were convoluted, meandering and went on for ever. In all his magnificence, he seemed so very, well, French.

The scale of the task Macron has set himself is daunting. He claims to want not just to reform France, but to transform it: into an ambitious entrepreneurial economy, which can be at the forefront of artificial intelligence, machine learning, big data and green technology, while preserving France's treasured sense of *art de vivre*. He also seeks to revive the European idea, defend post-war multilateralism, challenge nationalist tendencies and invent a 'new global compact' to respond to the failings of advanced capitalism. Failure to do this, he judges, will increase the risk of populist backlash and threaten the liberal order. 'The biggest risk for the next five years,' Macron told me in July 2017, 'is to do nothing.'

What the French president does will determine whether his election was a brief parenthesis of hope, or the beginnings of a reshaping of modern France, and with it possibly Europe. Macron's rise from nowhere to the presidency carried a powerful message that resonated well beyond the country. After the shock of Brexit it was an emphatic demonstration that it was possible to fashion a pro-European centrist response to populism and nationalism, and win. After the election of Trump, it was a resounding vote of confidence in the liberal order. Indeed, Macron is in some ways emerging as the world's anti-Trump, and France a test of whether liberal pluralism can hold.

France is a thrilling, seductive and maddening country. But it is also, time and again, a country that teaches deep humility. Every time the observer has the pretension to claim to understand France, the French spring another big surprise. The quiet bloodless political revolution of 2017 was one of them. But if the country under Macron's leadership cannot make tangible improvements to people's lives, particularly for the young, voters at the next presidential election, in 2022, may not be ready to give a liberal democrat another chance.

This book is not a biography of Emmanuel Macron. Nor is it an academic work. I am a journalist, and it is rather a story of how he rose from nowhere to overturn the French political establishment, and an analysis of what might happen next. Over the past six years, and through numerous conversations with Macron, I have watched the transformation of a cerebral technocrat into a savvy and calculating politician, who used his charm and seductive powers of persuasion to devastating effect in what became a quest for the presidency, and then an attempt to remake France. His remarkable ascent from obscurity to the Elysée Palace is both the dramatic tale of one man's personal ambition and the story of a wounded once-proud country in deep need of renewal. I have spoken to many of the protagonists in this drama, in order to piece together Macron's path to power. I have visited the places and people that influenced him, and chronicled his first year in office, trying to assess the underlying trajectory of the country that he now governs. My objective is to make sense of both the forces that shaped him and the way he is trying to reshape France.

The book is divided into two parts. Part One, 'Conquest', unpicks the factors that made Macron's improbable adventure work, and how he built En Marche into a force that toppled the mainstream parties and beat Marine Le Pen. Part Two, 'Power', turns to his time in office, the intellectual and philosophical origins of the presidential project, and the promise and the risks it carries. Throughout the book I have tried to maintain a balance between a desire to wish France well, after all these troubled years, and a need to keep a reporter's dispassionate eye on the way Macron handles the exercise of power. During the time that I have covered France for *The Economist*, nobody has accused me of an excessive indulgence towards the country – in 2012 I published a book called *Le déni français* ('France in Denial') – and in television studios and ministerial offices I have fended off accusations of 'French-bashing', however unfounded I thought they were, more times than I can count. France is a country that has welcomed, exasperated and inspired me, and brought some amazing, smart and generous people into my life. I hope, now that the country is undergoing a brave and difficult effort to transform itself, I can defend myself from accusations of excessive optimism and confidence. However it turns out, all errors of judgement are entirely mine.

PART ONE

CONQUEST

1

THE PARABLE OF AMIENS

'He puts his own liberty above everything.'

Christian Dargnat, En Marche

When history comes to recount the rise of Emmanuel Macron, it might begin and end in the city of Amiens. On the big-skied lowlands of the Somme, amid the woods and fields of beet and yellow rape that cover the former bloody battlefields of the First World War, this is where the future president was born and grew up. It is a city that is arresting both for its splendour and its banality. The soaring Notre-Dame cathedral, one of the biggest Gothic edifices constructed in the thirteenth century, rises magnificently above the city centre and surrounding floodplain. But Amiens is also a red-brick working city, built on a heavy industrial base, which has bled manufacturing jobs over the years, and is struggling to hold on to the ones that are left. By 2017 it had lost one big multinational tyre factory, but kept another. Whirlpool operated a plant that manufactured tumble dryers. Until 1989 the city had been run for nearly 20 years by a Communist mayor.

When you turn off to reach the city from the A16 motorway, you drive into the featureless suburban landscape that marks the outskirts of today's French cities: a Courtepaille fast-food restaurant; an Auchan hypermarket ringed by a vast car park; a Citroën car dealership; a Buffalo grill restaurant, topped with its insignia bearing giant red horns. Just as the surrounding flatlands of the Somme bear the scars of the First World War, the city centre of Amiens carries those of the second. Amiens was doubly bombed: by the Nazi Wehrmacht in May 1940, and then again by Allied forces on the Pentecost weekend of May 1944, as part of preparations for the D-Day landings the following month. Most of the centre of Amiens was devastated, its main thorough-fare rebuilt in charmless post-war style. This is the place that shaped Mr Macron, and the city he fled.

It was in a soulless exhibition centre on the edge of Amiens that Macron took to the stage to launch En Marche on 6 April 2016. The choice, he said that night, was 'not unintentional. I was born here. Part of my family still lives here, and I have a strong attachment to this place.' During his campaign Macron crafted a narrative that rooted him firmly in the industrial Picardy city, far from the parquet-floored salons of Paris, and in a family whose origins, he repeatedly underlined, were simple. It was a potent backstory. 'I wasn't born in a château,' he said while campaigning in Amiens. 'The history of my family,' he wrote in *Révolution*, the autobiographical book he published before the election, 'is that of republican ascent in provincial France.'[1] This meritocratic guiding idea was behind the compulsory, free, secular education introduced in the 1880s by Jules Ferry, a whiskered deputy who became min-ister for public education before serving as prime minister under the Third Republic. Macron's grandparents were among the bene-ficiaries. They came, he wrote, from 'a modest background': one was a teacher, another worked on the railways, a third was a social worker and the last a civil engineer. His paternal great-grandfather, George Robertson, was an English butcher from Bristol, who married a French woman in Abbeville, near Amiens, after World War One. His maternal grandmother, Germaine Noguès, known as Manette, was the first in her family to stay in school after the age of 15. Raised in Bagnères-de-Bigorre, in the foothills of the Pyrenees, she became a teacher and later a headmistress. Her own mother did not know how to read or write.

For Macron's grandparents, medicine was the preferred route into the professional classes. His father, Jean-Michel Macron, had once dreamed of life as an archaeologist, but his parents judged medicine to be the safer choice. A neurologist, he still practised at the time of writing at the Amiens public hospital. Macron's mother, Françoise Noguès, now retired, is a qualified doctor who formerly worked at the social-security agency in the city. Macron's two younger siblings each also followed their parents into medicine. His brother, Laurent, became a cardiologist; his sister, Estelle, a kidney specialist. During the election campaign, Macron returned often to this family journey into the middle class, which began with his grandmother, a 'child whose parents could neither read nor write'. 'I'm a child of provincial France,' he told a rally in Lyon in February 2017. 'Nothing predestined me to be here today.'

In reality, Macron grew up in a more comfortable, professional family than this campaign narrative suggested. The family home was in the quiet residential neighbourhood of Henriville, considered the bourgeois enclave of Amiens. First developed in the mid-nineteenth century, after the railways arrived and the old ramparts were torn down, this quarter lies just to the south of the city centre. An unkind observer in 1928 described Henriville as 'deathly boring, with its streets laid out in lines, its dreary appearance, its houses in the style of luxurious stables, its rare passers-by well dressed and its brick church pitifully ugly'.[2] Today, busy tree-lined boulevards frame the neighbourhood's northern and southern edge. Along them, a number of tall early twentieth-century villas rise behind wrought-iron gates. Other treeless terraces are more modest. Macron's childhood home in Amiens is to be found in one of these: an unpretentious two-storey red-brick house, which sits just back from the pavement, in a narrow street of flat-fronted terraced homes. The first time I saw it, while on a reporting visit to Amiens during the 2017 presidential election campaign, it seemed unremarkable. Purple hibiscus and white hydrangeas were growing in the little front garden. A narrow off-road parking space was fringed by a yew hedge.

It was a childhood of privilege by most measures, a world away from the forbidding tower blocks and housing estates of Amiens-Nord, on the rougher side of the city. In the Macron household there were piano lessons, foreign holidays and skiing trips. Emmanuel learned to play tennis at the club that lies down an alley in the street where he grew up. Macron's father, a reserved figure who later described himself as 'allergic' to the celebrity-style coverage of his son's political life, read widely and taught his son Greek, as well as introducing him to philosophy. His mother limited her working hours in order to spend time with her three children, driving them to music classes and sports lessons.

The three young Macron children attended the local state primary school, but were later sent to a private Catholic school, aptly called 'La Providence'. It was their grandmother Manette, by then a retired teacher, who persuaded the family to enrol them for a more academic secondary education at 'La Pro', as its pupils call it. A lycée run by Jesuits in Henriville, the school lies on one of the arterial boulevards within walking distance of their house. Destroyed in a fire during the bombing of Amiens in 1940, it was rebuilt in the late 1940s. When I went to take a look, the place from the outside resembled a boxy American post-war high school, fronted by symmetrical square lawns, and equipped – unusually for a French school of any sort – with an indoor swimming pool. It is a private institution, although not quite as exclusive a place as this might suggest. In 2017 its fees varied, according to family means, from €520 to €980 a year. The school runs an extensive bursary programme, and offers the technical stream of the *baccalauréat* for the non-academic.

A childhood spent around books, a private Catholic school, piano lessons, a local tennis club: Macron had a more securely middle-class upbringing than he hinted at on the campaign trail. Yet his version is not wholly disingenuous. To this day, the neighbourhood of Henriville feels comfortably bourgeois, rather than flashy, or glamorous. It is not Versailles or Neuilly-sur-Seine, those leafy quarters home to the moneyed French classes, nor is it a bastion of understated established wealth such as you find on the chic Paris left bank. When it comes to understanding Macron's origins, and the path he then travelled, this seems an important distinction. A former investment banker at Rothschild's, and a graduate of the Ecole Nationale d'Administration (ENA), the hyper-selective training school for elite civil servants, Macron appears to be in so many ways the embodiment of privilege. Ever since he entered public life, he has been the subject of caricature to this end. Jean-Luc Mélenchon, a fiery far-left class warrior who ran for election under the banner of a political movement called Unsubmissive France (*La France Insoumise*), accused Macron during the presidential campaign of being a '*grand bourgeois*'. Anne Hidalgo, the Socialist mayor of Paris, who preferred her party's candidate, Benoît Hamon, for the presidency in 2017, described Macron as 'the incarnation of the social reproduction of the elites'.

Yet Macron is not a member of what the French call the *haute bourgeoisie*. His childhood home is not grand. At the end of the street there is a neighbourhood *charcuterie-traiteur* on one corner, and a medical-supplies outlet on the other. A café-bar-tabac, selling cigarettes and lottery tickets, lies just across the boulevard. 'We were average parents,' Jean-Michel Macron told Macron's biographer Anne Fulda, describing it as 'a banal life'.[3] 'Of course it was a privileged background, but it depends what you mean by privileged,' Renaud Dartevelle, a close school friend of Macron's from the age of ten, told me. I had tracked him down in the southern suburbs of Paris, where he now teaches history in a high school. He had learned English by watching *Downton Abbey*. 'I come from the same kind of background,' Dartevelle said. 'His grandparents came from poor backgrounds; my grandparents did too. And that was not uncommon among this kind of *bourgeoisie* in Amiens. La Providence is not a school only for the very few.' When we met, Dartevelle was keen to underline this point about Macron. 'I don't think it's fair to say that everything was set up for him from day one,' he told me. 'He is sincere when he thinks that he owes what he has to his talents and efforts. Being part of the country's top elite is not an obvious outcome for someone of this kind of background.'[4]

Emmanuel Jean-Michel Frédéric Macron was born on 21 December 1977. It was a time of great uncertainty in France, after the end of the *trente glorieuses* (1945–73), those three fabulous decades of rapid post-war economic growth, industrialization and shared faith in the future. But it was also a time when the French were pushing the boundaries of modern science and taste. Concorde took to the skies with regular flights for the first time. The Pompidou Centre opened in Paris, and shocked architectural purists. TGV fast trains were under development, as was Minitel, the French connected personal computer and precursor to the internet, which was launched in 1982. For Macron's parents, it was a period of hope, as well as apprehension. Their first baby, a daughter, had been stillborn. 'Emmanuel's birth,' said his mother, 'was a moment of great happiness after difficult times.'[5] A chaplain who visited the new parents told them that they had given their baby son a name that in Hebrew means 'son of God'. Macron's father said that they chose the name just because they liked it.[6]

That Macron was an unusual child emerges unequivocally from the recollections of those who knew him during his childhood, as well as his own account in *Révolution*. Macron credits his grandmother, Manette, with his early interest in books and learning. With her lifelong passion for education, she taught him to read from the age of five. After school, he said, he would spend 'long hours' with her learning grammar, history, geography and French literature, and 'entire days' listening to her reading aloud from works by Molière, Racine or François Mauriac. At the first-round television debate during the presidential election of 2017, candidates were invited to bring along an object that held particular value to them; Macron chose the French grammar book his grandmother had used to teach him. 'I spent my childhood,' he said, 'in books.' In Macron's telling, his was an upbringing in which the world came alive through the written word, enchantments discovered through literature, poetry and soaring prose. Guided by the watchful Manette, he grew up in 'happy seclusion', he wrote, his nose in books, his mind transported elsewhere.

Others tell a rather less singular version of those early years. There were the long drives during the holidays across the country, from Amiens in the north of France down to Bagnères-de-Bigorre, which nestles in the valley beneath the snow-capped peaks of the Pyrenees, nearly 1,000 kilometres away. On holiday there, with his maternal grandparents, the young Macron would spend much of the day outdoors, chasing lizards, or off on fishing trips on the nearby stream with his grandfather, Jean Noguès. Nicole, Macron's mother's cousin, remembered them spending days playing pétanque or ping-pong, or out on walks. During the campaign, Macron recalled that it was in the Pyrenees, at La Mongie, that he learned to ride a bicycle up and down arduous mountain roads, and to ski. His world was not just one of books, and his discovery of it not purely through the enchantments and reveries of literature.

What does seem indisputable, though, is that Macron was a precocious reader, an eager learner, and that Manette loomed large in shaping those interests. 'He wanted to know everything about everything,' recalled Sylvie, his cousin, who today runs a clothing shop in Bagnères-de-Bigorre.[7] Manette, said Sylvie's mother Nicole, did not impose all these books and literary discussions on the young boy; the hunger to learn came from him too. 'His brother was more into toys, but he wanted to work; it was his nature,' she said. Tiphaine Auzière, Brigitte Macron's daughter from her previous marriage, who has her mother's petite frame and blonde hair and became a fervent supporter of En Marche, had no doubt about the towering influence of Macron's grandmother when I spoke to her during the election campaign. I wanted to know how much Amiens had shaped him. 'I would say that he was less influenced by the place he grew up than the person with whom he grew up, his grandmother, a very strong character,' she told me: 'He was very, very close to his grandmother, who was a teacher and gave him a taste for education and learning and also, I think, the idea that wherever you come from you should have the same opportunities to evolve.'[8]

The defining nature of Manette's relationship with her grandson was the way she cultivated him 'like a plant', said Antoine Marguet, who was also at La Providence at the same time as Macron. 'She saw how promising the plant was, and

ensured it had the right fertilizer: books and knowledge.'[9] In
Macron's account, his grandmother was at once his inspiration',
his guide and his refuge, during holidays as well as while he
was at school. This was not that unusual in France. With long
summer holidays and no school on Wednesdays, French children
often spend much time with their grandparents. Manette lived
in an apartment near the family home in Amiens, and during
term time Macron would go there after class, to 'drink hot chocolate, while listening to Chopin'. At one point, as a young child,
he asked his parents whether he could move in to live with her.
Renaud Dartevelle remembers meeting Manette for the first time.
'When I rang to see Emmanuel, who was at her place, she said
"Oh you must be Renaud." She was a very kind old lady, very
well mannered, smiling. I had this feeling of being special because
I was Emmanuel's friend, of course ... That gave me an insight of
how strong their relationship was.'

Macron's parents seem to have taken offence at the
overwhelming place that his grandmother occupies in his
own version of those early years. Reluctant to dwell on his
childhood, Macron wrote little about his parents in his book,
which in itself seemed to make a point. Yet he devoted pages to
Manette. 'Did he not have a family?!' his mother told Macron's
biographer Anne Fulda, evidently hurt. She did not dispute the
pair's closeness, but insisted on presenting a more balanced
account: 'We still contributed something.'[10] His father put this
one-sided version down to the media's urge to romanticize
and promote a story: 'It sells well.' Dartevelle, though, told me
that he did detect 'a sense of distance' between Macron and
his parents. He disputed the portrayal of Françoise Noguès as
remote, or distant. 'She was kind. She was caring,' he told me.
'She was not an absent mother, by any means.' But there was
a sense that the young Emmanuel did not fit in, and that he
found with his grandmother the space to be himself that he
lacked at home. His father, Jean-Michel Macron, was a discreet figure, 'more withdrawn' than his mother and 'not at all
interested in talking to an unknown teenager who came over',

Dartevelle said of his visits to the family home. When they were teenagers, Macron spoke little of his father, Dartevelle said, and when he did, it was more often in the context of the books that he had read, not the medical research he conducted, or the hospital work he carried out. 'I remember him once telling me that his father had read, over the summer, all of *Les Essais* by Montaigne,' Dartevelle told me, referring to the thick volume of collected essays by the Renaissance philosopher. 'He didn't used to talk about him as a surgeon, which he is, but as a reader of literature.' Their bond, such as it existed, was through books.

What nobody disputes is that the link between Macron and his grandmother was unusually intense, both emotionally and intellectually. She was a demanding tutor, a benevolent guide and an unconditional supporter of the choices he made long into his adult life. Manette died in 2013, when Macron was working as an adviser to President François Hollande at the Elysée Palace. He was devastated. 'No day goes by without my thinking of her,' Macron wrote. During the 2017 campaign a French reporter travelling with him in the rural department of Mayenne, asked Macron whether 'in the end, you're doing all this for her?' The young candidate, wiping the farmyard mud off his city suit and leather shoes, turned his head to look out of the window of the car. 'Yes,' he said, 'perhaps.'[11] 'She never brought me up with the idea that I had a destiny, but she undoubtedly armed me to have one ... I was unbelievably lucky. It gives you an immense self-confidence, an incredible liberty, but in the same way an obligation. I've always had the deeply rooted idea that the liberty that I secured for myself obliged me to do well. Because she was like that, my grandmother ... I headed into this battle when she was no longer there, she would have doubtless thought that it was mad.' But, he said, his voice trembling, 'she would have let me do it'.

Liberty, the sense of possibility, and the freedom to be different. This sense emerged from so many of the conversations I had over a period of months during 2017 with those who knew Macron as a child, teenager or student. Renaud Dartevelle told me that Macron 'always knew he had a special destiny'. He plainly outshone all his classmates, in almost everything. 'On the academic side, he excelled in all subjects, with a disconcerting facility,' said Father Philippe Robert, his physics and chemistry teacher in the lycée: 'In physics and chemistry, during written tests, I had to add extra exercises to keep him busy until the end of the exam.'[12] Dartevelle made the pupil sound like every classmate's nightmare: 'He was very bright. A very high achiever, from day one, always, in any subject, any year. Top grades. Between 18/20 and 20/20. He's the kind of student you have in your class once in a lifetime. I think the question for him from day one was: what am I going to do with all the gifts I have?'

During the parliamentary election campaign of 2017, I travelled up to the department of the Pas-de-Calais to report on the campaign for a constituency there. On a blustery afternoon in the inland village of Rang-du-Fliers, beside her yellow campaign bus, I found Tiphaine Auzière, Macron's stepdaughter. She was running for parliamentary elections as the deputy to the local En Marche candidate, having caught the political bug and become an enthusiastic advocate for the movement. A lawyer in the nearby town of Etaples, she turned up on a bicycle, dressed in jeans and trainers, her hair tied back in a ponytail. Improbable as it sounds, as a teenager her older sister Laurence was in the same class at La Providence as Macron. She was the one who first came home with stories about her unusual classmate. 'She said he was unbearable,' Tiphaine told me, 'because he knew everything about everything.' Antoine Marguet, the fellow pupil from the time, said that he had heard about 'this extraordinary guy' at school before he came across him. 'I wasn't in his class. But all the people I knew who were with Emmanuel told me that there was the grade he got, and then that of the others,' Marguet told me. 'He has always been different. He knows that he isn't like other people, and so sometimes he adopts a certain tone. People say he is arrogant, full of himself, a pain. But he has always had this intimate conviction that he is different ... I think this is very important. His intelligence, his knowledge, his culture: these put him somewhat on the sidelines.'

Out of the ordinary. On the sidelines. Different. A picture emerges of a young teenager who was set apart. He does not seem to have suffered as a school child from it. It is perhaps a reflection of his capacity for empathy that Macron does not appear to have drawn resentment from others for being clever. Father Robert said: 'He had absolutely natural relationships with his classmates. In his eyes, to be brilliant in all fields seemed normal.' Dartevelle recalled the same. 'He never showed off, never bragged, never made people feel sorry for themselves ... He was very careful. As far as I know, he was never resented for being so smart.' From the age of ten or eleven, Dartevelle remembered, Macron seemed to grasp how he was perceived by others. All the same, he was eager to see his gifts recognized. 'He's very talented, he's very bright,' Dartevelle told me. 'But what he's even better at is making people think he's a genius.'

This sense of difference was accompanied by an unusual degree of self-sufficiency. Everybody who has met Macron is struck by his ability to leave you with the impression that the meeting mattered to him. He is, as the French say, *dans la séduction*, and this trait was evident from an early age. Rare is the photograph from the time that does not show Macron with a broad sunny smile. Yet as a teenager he was at the same time not socially needy. 'He had a lot of friends. But not a group of friends,' Dartevelle told me. 'He was always very friendly, easy to connect with, but also, very private. Things were very cloistered between the various aspects of his life. He could connect easily with a lot of different pupils, but was never in a very exclusive relationship.' It was a pattern that continued into adulthood.

Perhaps the most startling way in which his singularity played out was Macron's quest to bypass the usual distractions and agonies of teenagerhood and step briskly into the adult world. His was not a rebellious adolescence. Not for the young Macron a heady embrace of counter-culture, nor the rejection of adult norms. Nor even much in the way of partying. Raised in a secular, agnostic family, he chose at the age of 12 to be baptized into the Catholic faith (although he later described his subsequent 'return to a certain agnosticism'). An adult before he had finished being a teenager, and serious beyond his years, Macron early on sought out the company and conversation of those older than himself, a habit he took with him into his later professional, and private, life. 'He was very conventional. He was only unconventional in the sense that he was reading adult literature when we were teenagers,' Dartevelle told me. 'But his were very classical choices. Gide's *Les Nourritures Terrestres* was his favourite book when we were teenagers. He wasn't even reading *The Catcher in the Rye!*' To this day, Macron has decidedly old-fashioned cultural tastes. A classically trained pianist, he favours French variety – Jacques Brel, Johnny Hallyday, Léo Ferré, Charles Aznavour – over anything released since the invention of the synthesizer. His vocabulary too, like the curses of Tintin's Captain Haddock, sometimes seems to belong to another era. Macron likes to dismiss nonsense with disparaging words such as *poudre de perlimpinpin* (snake oil), *galimatias* (gibberish) or *croquignolesque* (ridiculous). He addresses his friends as '*ma poule*', which translates as something between 'baby' and 'dude'. 'Emmanuel wasn't cool,' Dartevelle told me. 'He wasn't a partygoer. But I wasn't either. Maybe we were friends because I was a boring teenager too.'

This precocious maturity, and his uncommon teenaged ease with adult conversation, was to have unforeseen repercussions. 'What was most striking was his relationship with adults. He spoke to his teachers as equals,' Father Philippe Robert told *Paris Match*. One *prof* in particular caught his attention: a French and Latin teacher, with honey-blonde hair and an infectious smile, who ran an after-school theatre club: Brigitte Auzière. She was never Macron's class teacher. But the two school friends, Dartevelle and Macron, joined her drama club, having first acted together in a play, *Jacques et son Maître*, by Milan Kundera, when they were in their fourth year of secondary school. The following year, when Macron was 15, they signed up for Madame Auzière's theatre group. Macron got the part of a scarecrow, in the school's adaptation of *La Comédie du Langage*, an absurdist work by Jean Tardieu. A home video from the time shows the teenager, in patched baggy trousers and a straw hat, his arms outstretched, pacing about slowly onstage. Already then, as he lifts his head to look out and pauses before reciting his lines, he comes across as an unusually self-assured youngster, in control, unafraid of holding his audience with a long silence.

But it was the play that the drama teacher put on the next year, Macron's penultimate at school, that brought the teenager and the teacher 24 years his elder together. *L'Art de la Comédie*, written in 1964 by Eduardo de Filippo, was an intriguing, and with hindsight uncanny, choice. A play that explores the boundaries between art, theatre and politics, it sets a theatre director against a local prefect, and treats the audience to a procession of characters who may be local notables, or actors playing the part. It is both funny, and an exploration of the line between illusion and reality in public life. As the play lacked parts for all members of Madame Auzière's drama club, the young Macron suggested to his theatre teacher that they write in some new roles and adapt the play together. 'He was very good at making absolutely self-evident his leadership when it came to writing, and being good at school, or being the brightest in the group,' Dartevelle told me. 'I mean, nobody discussed the fact that he was writing the play for the whole group.'

A popular teacher known for her passion for literature, nurturing approach to teaching, as well as exacting demands of her pupils, Brigitte Auzière later gave her own version of their blossoming relationship. 'The writing brought us together every Friday, and created an incredible proximity,' she told *Paris Match*. 'I felt myself sliding; he did too.'[13] Dartevelle, with a lead role in the play, was well placed to watch this unfold. His discomfort was clear. 'When the thing became obvious, I was willing not to know, and I did my best not to know,' he told me. A teacher himself in adult life, Dartevelle subsequently saw members of his profession punished for less. Brigitte Auzière, the sixth and last child from the Trogneux family, a grand established Amiens name and brand of local chocolates, was married to a banker, André-Louis Auzière. They had three children. Macron was 16 years old.

31

The emerging liaison prompted consternation in the Macron family home, and gossip after Mass on Sunday in Henriville. Macron's parents implored Brigitte Auzière to keep away from their son until he was 18. Their reaction seems to have exacerbated the distance between him and his parents. At first, Brigitte's older brother, Jean Trogneux, tried to step in to put an end to it too. 'But Emmanuel insisted,' a family member told me. 'He never gave up.' Years later, when Macron had become president, Brigitte Macron reflected on the episode in an interview with *ELLE* magazine, suggesting that it was her idea for him to leave Amiens and finish high school in Paris. 'There was nothing between us at the time,' she insisted, presumably keen to dispel concerns about the legality of their relationship, 'but the gossip was already well underway.'[14]

Macron's determination to win Brigitte Auzière over – declaring to her, at the age of nearly 17, as he left for Paris, that 'Whatever happens, I will marry you' – was a breathtaking display of self-confidence for a teenager towards a woman more than twice his age. That he tried was audacious enough. That he succeeded, astounding. Brigitte Auzière's own three children, Sébastien, Laurence and Tiphaine, were all of the same generation as Macron. Laurence had been in his class at school. Like in any marital break-up, the children suffered. André-Louis Auzière, her first husband, steers clear of the public eye and has never given an interview nor spoken about it. 'But I couldn't not do it,' Brigitte Macron later said. 'There are moments in your life when you make vital choices. And for me that was one of them.'[15]

In his wedding speech, Macron thanked her children, acknowledging that it was 'not very simple' for them. Their future stepfather was their own age, and took on a precociously paternal role with them, advising them to take care when out partying. 'Nothing is normal in his life,' said Antoine Marguet, the fellow school pupil from Amiens. The way Tiphaine Auzière talks today about her stepfather, a mere five years older than her, suggests that such difficulties are long behind them. Macron refers to her and her siblings' children as his grandchildren; they call him

'Daddy'. 'He's really a stepfather who took on the role naturally,' she told me, 'by all the attention that he paid to all the members of the family. He is the head of the family. We have a father whom we adore, and who carries out his role as a father. But we are also lucky enough to have a stepfather who is always there to help us.'

So Macron left Amiens, his home town, behind him, allowing the school to hush up the affair. He was taken on, unusually, for the last year of school at Henri IV, one of the most selective and prestigious state lycées in France. Situated in the heart of the Latin Quarter of Paris, and originally founded in 1796, it counts among its alumni a former prime minister, government ministers, diplomats, ambassadors, novelists and philosophers. A more solid stepping stone into the Paris elite is hard to find. The distance Macron travelled from the battlefields of the Somme to the heart of the intellectual and power circles of the French capital was cultural as well as geographical. Like Julien Sorel, the protagonist in Stendhal's *Le rouge et le noir*, one of Macron's favourite novels, who arrived from the provinces to try to make it in Paris society, the teenager from Amiens found himself in a different world. The bookish student was at first in awe at the brilliance of the capital's brightest, struggled in maths, and was later wounded by his failure twice to win a place at the country's high-flying literary college, the Ecole Normale Supérieure.[16] He had stayed on at Henri IV for *classe prépa*, a post-*bac* preparation course, in order to take the entrance exam for Normale, but was by his own account too preoccupied by his relationship with Brigitte to put in the requisite revision. Despite his constant train trips back to Amiens to see her, Macron quickly learned the social codes of the French elite, winning instead a place at Sciences Po, an elite university focused on political science and public affairs, and taking in parallel a philosophy degree at the University of Nanterre. He went on to secure a place as one of fewer than a hundred French students in his year at the highly selective Ecole Nationale d'Administration (ENA) – whose alumni include three of the five past presidents – and with it access to the power-brokers of Paris.

The key to understanding Macron's departure from Amiens, his friend and best man Marc Ferracci told me, is 'a quest for liberty': 'In his speeches, in his policies and in the choices he has made during his life, there has always been this logic.'[17] If Macron outgrew Amiens, it was through a desire, as he put it in his book, 'to choose my own life'. The determination to do his own thing, to win for himself freedom, space and independence, marked both his escape from Amiens and the decisions he went on to take. Macron defied convention, family disapproval and the wagging tongues of the Amiens *bourgeoisie* with his relationship with Brigitte Auzière. He went on to win political independence by launching En Marche, securing himself the freedom he needed to flout the rules. 'I think he is somebody who puts his own liberty above everything,' Christian Dargnat, who became head of fundraising at En Marche, told me.[18] 'His decision to make a life with a woman 24 years older, breaking with his family, even if it wasn't a violent or definitive break; his choice to go to work for an investment bank, in order to give himself financial freedom: these are choices that fit the same logic, liberty,' said Ferracci. Each time, the gamble was immense; so was the freedom he procured.

Those early years revealed a rock-solid single-mindedness about Macron, mixed with extraordinary self-belief. This quest for freedom seems to have been partly about pursuing choices, but also about securing independence from others. Dartevelle made this point to me early on in our conversation. 'He doesn't like to owe people. Not the students, not the teachers. I think it has shaped his real self,' he said. 'He doesn't want to be owned.' The years between Macron's arrival in Paris and his marriage 13 years later were a time of stolen weekends in Amiens and Le Touquet and endless train journeys in and out of Paris from the Gare du Nord, of discovery and disappointment, and determination in the face of disapproval. Macron, presumably still wounded beneath that polished veneer, refers little to this period. But he told Anne Fulda, his biographer: 'It required the force of conviction.' His parents, he said, 'thought several times that it was going to stop. And did everything to make it do so.' The struggle 'was very hard', he said. 'There were family constraints on both sides ... That's what we lived through.'[19] The couple married on 20 October 2007 at the town hall in Le Touquet, a seaside resort of villas among pine trees and nautical-themed boutiques that lies on the northern French coast. His parents attended. But it was an elderly businessman named Henry Hermand, who had become a mentor to Macron in Paris, who sat at the top table and 'behaved like a father to him', noted his friend from ENA and fellow guest, Gaspard Gantzer.[20] In the speech Macron made at their wedding reception, held at the town's grand Westminster Hotel, he acknowledged the difficulties that he and Brigitte had gone through to get to this point. 'Every one of you has been witness over the past 13 years to what we have lived, and you have accepted it. You have made us what we are today.'

For a young man in a hurry, it took Macron more time than he had perhaps anticipated to settle on a professional track. Those who knew him when he first arrived in Paris expected the literary student to make a career as a writer, a playwright, or perhaps an actor. Something literary or cultural. To this day, Macron likes to keep a collection of poetry to hand, and can recite long passages from works of French literature, as he demonstrated to a surprised television reporter from Canal Plus when he was in government. Cornered after an event at the Finance Ministry, Macron was challenged to recite the part of the lovesick Alceste in the opening dialogue from Molière's *Le Misanthrope* – 'Leave me alone, I say, out of my sight!/I will be angry and I will not listen!' – and he did so on the spot. At the age of 17, living in a tiny *chambre de bonne* rented by his parents on the Paris left bank, Macron wrote an (unpublished) novel, *Babylone Babylone*, an epic set in Mexico in the sixteenth century at the time of the Spanish conquest that few have read besides his wife.[21]

Had Macron been accepted at the highly selective Ecole Normale Supérieure, his path might well have led in a more literary direction, as many of those who knew him at the time assumed it would. It was not until he arrived at Sciences Po that Macron was properly lined up for public life. By his third year, he had switched from international affairs to concentrate on public service, all the while studying in parallel for a philosophy degree at Nanterre. 'I wouldn't say then that he had the intention of pursuing a political career,' said Ferracci, his closest friend from Sciences Po days, whose first impression of Macron was of 'a Czech exchange student who hadn't seen a hairdresser in decades'.[22] Yet Macron was beginning to 'prepare for an engagement in public service', Ferracci told me, reading widely, and talking politics late into the night. As part of his philosophy degree, Macron wrote a dissertation on Hegel and the public interest and another on Machiavelli. His teacher on a course on 'the French state and its reform' at Sciences Po wrote in his report at the time: 'exceptional student from all points of view' and 'intellectual qualities out of the ordinary'. Not all of his friends were aware then quite what an encyclopaedic political knowledge he had also accumulated. A fellow student at the time was astonished to discover, on a visit to the National Assembly, that Macron knew the names of all the deputies and their constituencies.[23] Ferracci and Macron studied together for the entrance exam to ENA, staying up late discussing poetry, politics and their shared belief in a moderate social democratic centre-left. The bond lasted. Ferracci became a labour economist, policy adviser to En Marche and key architect of Macron's first labour reform as president.

By the time Macron left ENA, in 2004, the French machine for manufacturing its elite had taken over. Graduating fifth in his class, he was entitled to join the elite Inspection Générale des Finances, an inner corps of top *énarques* (ENA graduates) based at the Finance Ministry. This is both the core of the French techno-structure, the like-minded technical brains who run the country's administration, and a stable for a future high-flying career in politics, industry and finance. The list of *inspecteurs des finances* who have gone on to top posts includes Henri de Castries (former CEO of AXA), Frédéric Oudéa (CEO of Société Générale), Michel Rocard and Alain Juppé (former prime ministers), and Pascal Lamy (former head of the World Trade Organization). Alain Minc, yet another *inspecteur* and *eminence grise* of corporate Paris, told me that he first met Macron when the young *inspecteur des finances* sought his advice. 'I asked him where he would be in 30 years,' Minc told me. 'He said: president of the French Republic.'[24]

Some of Macron's friends at the time would have been surprised by such a boast. He has a way of compartmentalizing his interests and acquaintances. Some know little of the ambitions he confides to others. Whether or not Macron really believed it, or sought it, he spent the next decade building up a formidable network of contacts and mentors in Paris that would give him political options. 'It's extremely disagreeable to be with him in a crowded room,' another friend of his told me, 'because it's as if you don't exist.' Years later, in 2014, at a leaving party at the Elysée Palace for Macron after he had decided to quit his job as economic adviser to the president, François Hollande, who is disarmingly witty and self-deprecating in private, began his speech with the line: 'I am often introduced abroad as the man who works with Emmanuel Macron.'[25]

As is Macron's habit, the young *inspecteur des finances* charmed his elders, and this opened doors. Jean-Pierre Jouyet, whom President Macron later appointed French ambassador in London, was head of the *inspection* when the ENA graduate first turned up in the Finance Ministry, and told me that Macron was the one who stood out in what was a brilliant crop that year. He had as 'quick a mind' as the others, a 'better sense of empathy' and was 'the best all-rounder, with a knowledge of politics, literature and sport', Jouyet told me.[26] The pair soon developed what Jouyet fondly called a 'special relationship', sipping whisky together in the evening after work, and working out how to right France. The studied poise of the president belies an individual who is, in Jouyet's words, 'a real *bon vivant*'. What he avoided as a teenager he seems to have partly made up for as a student, or at least on certain mid-week evenings before he took off to see Brigitte. A friend from his time at ENA recalls evenings that began at a seedy bar near the campus, washed down with beer, cheap red wine and vodka.[27] Macron was known as 'the king of karaoke', said another student friend, and had a taste for French crooners and delivering heartfelt renditions of Johnny Hallyday's 'Que je t'aime'. He enjoyed lewd plays on words, and had no fear of acting like an idiot during karaoke sessions at Bunny's Bar in Strasbourg. Jouyet, the professional diplomat, put it to me this way: 'Emmanuel, he's not the sort to drink Coca-Cola.' When he joined the civil service, Macron was already toying, tentatively, with conventional politics. He raised with friends the possibility of standing for election to parliament as a Socialist, perhaps in Le Touquet, or alternatively in the Pyrenees, where his grandmother grew up. But, with candidate selection locked up by the barons of the Socialist Party, neither prospect came to anything.

Jouyet proved to be a powerful mentor for an ambitious networker who was learning fast how to operate the system. Before he turned 30, and on Jouyet's recommendation, Macron was appointed to be a *rapporteur* for a commission on economic growth set up by the newly elected President Nicolas Sarkozy in 2007. Run by Jacques Attali, one-time special adviser to President François Mitterrand, it was a golden opportunity to impress the capital's corporate and financial elite, from whose ranks its members were drawn. Serge Weinberg, a financier who sat on the commission, was among those who whispered Macron's name to David de Rothschild, who recruited him the following year to join Rothschild & Cie. The Attali Commission served at once as an incubator of policy ideas and an invaluable address book. 'It was obvious that he was bright, very cultured, had a deep mind, and that he would go far,' said Jacques Delpla, an economist at the Toulouse School of Economics, who first met Macron when they sat together on the commission: 'But it didn't cross my mind that he would go into politics. I saw him more as a future director of the Treasury.'[28] Mathieu Laine, a liberal intellectual and friend of Macron's who met him after he joined Rothschild's, had the same impression. 'He was smart and charming and we got on immediately,' he told me. 'But at the time I never thought for a moment that he'd become president!'[29]

In the four years that Macron spent at Rothschild's, on the Avenue de Messine in the 8th arrondissement of Paris, a neighbourhood of wide tree-lined avenues and Hausmannian corporate offices, Macron acquired the codes and applied the practices of the unforgiving world of corporate finance. He wore cufflinks, carried a Blackberry, and learned the hard way how to craft a deal. What did he take away from those years at Rothschild, besides a fat pay packet and the future political burden of having to defend his earnings? In an interview in 2010 with the Sciences Po alumni magazine, Macron said that he had been drawn to investment banking because it required 'analytical capacities, judgement and reactivity', and was 'more free and entrepreneurial' than a career industry would have been. Money, he claimed, 'isn't the alpha and omega of everything. I don't make a fetish out of money nor have a hypocritical relationship with it. I don't consider it scandalous to earn it.'[30] Rothschild & Cie Paris is an influential bank, with tight links to the French establishment. Georges Pompidou worked there for the better part of a decade before becoming Charles de Gaulle's prime minister and then successor as president. Run by the patrician David de Rothschild, who built it up after Mitterrand nationalized the original family banking group in 1981, it blends a cultural discretion with a corporate ruthlessness. François Henrot, the bank's managing partner, who said that he had been impressed by Macron's 'extraordinary' intellectual capacities when he interviewed him for the job, was less flattering about the nature of the work. At Rothschild's, he told a French documentary, 'you learn the art of negotiation' as well as how to 'communicate, that's to say, tell a story. So one learns here, in a way, the techniques of, how should I put it, not the manipulation of opinion but, well, sort of.'[31] Macron himself put it more bluntly in an interview when he was economy minister: 'You're a sort of prostitute. Seduction is the job.'[32]

The timing of Macron's arrival at Rothschild's, in September 2008, was awkward. Ten days later, Lehman Brothers collapsed. The banking world was in turmoil. Work in mergers and acquisitions dried up as finance went into crisis mode. The debutant banker spent months working on ideas that went nowhere.

Macron was 'bullied' by some of the partners, one fellow banker from the time told me, because of their misgivings about the know-it-all technocrats they would see turning up from the Finance Ministry. He was also thoroughly ignorant about corporate financial analysis. 'He knew nothing about financial modelling, or accounting, and had a hard time from many of the partners who distrusted the bright young things from the Finance Ministry,' the same banker told me. A former colleague recalled that 'He didn't know what EBITDA [earnings before interest, tax, depreciation and amortization] was. He didn't try to hide it. And instead of looking it up in a corporate finance book, he asked around, which was disarming.'[33]

Yet Macron, it turned out, was good at the job. He employed his charm, leveraged his contacts, and revelled in the liberty that Rothschild's gave its young associates. Colleagues from the time recall, among other things, his courteous and friendly manner towards staff, whether on the front desk or in the boardroom. He was also quite capable of playing the cynical game, to the consternation of journalists from *Le Monde*, whom he had promised to help find a financial backer for the paper.[34] Believing him to be on their side, they were persuaded by Macron to delay a decent takeover option, at a time when he was also close to those preparing a rival bid. By the time Macron decided to leave Rothschild's, in 2012, he had a mega deal under his belt, having helped to negotiate Nestlé's purchase for $11.8 billion of Pfizer's baby-food business, using a connection with Nestlé's boss, Peter Brabeck, that he had made on the Attali Commission, and pocketing around €1 million that year for himself in the process.

Those four years revealed qualities that Macron went on later to employ in public life: an ability to think ahead and see the big picture; a capacity to create and exploit opportunities, and take risks; and a determination, bordering on ruthlessness. While at Rothschild's, Macron was also beginning to engineer a move into political life. He had acquired a priceless Paris address book, and was proving deft at using it. His friend

Jouyet, who had graduated from ENA in the same year as François Hollande, a long-time Socialist Party hack with the look of a provincial accountant, encouraged the young banker to consider Hollande's chances of winning the presidency. Macron took the tip, made himself indispensable to Hollande and, in 2012, stepped into his top-floor corner office at the Elysée Palace as deputy secretary-general to the newly elected Socialist president.

Number 55 rue du Faubourg Saint-Honoré, the seat of the French presidency, was a long way from Henriville, Amiens. The two years that Macron spent as presidential adviser under Hollande, during which I first met him, followed by another two as his economy minister, served as confirmation that the provincial outsider had become the ultimate insider. In his professional life, Macron had put himself at the heart of the French establishment. In his private life, he divided his time between Paris and the seaside villa at Le Touquet. Most members of his family no longer lived in Amiens. His mother had moved to Paris after her divorce from Jean-Michel Macron, long after their children had grown up. His father, who remarried, was the only one of his immediate family to still reside in Amiens, in the house at Henriville where Macron grew up. Various members of Brigitte Macron's family remained in Amiens, and indeed still run the Trogneux chocolate business, which has a boutique in the city centre selling ribbon-wrapped boxes of homemade truffles and macaroons. But her adult children also left to settle elsewhere, and family reunions usually took place in Le Touquet. Macron, said one acquaintance from Amiens days, 'became more of an Auzière than a Macron'. Amiens belonged to the past. 'Macron rarely comes back. He launched his campaign here, but it was just publicity,' Brigitte Fouré, the centre-right mayor of Amiens, declared during the 2017 election campaign. Macron had left too young to have had any involvement in local politics. He seldom visited. The connection to the town was remote.

It was politics, in the end, that brought Macron back to Amiens. On 6 April 2016 he launched En Marche in this Picardy city, a place it suited him to reclaim. A year later, Amiens was again the backdrop for Macron's political ambitions, during a visit between the two rounds of the presidential election that became a turning point in the campaign. I went up to cover the visit; what happened that day felt then like the moment that finally revealed the full measure of the candidate.

Macron was in a duel against Marine Le Pen, the gravelly-voiced far-right leader. Champion of working-class voters, she promised to stop factories from closing, and jobs from disappearing, by shutting France's borders. The city's gritty industrial vulnerability made it an awkward home turf for Macron. Le Pen pilloried him as the agent of 'savage globalization', 'arrogant finance' and the rootless metropolitan elite, ill-placed to understand the working man's troubles. Amiens was fast becoming part of left-behind France, a reminder of a once-muscular industrial past. Its unemployment rate, at 12 per cent, was above the national average. The city had lost a mattress factory and a tyre plant. The Whirlpool factory, where 286 workers manufactured tumble dryers, was threatened with closure too. Over the previous 15 years, the plant had already shed three-quarters of its workers. Now it planned to shift production to lower-cost Poland, leaving workers angry and betrayed. The city's troubles, in short, put Macron's pro-European creed of open borders and corporate freedom sorely to the test.

Earlier in the campaign, Macron had said that he was not in the business of making false promises about keeping factories from closing: 'we need to protect individuals,' he said, 'we shouldn't protect jobs'. But pressure was building on the candidate to show that he nonetheless cared about the plight of '*les Whirlpool*', as the workers at the plant in his home town were known. So Macron scheduled a campaign stop in Amiens on 26 April, and I went along. The day began dismally. As he sat down with union leaders in a meeting room at the Chamber of Commerce in the city centre, Le Pen staged an ambush. Turning up unannounced at the Whirlpool factory gates on the outskirts of the town, she claimed to be fighting for 'the workers' while Macron was defending 'the oligarchy'. Triumphant images of her on the picket line with delighted unionists began to fill the 24-hour news channels, and selfies of her with Whirlpool employees spread on Twitter.

Macron was livid. Behind closed doors, his team thrashed out a plan. They could not let Le Pen's visit upstage his. But security worries made it too dangerous for Macron to go to the factory, an adviser warned. Macron was having none of it. 'It's not the security guys we should be listening to,' he declared furiously. 'I will never be safe, because that's how the country is right now. So we need to take the risk. We need to go to the heart of the beast each time.' Then he dealt a cruel blow. 'If you listen to the security guys you end up like Hollande. Maybe you are safe, but you are dead.'[35]

So a campaign stop was hastily scheduled at the factory that afternoon. It was a brave decision. The gates to the plant lie down a side road, wedged up along the railway tracks. As I and the other reporters there that day approached on foot, plumes of black smoke rose from burning tyres. Unionists in fluorescent jackets awaited Macron's arrival in a menacing, muscular block. The acrid stink of charred rubber hung in the air. Angry workers were blowing whistles, distributed by FN activists. They had installed an effigy of a coffin. 'We don't expect anything of Macron, he's just the continuation of Hollande,' Jean Santerre, a worker at the factory for 23 years, told me angrily. 'What's he going to do for us? Nothing.' He and his colleagues would vote for Le Pen, he said, because at least she had a solution: 'shut the borders', and stop foreigners taking French jobs.

Sure enough, when the besuited Macron stepped from his car, he was jeered and whistled. His security team slowly reversed his black official car all the way down the narrow lane leading to the picket line, just in case. 'I was watching on my screen and I said to myself: it's not possible, he's going to get punched in the face,' Christian Dargnat, En Marche's fundraiser, told me months later. Yet what happened next surprised most of those present. For nearly an hour, and to the clear discomfort of his security guards, the candidate, still in his dark suit and tie, waded into the edgy crowd. Visibly wound up, his voice indignant, he took on the abuse, arguing his case, refusing to make empty promises. 'I can't tell you I'm going to save your jobs,' Macron told them. 'The response to what is happening to you is not to stop globalization nor to close our borders … Don't make this mistake. People who say that are lying … After closing the borders, what happens? Thousands of jobs that depend on them being open are lost.' Retraining would be improved, he said, buy-out options would be examined. By the time Macron drove off, Santerre and his friends had not changed their minds. But calm had returned, and with it a certain respect for the candidate.

That evening, Le Pen's selfies with smiling workers did grab the news headlines. Yet the moment seemed nonetheless to offer a telling insight. Although a poll suggested that 60 per cent of voters would vote for Macron, only 37 per cent thought at the time that he had presidential stature. He had often appeared more ambiguous than decisive, more cerebral than tough. Even in France, which treats public intellectuals like national treasures, his erudite vocabulary and measured reasoning were much mocked. At rallies, Macron had a tendency to drown his audience with abstract nouns. When he finally told an anecdote onstage in Paris during a long speech just days before the Amiens visit, it had been all about a philosopher. Nobody doubted Macron's intellectual capacities. If there were reservations about his ability to lead France, they concerned, rather, his untested political resolve. Faced with a fractured country and restless unions, would he have what it took to stave off, or withstand, revolt?

Macron's return to Amiens that spring day in the closing stages of the campaign hinted at an answer. It revealed a steelier, more fearless leader than many had reckoned with. A fraught encounter at the Whirlpool factory in the campaign's dying moments, between a former banker in a tailored suit and the victims of the forces of globalization, could so easily have turned to disaster. He put his physical security on the line, and did not flinch. He laid out his economic reasoning to those least likely to accept it, and stuck to it. This was a risk Macron was prepared to take, and one that turned out to his advantage.

So Macron did return to Amiens. His home town that day transformed a candidate into a president-in-waiting. Amiens was indeed too small for Macron. He outgrew the city, and its conventions. Yet in the end he needed it, a contradiction that seems apt for a scholar-president who embodies so many. Macron's journey from the working Picardy city to the heart of the capital's political elite was one of defiance, of tension between convention and rebellion, and a quest for total liberty. In the end, a refusal to play by the rules, and a resistance to the disapproval of others, pushed Macron out of provincial Amiens – and into the most improbable political adventure that France had witnessed for over half a century.

2

LE DISRUPTEUR

'If we want a modernizing agenda, we need to put together two-thirds of the Socialist Party, all of the centrists, and part of the centre-right. That would give us a pro-European market-friendly majority in favour of modernizing the social model.'

Emmanuel Macron to the author, June 2015

The annual Bastille Day military parade along the Avenue des Champs-Elysées, to mark the country's founding revolutionary moment, is a tightly choreographed and usually sober display of troops, tanks and fighter planes. It is France's opportunity to put on an unapologetic muscular parade, and remind the world, or perhaps itself, that it is still a country to be reckoned with. When Emmanuel Macron invited Donald Trump to be his guest of honour for his first parade as president in 2017, he treated his guest to a surprise finale that seemed to delight the host as much as it left his American visitor baffled. The top French military band, their trombones and trumpets darting about in a frantic dance sequence, broke into an improbable, hilarious and high-camp rendition of Daft Punk's 'Get Lucky'. It could have been the soundtrack to Macron's run for the presidency.

Macron owed his election, in part, to an incredible run of good luck. At the end of 2016, just eight months after he launched En Marche and with only four months to go before the first-round vote, the electoral novice was languishing far behind the two leading contenders for the presidency. François Fillon, a tweedy former prime minister standing for the conservative Republicans, was firmly in the lead on 26 per cent, followed closely by Marine

Le Pen, on 24 per cent. Macron was trailing on 13 per cent, merely one of a cluster of possible third-placed candidates. After the disappointments of the Hollande Socialist presidency, the election at that point looked set to turn into a run-off between the right and far right. Indeed, this was precisely the calculation that Sarkozy had made, and which prompted him to return to politics in 2014 from the lecture circuit to mount what turned out to be a failed bid for the Republican primary. Since no poll at the start of 2017 suggested that Le Pen would be able to beat Fillon, the boulevard, as the French would put it, was wide open for the Republican candidate.

Yet towards the end of January 2017 a parliamentary pay-roll scandal broke that was to damage fatally the poll favourite. Fillon's candidacy collapsed, Macron established himself as a credible contender, and by the end of that month he had over-taken the Republican in the polls. From early March the gap he opened up would never close. On 23 April the debutant out-sider who had never run for elected office topped the first-round voting with 24 per cent. In second place on 21 per cent came Le Pen. Fillon crashed out of the race altogether. The liberal inter-nationalist with the upbeat message faced the glowering far-right nationalist in a second-round run-off that upped the stakes, but also narrowed the odds on Macron. Two weeks later, after she put in a disastrous performance during a televised debate, he was elected president.

* * *

Before appointing his generals, Napoleon would ask whether they were lucky. Macron's 'coup d'état against the party system', wrote Jean-Dominique Merchet, a military analyst, referring to the power grab that brought Napoleon Bonaparte to power as First Consul of France, 'was a slow-motion 18 Brumaire, with its dose of lucky amateurism and muddled opportunism'.[1] Fortune indeed seemed to favour the young man from La Providence. He appeared to know it too. With Macron, no symbol is without its purpose, and the choice of 'Get Lucky' on Bastille Day seemed to say it all.

Macron's run of good luck had in fact begun three years before the 2017 election campaign, on a hot August day in a quiet corner of rural Burgundy, when a tall, dashing politician taunted President Hollande. Over dishes of locally reared chicken at a summer festival in the village of Frangy-en-Bresse, known as the Fête de la Rose, Arnaud Montebourg was in his element. The jovial economy minister was far from the corridors of government. The sun was strong, and the local burgundy was flowing. The wine list that day included bottles of specially labelled *cuvée du redressement*, a mocking reference to what Montebourg denounced as his government's budgetary austerity policy and its alignment with the 'obsessions' of the German centre-right. 'I'm going to send a good bottle of *cuvée du redressement* to the president,' declared Montebourg to the assembled television cameras, visibly amused by his own joke. It was 'a declaration of war', said an adviser to Hollande.[2] The next day, on 25 August 2014, Montebourg was fired, and Macron was summoned from holiday to take his place.

Montebourg's reckless moment of irreverence in the heat of the Burgundy summer opened up space for Macron in government, and propelled the unknown technocrat into the public eye. At that time, three years before the presidential election, the script looked set for the ballot in 2017 to end up as a re-run of 2012, and a contest between the same three main candidates: Hollande, the unloved portly president who took office promising to be 'normal'; Nicolas Sarkozy, the indomitable former president who had earned a reputation as the 'king of bling'; and Marine Le Pen, the strident, peroxide-haired daughter of Jean-Marie Le Pen, founder of the far-right National Front (FN). Macron, like many of his generation, was disturbed by this prospect, and what it said about political paralysis in France. When I went to see him at the Elysée Palace in June 2014, as he was packing up his boxes, he said: 'If Sarkozy and Hollande are the two candidates in 2017, there will be a political crisis in France.'[3] Perhaps Macron was already thinking about the opportunity for an upset that such a crisis might bring. If he was, he certainly didn't say so. In any case, for most observers at the time, the candidates in reserve on the left and the right, should Hollande or Sarkozy flounder, were already identified. If there was a young, modernist challenger to Hollande on the left, it was Manuel Valls, the reformist centre-left moderate and brooding Spanish-born prime minister, who had been plucked from the Interior Ministry to run the government earlier that year. If there was a less abrasive alternative to the hyperactive Sarkozy on the centre-right, it was Alain Juppé, the aloof, rather stiff former prime minister and popular mayor of Bordeaux, the elegant city on the Garonne river.

What happened, instead, was a catalogue of twists beyond the hopes of any of Macron's campaign team. It involved a serial run of unexpected decisions, judgements and events that, one by one, turned out to the young minister's advantage.

For the first time ever, both the Republicans and the Socialists, the two political families that had between them shared power over the previous six decades, chose to hold presidential primaries open to the general public, in order to select their candidate for 2017. Each did Macron a huge favour, selecting an unlikely nominee, more suited to the extreme wing of their respective base. In November 2016, against all the odds, Republican voters selected as their nominee François Fillon, an inscrutable third man who had been considered a rank outsider only weeks before the vote. To understand his appeal, and how the secretive figure with the look of a country squire had seized the nomination, I went out to the little town of La Ferté-Bernard in La Sarthe, in rural western France. With its gently sloping hills and medieval churches, the charms of La Sarthe, where the son of a provincial notary grew up, are as discreet as its people. La Ferté-Bernard has an active parish and scout group, and rabbit was on the *menu du jour* at Le Dauphin restaurant. Volunteers at Secours Catholique, a charity, helped to distribute warm clothes, tinned food and weekly homework for families in difficulty. 'People here say that they know things have to change, and that it will be difficult,' Jean-Carles Grelier, then the town's centre-right mayor, told me: 'They are fed up with being sold dreams, and then being disappointed.' In the café opposite the church, locals mentioned Fillon's 'common sense' and 'honesty'. On the wall of the mayor's office hung a photo of the visit to La Ferté-Bernard by Charles de Gaulle, the last French president to come to the town, and whose image Fillon kept on his bedroom wall as a child.

With his thick eyebrows and forlorn gaze, Fillon had stood out during his time as prime minister in 2007–12 under Nicolas Sarkozy for his loyalty, and his ability to endure life in the shadow of a hot-blooded president whose aides nicknamed him 'Mister Nobody'. He was both a solid rural traditionalist – a wife, five children, a manor house, horse and stables – and an adrenalin-seeker. His brother ran the Le Mans racetrack, and Fillon was an amateur racing driver, drawn to the thrill of top speeds. In some respects, he was an odd choice in 2016 for an essentially conservative Republican party. He ran on a radically liberal economic programme, vowing to shrink the country's labour code from over 3,000 pages to just 150 and end the 35-hour working week, unapologetically invoking Britain's Margaret Thatcher, an unusual reference point in a country with a lingering suspicion of free markets and a deep reverence for the state. During the primary campaign, his rival Juppé, who was by then the favourite to win both the nomination and the presidency, warned of the 'brutality' of Fillon's economic programme.

Yet Fillon's promises to restore respect to the presidency, freedom to the economy and firmness to social policy resonated with the traditional right, which turned out en masse during the primary to make sure that his name would be the one on the presidential ballot. The election was open to anybody who turned up on the day, paid two euros, and signed a charter supporting the values of the 'right and the centre'. Fillon's parliamentary vote against the legalization of gay marriage in 2013, his disapproval of adoption by gay couples, and his declaration of war against 'Islamic totalitarianism' all chimed in particular with the party's highly mobilized conservative wing, and Sens Commun, a Catholic ultra-traditionalist movement active in politics. For this provincial conservative part of the electorate,

Juppé was too socially liberal and centrist, Sarkozy too volatile and rough-edged. The mood at Fillon's rallies, which drew disproportionate numbers of grey-haired supporters and Barbour jackets, was polite rather than feverish. The candidate, a model of self-control and poise during the primary debates, was above all regarded on the right as a safe pair of hands for France. He eliminated the former president, Sarkozy, in the first round of voting, and then the 71-year-old former prime minister, Juppé, in the second.

Two months later, the Socialists sprung their own surprise. Until the autumn of 2016, Hollande kept his option to seek re-election open. No healthy modern French president had failed to run again. Every one of Hollande's four predecessors had done so: Valéry Giscard d'Estaing (defeated in 1981), François Mitterrand (re-elected in 1988), Jacques Chirac (re-elected in 2002) and Nicolas Sarkozy (defeated in 2012). As late as October, close aides urged Hollande not to give up, telling him: 'François, you no longer have a choice. You have to be a candidate.'[4] Yet the Socialist president's chances were evaporating fast. His popularity had sunk to record lows. No poll suggested that Hollande could even make it into the presidential run-off in 2017. He faced a choice between two humiliations: declining to run again, or standing and facing first-round defeat.

In the end, Hollande was disqualified not only by the mediocrity of his performance, and the plunge in poll ratings this generated, but by his own indiscretion. In October 2016 two French reporters published a 662-page book, *Un président ne devrait pas dire ça* (*A President Shouldn't Say That*), based on over four years and a hundred hours of recorded interviews with the Socialist president, for which they had met him at the Elysée Palace, or over dinner at their homes.[5] In the book, Hollande insulted fellow Socialist politicians, called the judiciary a 'cowardly institution' and the national football team 'badly brought-up kids'. *En passant*, he admitted to having authorized four targeted killings by the French secret service. Friends of Hollande say he had been too trusting of the reporters, too happy to gossip with them, persuaded that the book would be a flattering testament to his record. Instead, it destroyed him.

Within days, the president had dispatched eight letters of apology – to bodies representing judges, magistrates and prosecutors – claiming that his comments bore 'no relation to the reality of my thinking'. A poll by Ipsos, taken just after the book's publication, recorded Hollande's approval rating at a staggeringly low 4 per cent. His friends, seeing him in a hole, handed him a spade. Manuel Valls spoke publicly of his 'anger', and his deputies' 'shame'. That a president seeking re-election could engage in such a politically suicidal exercise left his allies dumbstruck, and his political future in freefall. On 1 December 2016 Hollande delivered a live television address. He was 'conscious of the risks' that his candidacy would present, he said, and so would not be seeking re-election. His aides watched the sad spectacle in silence; his assistants were in tears. Days later, Valls confidently gathered his supporters in Evry, the multicultural *banlieue* south of Paris where he had cut his political teeth as mayor, and threw his hat into the ring. The En Marche team met at headquarters to listen to their boss via speakerphone: 'This was an impeachment from the inside,' Macron judged. 'If there's a traitor, someone who shot Hollande, it's Valls.'[6]

Just as the Republicans handed Macron the gift of a divisive rival candidate who leaned towards their party's extreme right, so the Socialists followed suit. In January 2017 seven candidates ran for the nomination, three of them with a good chance of victory. One was Valls, who led the first-round polls but struggled to fill his town-hall meetings. The other two were left-wingers: Arnaud Montebourg, the insubordinate former economy minister who had promised to send Hollande the bottle of burgundy, and Benoît Hamon, a former education minister advised by the economist Thomas Piketty, who believed in a post-productive economy and advocated a universal minimum income financed by a tax on robots. Had Valls, with his Blairite economic policy and tough line on law and order, secured the Socialist nomination, his reformist centre-left pitch would have cramped Macron's space. Yet, as ever, Macron got lucky. Carried by a wave of left-wing Socialist protest at Valls's authoritarian streak, Hamon squeezed out Montebourg in the first round, and then roundly beat Valls in the run-off. Over the course of just two months, between November 2016 and January 2017, a presidential election that had been shaping up to offer a re-run of 2012 was defying every page of the script.

The upshot was an unusually wide empty space in the unfashionable political centre, and a broad swathe of the centrist French electorate – those drawn to Juppé on the right, or to Valls on the left – who felt thoroughly disenfranchised. This opened up improbably promising territory for the En Marche candidate. On the left, Hamon led a pallid campaign, which spoke chiefly to his narrow metropolitan, environmentally friendly base – those who cycled and recycled – but failed to catch the broader electorate's imagination. The Socialist ended up with just 6 per cent of the first-round vote at the presidential election, the party's worst score since 1969. On the right, meanwhile, Fillon supplied Macron with his next, and most stunning, piece of good luck – by driving into a wall.

In a series of articles beginning on 25 January 2017, *Le Canard Enchaîné*, a satirical newspaper, dropped a bombshell. Over the years, it revealed, Fillon had employed on the parliamentary payroll his wife, Penelope, and two of his adult children, to the total accumulated tune of nearly €1 million, in what became known as *Penelopegate*. The former prime minister protested his innocence, charged his accusers with 'misogyny', yet failed to come up with convincing evidence that his wife had done substantial work for all these payments. It was a devastating revelation. The solemn Fillon had not only been the favourite for the presidency, but had based his campaign on moral probity and economic rigour. One cannot lead France, he declared during the Republicans' primary campaign, unless one is 'beyond reproach'. Now he was himself the subject of a judicial investigation. His electorate were dismayed. 'We're all in shock,' Sylvianne Bessière, a retired air hostess told me, at a Fillon rally on the outskirts of Paris in late

January. 'I didn't expect it from him. I thought he was a man of integrity. And he's got the best programme.' As more revelations followed, including the news that Fillon had accepted the gift of tailored suits worth €13,000 from a lawyer known for his web of links to African leaders, the party was speechless. His resignation as Republican candidate, just months from the election, was suddenly on the cards.

Yet, as the revelations rolled in, Fillon continued to insist that he had done nothing wrong. He would not resign as nominee, he told TF1 television evening news, unless he was *mis en examen*, meaning that preliminary charges would have to be brought against him. On 1 March, less than two months before voting day, judges informed him that this would happen; Fillon clung on all the same. His team began to fall apart. Fillon's priestly-looking campaign director, Patrick Stefanini, resigned in dismay. Leading Republican figures, including Bruno Le Maire, who went on to become Macron's finance minister, deserted him. A senior Republican told me that he and a colleague went to see Fillon to try to 'unplug him'. But Fillon would have none of it. Nor was Sarkozy willing to push him out because, a friend of the former president told me, he did not want his lifelong rival Juppé to step in. There was too much bitterness between them all. On 5 March 2017, Fillon mounted a last-minute show of force at an open-air rally at the Trocadéro in Paris, the Eiffel Tower as a backdrop, and with the help of Sens Commun and the anti-gay-marriage movement. The turnout was impressive, kept Fillon in the race, and prompted Juppé to rule himself out as a back-up. But it was too late to rescue Fillon. Macron had overtaken him in the polls. By April, Fillon was ignominiously eliminated in the first round, beaten by Le Pen.

It remains a mystery how exactly *Le Canard Enchaîné* got hold of the Fillon revelations. Old-fashioned digging in Fillon's constituency, claimed the satirical paper. Unbeknown to Fillon's own campaign director, its reporters had started to question the Republican candidate back in November 2016. Robert Bourgi, the Franco-Lebanese lawyer close to Sarkozy who had offered

Fillon his tailored suits, told a French documentary that he fed the information about the suits directly to the press in order to destroy Fillon. Whatever the manoeuvrings and intrigue that led to Fillon's demise, Macron was the clear beneficiary. After eliminating Fillon, Macron found himself in a run-off against Marine Le Pen, France's deadliest but most beatable candidate.

In the preceding years, the third and last daughter of Jean-Marie Le Pen had emerged as what looked like a politically classy act, and was all the scarier for it. Her bombastic father, all bluster, paranoia and red-blooded xenophobia, was always ready to launch into an offensive diatribe, repeating as recently as 2015 his claim that the Nazi gas chambers were a mere 'detail' of the history of the Second World War. In a dual attempt to free herself from her father's shadow, and her party from his jack-booted and anti-Semitic thugs, Marine Le Pen had embarked on a strategy of *dédiabolisation* (de-demonization) to try to turn a toxic fringe movement with neo-Nazi links into a 'patriotic' party of government. To that end, she was generally more careful in her use of language than other European ultra-nationalists. Geert Wilders, her counterpart in the Netherlands and leader of the anti-immigrant Party for Freedom (PVV), called Islam 'the ideology of a retarded culture', and the Koran 'fascist'. Marine Le Pen, by contrast, appealed to shared French secular values by denouncing 'Islamification', rather than Islam. 'I don't believe that Islam is incompatible with Western values,' she said in 2011. 'But sharia law is, and that's what fundamentalists want to impose in France.'[7]

Marine Le Pen knew full well the power of the symbol. She was taken to court, although acquitted, for comparing Muslims praying in the street to the Occupation. But for the most part she focused on building a veneer of respectability. She dressed in sharp skirts and high heels, stepping from her black car like a rock star when she turned up to campaign. The girl who grew up in a mansion behind wrought-iron gates in Saint-Cloud, perched on a bluff west of Paris, turned into a champion of the forgotten. Her ear for a simple slogan –'They built Europe on

coal and steel; now there's no more coal and no more steel!'
or 'While they are fighting against the FN, we are fighting for
the French!' – turned her rallies into a strange form of family
entertainment. On a Saturday evening in 2015 at the municipal
theatre in Saint-Quentin, a town in the flat plains of the Somme,
I watched Marine Le Pen onstage. 'Left, right, right, left,' she
called out, mimicking the beat of a metronome: 'They both want
to put France to sleep!' About half the faces in the audience were
female, and almost all white. One couple had brought their three
little girls, who sat patiently twirling their hair as the FN leader
did her stand-up routine. Backstage after her speech, while FN
activists sipped champagne from white plastic cups, and anti-FN
protestors gathered in the street outside, she sat nonchalantly on
the dressing table, swinging her legs and puffing on an electronic
cigarette. Three satsumas were perched inside her open black
handbag. Was she ever worried about her own safety, I asked
her? With a chillingly steady gaze, she replied: 'I am imperme-
able to fear.' Jean-Marie Le Pen sought controversy, not power.
Marine Le Pen, it seemed, wanted to govern.

Until the last moment, she ran a smart presidential campaign
in 2017, taking her message to small villages and rural areas,
winning over the working-class vote, although her position on
the euro – did she really want to take France out of it? – always
looked deeply confused. At any rate, her performance was good
enough to carry her into the run-off. Then on 3 May, during the
second-round televised presidential debate, she self-destructed.
Dressed in a navy trouser suit, a pile of multi-coloured paper files
before her and a rigid smile on her face, Marine Le Pen seemed
to lose it. Like the Dobermans her father keeps in the garden
of his villa, and which she once accused of killing one of her
beloved cats, Le Pen attacked, putting on a display of increasingly deranged aggression that cruelly exposed how unfit she was
to govern, and left even her own team baffled. Macron's campaign arguments had been 'shameful', she said, and revealed
the 'coldness of the banker' he had never ceased to be. He was
the candidate of 'savage globalization' and 'indulgent to Islamic

fundamentalism'. 'I hope we won't learn that you have an offshore account in the Bahamas!' she declared. Macron pushed back, but kept his calm. 'Don't play the professor with me,' Le Pen pleaded at one point, while he pointed out that she had confused two big French industrial firms: 'one makes phones, the other makes turbines'. 'France,' he told her, 'deserves better than you.'

Months later, Le Pen recognized that she blew it. What made the former lawyer put on such a display? Was she exhausted? Did she panic at the prospect of having to defend France's withdrawal from the euro, a policy her party subsequently dropped? Had she been too much under the sway of advisers who told her to provoke Macron to lose his nerve, as reports subsequently suggested? Or, in the end, did she find the prospect of power too frightening? Whatever the reason, she put in a calamitous performance, and Macron held steady. Four days later he was elected president.

So fortune favoured the candidate more than he could have reasonably hoped. 'He is phenomenally talented and stands head and shoulders above the others of his generation. But to this day I tell him: never forget that you've had a lot of luck,' Mathieu Laine, the liberal intellectual and early backer of Macron's bid, told me. 'It's never just a matter of talent.' As an insurgent outsider, Macron was also the beneficiary of the French two-round presidential system that makes it possible, in a crowded field, to get into the second round with just a fifth of the total vote. A place in the run-off can hinge on a tiny number of votes. When Jean-Marie Le Pen beat the Socialists' Lionel Jospin into the second round in 2002, he did so by a margin of fewer than 200,000 votes. In 2017 Macron secured 24 per cent – less than his two immediate predecessors, but more than Chirac managed in both 1995 and 2002, and only a little below the 25.9 per cent that François Mitterrand scored when the Socialist made history in 1981. The lucky gambler became president under a system in which he was the first choice of less than a quarter of voters.

Yet, for all the luck that came his way, it would be a misreading of the presidential election of 2017 to argue that Macron owed his victory only to chance. The candidate was dealt a good hand.

But he also shaped his own chances, seized opportunities as they opened up, and created new ones when he needed them. In this sense, he was a gambler too. 'There were a lot of people who argued that French society was ready for change. But the only one who actually did it, and knew he had to do it differently, was him. He dared to take risks where others didn't,' Christian Dargnat, the fundraiser, said: 'A lot of people accept the existing framework, are used to the fact that there is one. Emmanuel dared to break out of the framework. His life is a series of transgressions.'[8]

Macron's path to the presidency was in fact marked by five audacious bets, placed over a period of six years, which positioned him for the lucky turns that came his way. Had Macron not moved early to put himself in the race, the weaknesses of the mainstream candidates in early 2017 might have led to a far darker outcome for France.

The first of these dates back to 2010, when the young investment banker was making his mark at Rothschild's, and considering a possible return to public service, or a run for parliament. At a dinner hosted by the Paris financier Serge Weinberg – which was attended by members of the capital's *gauche caviar*, or left-leaning financial elite – Jean-Pierre Jouyet, Macron's former boss, came across his protégé. Jouyet took him into a corner and asked him what he wanted to do. Macron replied that he was thinking of looking for a constituency in which to run for parliament as a Socialist candidate, possibly in the Pyrenees, where he had family roots. Jouyet was supportive. But, he told me, 'I recommended that he join François Hollande'. The prospects and political skills of the man who had been the leader of the Socialist Party for 11 years until 2008, Jouyet judged, were underrated and could make him a smart bet.

At the time, the expectation in France was that Dominique Strauss-Kahn, the wealthy silver-haired former finance minister with rock-star appeal in Paris, would quit his job running the International Monetary Fund in Washington D.C., and return to France to run in the primary. Polls consistently showed that, with his international stature and reputation for centre-left reformism, the IMF boss was well placed to win the nomination, and beat Sarkozy in the 2012 presidential election. Hollande, by contrast, looked like a primary loser. A balding, portly party hack, he was dismissed by one colleague as a 'woodland strawberry' and nicknamed 'Flanby' after a caramel pudding. One poll, in December 2010, put Hollande on just 3 per cent for the Socialist primary the following year. 'The key weakness of François Hollande is inaction,' Ségolène Royal, his former partner and herself a defeated presidential candidate in 2007, sneered to *Le Figaro*: 'Can the French point to a single thing that he has achieved in 30 years of politics?'

Jouyet and Hollande had been friends since their days together on the benches of ENA, in the graduating class of 1980 that included Royal too, and Macron had already met the former Socialist Party boss at a dinner at Jacques Attali's home. Macron had also suspected that Strauss-Kahn's personal wealth would make him a problematic candidate for the Socialist Party. So he offered his services to the Socialist outsider, Hollande. 'He's a risk-taker,' Alain Minc told me, and one with a preference for a particular sort of punt: 'He prefers to put a bet on a high-risk, high-return option.'[9] The gamble paid off, and sooner than expected. On 14 May 2011, Strauss-Kahn was arrested in New York, hauled off a plane, and later charged with the sexual assault of a maid in a Manhattan hotel room. The charges were later dropped in return for an undisclosed agreement, but the affair wrecked his political future and threw the Socialist primary race wide open. That October, at a popular primary vote that was open to any Socialist supporter for the first time, Hollande secured the party nomination with 57 per cent of the second-round vote, putting himself well ahead in the race for the presidency the following year. Macron made himself indispensable to the nominee, organizing his working groups on economic policy, which would meet after hours in La Rotonde, Macron's local brasserie on the boulevard du Montparnasse. When Hollande was elected, Macron was the natural choice to become economic adviser at the Elysée Palace.

Backing Hollande early on was either far-sighted, or lucky, or both. But it was only one of several high-risk punts that Macron took. The second was his decision two years later, in 2014, to leave his plum job as deputy secretary-general at the Elysée, considered to be among the best posts in the French administration. It was a surprising choice for a driven young aide with ambitions for office, and I recall thinking at the time that something about the decision just didn't quite add up. In his coveted position at the heart of French power, Macron had the ear of the president, and belonged to a small circle of three or four advisers who took pretty much all the decisions between them. At a young age, he also acted as 'sherpa', preparing the big international leaders' meetings, a position that secured him vital contacts in the chancelleries and cabinet offices of the world's biggest powers, as well as a ringside seat from which to observe global affairs. It was a job of unusual influence. Yet Macron sensed that his prospects under Hollande had narrowed. He felt that it was increasingly difficult to make his voice heard. 'We need finer execution, and a more precise and clearer line,' he told me in 2013, visibly dissatisfied.[10] The following year he was passed over for two big jobs – as chief of staff to the president, a post that went to his former boss Jouyet; and as budget minister under the new prime minister, Manuel Valls – and had grown frustrated. Moreover, Macron's relationship with Hollande was no longer as close as it had been. He was particularly wounded by the president's indifference to the death of his grandmother, Manette, an event that shook the young adviser. 'It's finished with Hollande,' he told a friend at the time.[11] Macron, says another acquaintance, has built a hard shell around him, but it masks a sensitive core. When the mother of his press attaché, Sibeth Ndiaye, died in 2015, he offered her a copy of *Journal de deuil* (*Mourning Diary*) by Roland Barthes. Hollande showed no such understanding.

With a couple of associates, Macron decided to move on to other things. He had some lectures lined up at the London School of Economics, and a plan to launch a boutique advisory business under the name Macron Partners, as well as an e-learning start-up.

A friend had lent him office space in Paris. He had registered the domain name. He was heading to California with Brigitte, for a holiday and to talk to tech contacts in Silicon Valley. 'He always had political ambitions. But I don't think he thought then that a job in government was an option,' said Shahin Vallée, an economist who was planning to join his business venture: 'Hollande's message was clear; he did not want technocrats as ministers. Macron planned to set up this company, and then return to politics later on.'[12] After Montebourg's provocations in Burgundy that August, Vallée sent Macron a text message to say: 'I'm guessing this might change your plans'. 'No,' Macron texted back, 'let's keep going as planned.'

When I went to see Macron in his office at the Elysée Palace in June 2014, he looked unreasonably cheerful, as if relieved to be leaving it all behind. He had become particularly frustrated with the difficulties of implementing a more business-friendly policy on the back of a presidential election campaign that never made this explicit. 'Our problem was that we didn't abolish Clause Four before the election,' he told me, referring to the British Labour Party's statutory promise to nationalize industry, which Tony Blair expunged before his election in 1997. 'The Socialist Party hasn't moulted its old skin. It's pretty retro. Valls will have to fight for every vote. The real point is that there wasn't an ideological renovation ahead of political action.'[13] If Hollande was not ready to trust him with better things, Macron had other things to do. Arguably, had Macron stayed on at the Elysée, Hollande might have called him into government that summer anyway. At any rate, his loss was felt. When a last-minute replacement was needed for Montebourg in late August, Valls and Jouyet – ever the mentor – pushed for Macron. 'He wasn't expecting it, and said he'd think about it,' Jouyet told me years later. 'An hour later, he rang back and accepted.'[14] As chief of staff, Jouyet had the job of standing on the steps of the courtyard at the Elysée Palace, to read out the names of the reshuffled government before a bank of television cameras. When he got to Macron's name, he could not stop himself smiling.

At the Finance Ministry, Macron soon carved out his own brand, as an outspoken, liberal-minded, tech-embracing maverick. Some of his comments were clumsy, offensive and downright rude. After drawing up plans to deregulate the coach industry, he declared that this would help 'the poor' to travel. The minister at one point apologized in parliament after calling workers in an abattoir 'illiterate'. When he told a striking worker that 'the best way to pay for a suit is to work', though, he refused to apologize. Macron was turning out to be independent-minded, and stubborn. Perhaps this was impatience, mixed with arrogance. Or an uncommon belief in his own destiny. Or the sense of freedom gained from confidence that other options would be open to him if politics did not work out. Whatever the reason, he exasperated ministerial colleagues, delighted tech types, and seemed to impress the French. Polls started to test his popularity, and it steadily climbed. All the while, he used the job to expand his network. With a need for very little sleep – he manages, his friend Ferracci said, on four hours a night – Macron would linger late after dinner, standing as guests gravitated towards him, displaying little of the usual ministerial arrogance that tells others in the room that his time is not worth theirs.

Just over a year after he entered government, Macron began preparations for his boldest move: the decision to set up a political movement outside the Socialist Party, with only a year to go before the presidential election. This involved months of secret talks and clandestine planning, which is covered in detail in chapter four. The point here is to measure the nature of this gamble. The decision to launch En Marche set Macron on a collision course with the Socialist barons, marginalized him from all the power networks on the left, and deprived him of any party funds. At the time of the launch, Macron was an unconvincing public speaker, suffered from his image as a well-paid former banker and member of the capitalist elite, and seemed to lack the common touch. His chances of mounting a presidential campaign seemed utterly remote. Nobody was even sure when he launched En Marche what it was supposed to be for. Much of the Paris commentariat assumed that it must be some sort of vehicle to prepare the way for Hollande's re-election campaign. 'If he's elected president of the republic in 2017,' said a wide-eyed Christophe Barbier, editor of *L'Express* magazine, in August 2016, 'it would be a quasi-revolutionary phenomenon.' Renaud Dartevelle, Macron's old school friend, put it to me this way. 'If he can't see how to win, the conclusion for him is that the system is broken. So he says: "Let's change the rules." He thought outside the box,' Dartevelle said. 'That's what he does.'

At times, Macron's touch faltered. Having launched En Marche, he wavered, hanging around in government for months, leaving outsiders confused about what he was up to, and whether he really had the guts to run. A fellow minister told me at the time that the rest of government had had enough of Macron and his self-centred projects. He was no longer a team player, and it would be better for him to go. Some of his advisers urged him to quit right away. But Macron couldn't quite let go. 'He feared disappearing, just like Montebourg had,' one of his aides told me. Once outside government, with no portfolio, staff or chauffeured car, Macron would no longer be guaranteed air time or column inches. He would have to rely on his own brand, and fundraising, to keep himself in the public eye. Macron 'wants to leave, but has trouble making a move', noted a presidential adviser in August that year.[15] For somebody who did not like to owe anybody, the minister seemed to feel the unusual burden of his debt to Hollande. 'He owes nothing to Valls,' another adviser told me while Macron was still in government, and mulling over his options. 'But it's thanks to Hollande that he returned to public life.'

Finally, Macron made the break, resigning at the end of August 2016, eight months before the election. When Gaspard Gantzer, Hollande's communications director, and a former drinking buddy and football teammate of Macron's from ENA, learned late that month that the minister was about to quit, he saw red. Gantzer knew his old friend too well. 'He is putting his own personal destiny over collective success,' he noted at the time: 'A stabbing. It's intolerable.'[16] Hollande was dismayed. Macron resigned by sending the president a text message – like a teenager jilting a girlfriend, noted Gantzer. After summoning Macron to the Elysée Palace to say it to his face, Hollande reported back: 'He told me that he was leaving because there was no more space to act, that it wasn't against me, that he would still support me.' This time, for once, the president had no illusions: 'I didn't believe him. He has chosen to play a personal card.'[17]

The adviser was right. Macron's strategy, another friend of his told me then, 'is to make it impossible for Hollande to stand. I'm not sure it will work, and I'm not sure that Macron really will stand against Hollande.' This was the last risk, and it was arguably the most opportunistic, and treacherous, of all. On 16 November 2016, Macron announced his decision to run for president before Hollande had unveiled his own plans. Throughout much of 2016, the prospect of running against Hollande had seemed to bother Macron. He was the one who for years had carried Hollande's bags, passing him briefing notes in meetings, preparing his international summits. I had watched him in that role, and they seemed unusually close. 'He's loyal to Hollande, just not to his ideas,' a friend of his told me in July that year. Yet Macron is also cunning and cold-headed, and was never completely straight with Hollande about his plans for En Marche. The president had been warned by some Socialist elders to watch out for his ambitious young minister. They worried that Hollande was too indulgent, blinded to the risks he posed. As early as the autumn of 2015 Hollande dismissed such alarmism: 'Macron is not somebody who seeks to exist politically to the detriment of government … He's a decent guy, he's not duplicitous.'[18] Shortly before the launch of En Marche, Macron went to see the president at the Elysée Palace to explain his plans. 'I want to do something,' he told his boss.[19] 'There are people who are asking me. I can connect with voters, far from politics.' Hollande replied: 'Yes, go ahead. But be careful, don't surround yourself with politicians, because that would be perceived as an operation within the Socialist Party, or worse, as competition.' Macron told Hollande not to fret. 'No, no,' he reassured him, with brazen disingenuousness, 'it's going to be citizens.'[20] Even after En Marche was born, the president continued to underrate the threat. 'You will finish with 7, 8, perhaps 10 per cent,' he told Macron, who replied: 'We will see.'[21]

Instead, En Marche turned out to be a vehicle for the destruction of the Socialist Party and the crushing of Hollande's options. The president's misjudgement was total. Macron may have called Valls the traitor. But Hollande told colleagues that by leaving government when he did, Macron 'betrayed me methodically'.[22] On a wintry Wednesday morning, before the deadline for the Socialist primary candidates to declare, the former banker chose a hangar-like vocational training centre in Bobigny, a *banlieue* north of Paris, to announce his presidential bid: as an independent, for En Marche, and outside the Socialist primary. It was a heavy pre-emptive strike. Hollande was trapped. Not a single poll suggested that he could retain the presidency, nor even make the run-off. Macron's decision to run made this prospect even more remote, as he had known it would. Manuel Valls, by repeatedly voicing his shock at the president's indiscretions, hammered in the final nail. Two weeks after Macron declared his candidacy, Hollande announced that he would not run again.

So Macron was lucky, but he also created his chances and took his own risks. Why did those risks pay off as they did? How did Macron manage to make a success of campaigning on the liberal centre ground with a party that was barely a year old and at his first attempt at running for elected office? Four factors help explain this victory. One was his reading of the unstable, shifting forces of French party politics. The second was the underlying historical changes in France that made insurrection possible. Third was the engineering of En Marche as a movement to wage the campaign. And the final factor was the compelling personality of the candidate himself. The first of these factors will be explored in the rest of this chapter. The others each form the basis of the three chapters that follow.

* * *

In one sense, En Marche was born during the 18 hours that Macron spent speaking in parliament about shopping. Or, to be precise, the possibility for shops to stay open on Sundays and into the evenings. The year was 2015, he was economy minister, and he had put together a piece of draft legislation designed to deregulate the economy, which became known as the *loi Macron* (Macron law). This was his flagship bill, which the enthusiastic novice minister presented to parliament in January 2015, five months after he first joined government. Designed to stimulate economic activity, it was a mixed bag of measures: the loosening of Sunday-trading and late-opening rules; the liberalization of the country's inter-city coach industry to try to create more cross-country services; and the deregulation of certain protected professions, such as notaries. For the minister, the many long hours that he spent in the National Assembly prompted a central insight: the French system was blocked, and political parties were the problem.

By international standards, many of the measures wrapped into Macron's bill were meagre. He wanted to allow shops to open on one Sunday a month, up from five times a year under rules in place at the time, and those in certain tourist areas to open on Sundays all year round. He would allow coach companies to launch services between French cities, in competition for the first time with the country's mighty SNCF railway. Such plans hardly constituted a full response to the country's stagnating economic growth. Yet a measure of the bill's boldness in France, a nation built with the *dirigiste* hand of the state, was that it upset both the political right and the left. Before Macron's draft was even unveiled, pharmacists and notaries – the backbone of provincial conservatism – took to the streets to protest. Left-wingers denounced it as a betrayal of the concept of social progress. Macron's law 'calls into question all the historic battles of the left', declared Marie-Noëlle Lienemann, a Socialist senator. A stinging letter to *Le Monde* from Martine Aubry, the mayor of Lille and standard-bearer of the Socialist left, captured the indignation in her camp. 'What kind of society do we want to live in?' she wrote. 'Has the left nothing better to propose for the organization of life than a Sunday walk in a shopping centre and the accumulation of consumer goods?'[23]

Macron had his hands full defending the bill. Despite the wariness of many Socialist backbenchers, he thought, perhaps naively, that he could win round enough deputies through force of persuasion. During those weeks in late January and early February 2015, a politician who had never been elected to parliament spent weeks at the National Assembly, speaking in the chamber and in committee rooms, eating at the parliamentary brasserie, known as the *buvette*. By the time deputies had finished debating all articles of the bill, at 5.54 a.m. on Sunday 15 February 2015 after a sitting that ran all night, there had been no fewer than 111 hours of parliamentary debate in the chamber. Altogether, Macron had spent a cumulative total of 18 hours speaking. 'During those debates,' one of his advisers told me later, 'the minister acted in a way that was, for us, self-evident: that is to say, he answered questions on matters of substance, refused to reject an amendment just because it came from the opposition. Not falling back on traditional partisan roles seemed to be an absolute novelty.'

Macron's hope was that there was a consensus to be found among both Socialists and those on the centre-right, which could defeat left-wing backbench rebels. 'He also wanted to win over public opinion, and to make sure it was perceived as a French initiative, not something imposed by Brussels,' an adviser told me at the time. Maybe this was inexperience, or excessive ambition. Perhaps Macron placed too much faith in his own capacity to get things done. Either way, his efforts were in vain. Centrist-leaning deputies from the right might have shared his views but, he said later, they were 'prisoners of the logic of party machines'.[24] On 17 February, Manuel Valls, the prime minister, judged that a parliamentary majority was not possible; ministers were summoned to an emergency cabinet meeting and told that the law would be forced through by an accelerated procedure, under article 49.3 of the constitution. It was both a display of authority by Valls, and a defeat of Macron's efforts at trans-partisan politics. When Gantzer caught his old friend as he left the cabinet meeting, he noted 'a fold of bitterness in the corner of his mouth'. That evening, the economy minister appeared on the television evening news, deflated. Later, to calm himself down, he went home and played the piano until three in the morning.

Bruised, Macron took away from this episode a number of lessons. Among them was the conviction that the party-political system as it had existed in the post-war period was impeding the creation of a reforming consensus in France. 'I've seen from the inside the emptiness of our political system which prevents a majority of ideas on the grounds that they undermine the political machines,' Macron declared the following year, when he announced he was running for the presidency. France was blocked not because of its deputies, but by the parties they were beholden to, which 'paralysed' the country's capacity to move forward. 'That law turned him into a politician,' said Laurent Bigorgne, the director of the liberal Institut Montaigne, and a friend.[25] The debates taught Macron that legislators from the moderate centre-left and centre-right had more in common with each other than either side did with the extremes within their own parties. This consensus, Macron judged, reflected public opinion too. 'My view is that public opinion is in advance of politicians,' he told me in January 2016, when En Marche was still a secret project: 'I think you can mobilize by creating a consensus for reform during a presidential election.'[26] A majority of the French were in favour of Sunday trading. France was held back, in other words, not because of an innate resistance to change, nor an inclination to protest, but because the party system no longer reflected underlying divisions. 'If we want a modernizing agenda,' Macron told me when I interviewed him in June 2015, a few months after Valls's decision to abandon a parliamentary vote, 'we need to put together two-thirds of the Socialist Party, all of the centrists, and part of the centre-right. That would give us a pro-European market-friendly majority in favour of modernizing the social model.'[27] Although I didn't realize it at the time, he was already beginning to think through a potential disruption of the party system, which would give birth formally less than a year later to En Marche.

A second episode later that year stiffened Macron's resolve to go ahead. This was the government's controversial response to the harrowing terrorist attacks of 13 November 2015 at the Bataclan theatre, Paris terrace cafés and the Stade de France, a bloodbath in which 130 were killed and scores wounded. The attack took place towards the end of a year that had put France on edge. After the *Charlie Hebdo* terrorist attacks of January came a series of further bloody assaults. On 26 June, Yassin Salhi, a French citizen, strangled his employer to death in the back of a van, hacked off his head with a kitchen knife, and attached it to the gates of a chemicals factory near Lyon. On 21 August a passenger armed with a Kalashnikov opened fire in a high-speed Thalys train between Amsterdam and Paris, injuring two passengers, before being overpowered by three others, two of them off-duty American military personnel. Among European countries, France felt particularly vulnerable. A pretext for jihadists seeking to stir violence against the country was not hard to find. France had dispatched troops to Mali in early 2013 to beat back an Islamist incursion in the Sahel. The country had banned the veil in state schools, and the burqa on the streets. Its fighter planes had been helping to bomb IS targets in Iraq and Syria. Online French-language jihadist videos were calling on the faithful to strike French infidels. Home to Europe's biggest Muslim population, some five million strong, France was supplying more jihadist fighters to Syria and Iraq than any other. In January 2015, in a chilling address, Manuel Valls had told lycée students that they would have 'to learn to live with' terror.

The November terrorist attacks shook the nation, and darkened the mood. The government put in place a state of emergency. 'France is at war,' Hollande declared gravely to a joint sitting of the lower and upper houses of parliament in Versailles, in a martial speech that carried echoes of George W. Bush's 'war on terror'. In what was to become the most contentious element of the speech, Hollande announced that he planned to write into the constitution the power to strip nationality from French-born dual citizens convicted of terrorism, a measure known as *déchéance*.

The Socialists were aghast. So were Republicans on the liberal centre-right. The proposal flew in the face of the French legal tradition of *droit du sol*, or the right to nationality based on birth on French soil, and created the impression that those of dual citizenship would become a second-class category of French nationals. Thomas Piketty, the economist on the left, accused the government of 'running after the National Front'. Alain Juppé, on the centre-right, described its likely effectiveness as a counter-terrorism measure as 'feeble, if not zero'.

This episode was the moment at which Macron's plans accelerated. Not only did political parties no longer reflect underlying divisions on economic policy – the lesson the minister drew from the debate over his Sunday trading bill – but the same was also true for questions of citizenship and identity. Later that month, Macron decided to speak out. At a conference in Paris organized by Bernard Spitz of the Gracques, a centre-left pro-European group, he strayed off his ministerial territory. The terrorist bloodshed in Paris, Macron said, was not just the result of propaganda and madness. The French, he said, also had to recognize 'our responsibility' in creating a 'fertile ground'. Abandoned by the state, some areas of the country had been left vulnerable to those recruiting for jihad. France, argued Macron, had to face the fact that this was a home-grown phenomenon, not just the work of mad men. Valls was irate. 'There is no social, sociological or cultural excuse for terrorism,' he seethed in parliament, adding, a few weeks later, that 'To explain is to want to excuse.' As the debate raged within the party, Macron became increasingly outspoken over his 'philosophical discomfort' with his government's line on *déchéance*. He considered resigning, but couldn't quite bring himself to go. In the end, Hollande realized that he lacked the support necessary to amend the constitution, and abandoned the text. But it was too late to mend the divisions within the party.

Such were the frustrations in government in 2015 that shaped Macron's vision of a realignment of party politics. His emerging analysis, which formed the basis of the design of En Marche, was that the new politics should be fought not on the centre ground, but forced onto a different axis altogether. 'If it had just been centrism, I don't think we would have won,' Macron told me in July 2017. 'In France, the political families of the left and the right, structured in the post-war era, are exhausted because of their own divisions and inconsistencies, and no longer have answers to today's challenges.'[28] To get France moving, politics needed to be disrupted along a different fault line: between those broadly in favour of an open society, trade, markets and Europe on the one side; and Eurosceptic nationalists advocating protectionism and identity politics on the other. The underlying idea was that the big forces shaping the future – technology, the freelance economy, the environment, Europe, inequality, globalization – no longer fell neatly into the old ideological divide between left and right. 'The biggest challenges facing this country and Europe – geopolitical threats and terrorism, the digital economy, the environment – are not those that have structured the left and the right,' Macron told me in July 2016, shortly after launching En Marche. 'The new political split is between those who are afraid of globalization, and those who see globalization as an opportunity, or at least a framework for policy that tries to offer progress for all.'[29]

These new fractures were emerging across Europe, but were particularly apparent in France. The French have long been more hostile in polls to globalization than others. In 2016, 54 per cent of the French judged that globalization was a threat, compared to 45 per cent of Germans and 39 per cent of Spaniards and Italians, according to a study by the Bertelsmann Stiftung, an independent foundation. Yet this average masked a wider divergence: 76 per cent of National Front voters on the far right, and 58 per cent of Jean-Luc Mélenchon's party on the far left, considered globalization to be a menace. Those figures dropped to 43 per cent for Socialist voters and 39 per cent for Republicans. The same applied to French attitudes to Europe. Asked in a poll by TNS Sofres in June 2016 whether they were in favour of remaining in the European Union, a large majority of French Socialist (72 per cent), Green (80 per cent), centrist (70 per cent) and Republican (62 per cent) voters agreed. But only a minority of those on the far left (48 per cent) and far right (13 per cent) did. The former, drawn from across the party divide, made up the pool of post-partisan support that Macron sought to mobilize.

Moreover, former collective identities, forged in industrial societies, were beginning to split and fragment. Hyper-connectivity, digitalization, the hollowing out of middle-class jobs, the mobility of capital, the spread of the freelance economy, the decline of unionized heavy industries: all were combining to undermine the common interests of the left, and fracture values on the right. These changes were prompting new insecurities and fears. Most notably, the working-class vote – once the backbone of the post-war French Communist Party – began to shift. It had been allied under Mitterrand to that of the public-sector middle class, which supported the Socialist Party, enabling his election in 1981 on a common programme. Over the years, a big chunk of the working-class vote drifted from the Communists to the National Front. By 2017, Marine Le Pen's far-right was the favourite party of blue-collar workers. Amid such fluid allegiances, there was space for a new sort of political identity, defined by different values. This evolution was taking place in other Western democracies too, whether those with polarized party systems, as in Britain and America, or those where party politics was fragmenting, including the Netherlands and Germany.

En Marche in other words did not seek merely to conquer and occupy the centre ground, but to upset the landscape. Its political position was 'not centrism', Ismaël Emelien, one of Macron's closest advisers and co-founder of the movement, told me: 'The challenge for us was to get away from the left-right analysis. Not because it has no value, but because we observed that, within the left and the right, nobody agreed on the matters we considered important: Europe, work, immigration, the future of the environment. These entities that we call left and right are artificial relics. For us, they contributed to the divorce between politics and the rest of the country.' En Marche, argued Emelien, was 'not an attempt to reinvent the centre, or create a new radical middle. To be at the centre is by definition to position yourself in relation to others. We reject that. We don't want to be centrist.'[30]

Precedent, in any case, taught that French presidential elections could not be won from the political centre. France had a minor history of centrist leaders who came to nothing. In 1965, Jean Lecanuet, a dashing young senator, campaigned for the French presidency promising a 'great democratic movement reaching from progressive liberals to reformist socialists',[31] with a slogan that seemed oddly to presage Macron's: '*Un homme neuf, une France en marche*' ('A new man, a France on the move'). Lecanuet failed to make it into the run-off, in which Charles de Gaulle that year defeated François Mitterrand. A decade later, in 1974, Jacques Chaban-Delmas, Georges Pompidou's prime minister from 1969 to 1972, ran for the presidency based on politics he too defined as 'neither on the one side, neither on the other'. He failed to make the second round, crushed by the savvy campaign of a younger, more dynamic, figure from the centre-right, Valéry Giscard d'Estaing, who went on to defeat Mitterrand. François Bayrou, a centrist former presidential hopeful and horse-breeder from south-west France, ran three times for the presidency (2002, 2007, 2012), but never got through to the run-off. The centre ground, in short, was seen as electorally unfavourable under the French two-round system, and a place of soft, squishy compromise and moderation.

Emmanuel Macron was not the only French politician to have identified the potential for a political realignment. Paradoxically, he shared his reading of the tremors remaking party politics with another insurgent from the opposite end of the political spectrum: Marine Le Pen. At a local level, under her leadership, the FN had begun to take hold of town halls and municipal councils. By 2014, at elections to the European Parliament, it had become the top-scoring party in France, securing 25 per cent of the vote. As Le Pen prepared her own assault on the French establishment, she too sought to force open a new political fault line, exploit the fragility of the traditional parties, and engineer their collapse.

Before Macron began to spell out his ideas about a new political alignment, Le Pen was already detailing hers. The 'left-right split is artificial', she told me when I went to interview her in November 2013, two years after she won the FN leadership, because 'the left and the right are the same thing'.[32] Swivelling on a black leather chair, behind a glass-topped executive-style desk in her office at the FN headquarters in the Paris suburb of Nanterre, Marine Le Pen was by turns disarmingly witty and icily caustic. In her view, a new political fracture would put an end to the cosy duopoly that had ruled France for the past six decades: an 'inbred world of politicians, the media and big financial powerhouses' that she said formed a 'sort of oligarchy, which has grabbed hold of power without ever being elected'. The new party division, she declared, would instead pit 'globalists, who think that the nation state is passé and that the future is about supra-national structures, against those who consider that the nation state is the guarantor of sovereignty'. It was curiously prescient, and such a line could be readily revived, by Le Pen or her successor, as a powerful counterpoint to Macron and his rootless metropolitan supporters in 2022. She outlined a long-term plan to widen the FN's electoral base, by appealing to 'patriotic' voters both on the left and on the right. 'We have emptied the Communist Party,' she said to me triumphantly, 'now we're going after Socialist voters.' The Republicans, she implied, would be next.

Macron and Le Pen, of course, were on diametrically opposing sides of this new fracture. But they shared an understanding that the issues dividing them were the ones that would frame future politics. That they ended up facing each other in the run-off in 2017 was a reflection of the yearning for something different, as well as the appeal of these two contrasting forms of post-ideological allegiance. Le Pen's version, in her telling, was a 'patriotic' mission to defend France from an army of perceived outside threats: the euro, globalization, competition, immigration and Islamification. She promised to give 'preference' to French nationals, withdraw France from the euro, raise protectionist tariffs, curb immigration and reinstate welfare privileges. Hers was a blood-and-soil nationalism mixed with economic protectionism. Macron, by contrast, was an unapologetic champion of the EU, favouring (mostly) open borders, global trade, technical innovation and the adaptation of France's welfare system to a less stable future job market. 'At a time when some people believe that raising walls is a solution, we do think that openness is the right path,' Macron declared soon after his election.

Each was the antithesis of the other. Le Pen was the favourite among blue-collar workers; Macron drew disproportionate support from university graduates. She climbed to the top of the polls on the back of dire warnings of an immigrant invasion and Islamist infiltration; he praised Angela Merkel for 'rescuing our dignity' over refugees. Their mutual antipathy was unambiguous. Le Pen called him an 'ultra-liberal' globalist, a sort of citizen of nowhere, who was 'surfing on air'. Macron said that she pretended to speak 'for the people', but in truth spoke only for her clan. During their head-to-head televised presidential debate before the run-off vote, Le Pen accused him of being the candidate of 'savage globalization'; he retorted that she was a 'product of the system you denounce; you are its parasite' and the 'high priestess of fear'.

Macron and Le Pen held irreconcilable views, and were repugnant to each other. But they shared an analysis of the new French political divide. And Macron's efforts to force a new fault line were in some ways served by hers. In 2016, when En Marche was still in its infancy, I asked him whether he worried that his strategy lent Le Pen legitimacy. He was unapologetic. It was 'time to face up to reality', he replied: the FN was 'already the leading party in France'.[33] The way to take on her party was neither to pander to it, nor to try to tame it by bringing it into the fold, nor to scare voters with the prospect of its victory. It was rather, he told me, 'to propose an alternative political project with a pro-European narrative that is not based on fear'. Macron's attempt to fashion a progressive, European alternative, infused with a message of hope, was both a means of remaking party politics and a response to the populist threat.

So, yes, Macron was lucky, and how. But not only. Plenty of obstacles were also placed in his way. Throughout the campaign, the candidate faced his share of personal attacks, sabotage, fake news and orchestrated rumours. During the campaign for the presidential run-off, Jean-Luc Mélenchon refused to call for a vote for Macron, and far-left demonstrators took to the streets with the anti-Macron and anti-Le Pen slogan, 'Neither a banker nor a fascist'. After his election, and with Putin standing by his side, Macron accused Sputnik and RT, two Russian media, of being 'organs of propaganda'. En Marche was also the victim of repeated hacking, which it suspected was organized by Russia-linked operatives. En Marche's small cybersecurity team mounted a counter-sabotage manoeuvre, flooding phishing emails with false information to minimize the damage. Even so, a last-minute scare kept them up all night. On the evening of 5 May, just two days before the presidential run-off, the party announced that it had been the victim of a 'massive and coordinated' hacking operation, which 'clearly amounts to democratic destabilization as was seen in the United States'. A digital dump of 9 gigabytes of internal emails and accounting files looked designed to upset Macron's campaign in the final stretch.

In the end, Macron turned out to be a finer political analyst than many observers had imagined the former technocrat and one-time investment banker to be. For months he had been dismissed as an upstart, a kid, an intruder, a traitor, a media fantasy or a hologram. Yet Macron's hunch that the old party system was exhausted was right, and this opened up the possibility for something new. What he also realized was that the opportunity would not last. Alain Minc, who had backed Alain Juppé for the Republican primary in 2016, recalled a conversation he had with Macron in early 2012. The two *énarques*, both belonging to that inner elite corps of *inspecteurs des finances*, discussed his possible future political ambitions, and aspirations one day to run for the presidency. 'I told him to aim for 2022,' Minc told me. 'I got it totally wrong on timing. He told me that I was an old man, and didn't understand the new world. And that I was part of the system, and that the system was dead.'[34]

3

THE ROOTS OF *DÉGAGISME*, 1995–2017

'There are moments of great acceleration of history and I think that we are living through one of them.'

Emmanuel Macron, March 2017

In the summer of 2015, while Macron was pondering his political options, Courtney Love, widow of Nirvana lead singer Kurt Cobain, arrived at Charles de Gaulle airport in Paris, and posted a message on Twitter: 'they've ambushed our car and are holding our driver hostage. they're beating the cars with metal bats. this is France?? I'm safer in Baghdad.' The singer was one of the many passengers caught up in violent anti-Uber protests at the capital's main international airport, and couldn't believe her eyes. The previous year, the American ride-sharing firm had launched UberPop, a service that matched unregistered car drivers with passengers and which was ultimately ruled illegal in Paris. The capital's taxi drivers, already exasperated by the arrival of ordinary Uber cars, did what protesters do. Roads were blocked, passengers intimidated, drivers threatened and tyres slashed.

It was a familiar, theatrical defence of producer interests in France. Incumbent operators defend their markets against newcomers. Lobbies intervene. Farmers dump rotting cabbages or bleating sheep on the streets. Protesters hold *manifs* (demonstrations). France had earned a reputation as a tough market to break into, and the taxi industry was no exception. It may have been all but impossible to find a cab on the streets in Paris. Yet each time there was talk of expanding the number of licences, taxi drivers responded with paralyzing blockages.

A favoured technique was the *opération escargot*, by which taxis crawled three abreast in convoy around the capital's *périphérique* ring road, disrupting rush-hour traffic. The Paris town hall issued taxi licences at no cost. But because existing drivers resisted any planned increase to the number of licences, their value on the informal market soared. By 2015 they were worth €200,000, turning a taxi licence, in effect, into a retirement policy for a taxi driver. No owner of this precious resource was going to give it up without a fight.

The upshot was gridlock. Back in 2008, the bipartisan Attali Commission, for which Emmanuel Macron was a *rapporteur*, had argued for a deregulation of the taxi industry. But, thanks to its mighty lobby, the advice came to nothing. Such was the scarcity of taxis on the streets of Paris that the concept of Uber was actually dreamt up in the French capital, one wintry evening in 2008, when Travis Kalanick and Garrett Camp were in town for a tech conference, known as Le Web, and couldn't find a cab. They hit upon the idea of a ride-hailing app, and a year later launched Uber in America. When the French government finally deregulated the chauffeur-driven car sector, it initially put in place a raft of restrictions, which Uber proceeded to breach. Exasperated, the police raided Uber's premises. Two Uber executives were detained. Only one French minister at the time dissented. The law concerning UberPop had to be respected, Emmanuel Macron declared, but he went on to defend the principle of allowing Uber to operate its regular service. 'There's potential here to create thousands of jobs,' he said. 'What should we do? Should we only defend those who have a job? Or try to open up this economy to give a place to other people who also want work?'[1] 'Uber', he concluded, 'has its place in France.'

What Macron saw up close in the digital economy he went on to apply to his political ambitions. Disruption was throwing economic certainties sideways, and at an increasing pace. This created unexpected chances for sudden, dislocating change. As economy minister, he spent a large amount of time with the tech world, watching the way that start-ups were challenging incumbent firms and taking risks, travelling to San Francisco, Las Vegas, London and Tel Aviv. 'Young people in France will take risks, but sometimes French society doesn't back them enough,' he said on a visit to Israel in 2015 to support French tech.[2] 'We need, collectively, to be able not to be jealous or to sneer at success, but to say: it's great, this person, this young person, has succeeded and is transforming things in the world.' Through conversations at tech fairs, start-up events and investor meetings, Macron saw how fast digital was transforming the economy and how quickly social expectations, behaviour and communication were being upturned. He was not the only one thinking that this could also disrupt politics. Guillaume Liegey was a young McKinsey consultant who had been seconded to the Attali Commission when he met Macron. In an article in July 2015 entitled 'If Political Parties Were Start-Ups', Liegey argued that tech firms could show parties how to reinvent themselves, and that start-up tools could be used to build a political movement. New technology made change possible, and fast change more possible still. 'There are moments of great acceleration of history,' Macron said in early 2017, 'and I think that we are living through one of them.'[3]

In some ways, France looked like one of the least likely countries in Europe to witness massive political upset. All Western democracies were living through the same sense of technological disorientation. Political parties elsewhere too, including in Britain, were split internally over Europe, globalization and immigration, between metropolitan liberals and Eurosceptic nationalists. British centrist politicians dreamed in vain of establishing a radical political middle that could forge a post-partisan consensus. Party politics in other Western European countries, including Italy, Spain and Greece, had long been far more turbulent. Italy had seen parties – Forza Italia, the Five Star Movement – emerge from nowhere, sometimes to seize power and then fade away again. Greece, under military rule between 1967 and 1974, was taken to the brink of ejection from the eurozone over the sovereign-debt crisis, which saw the virtual annihilation of its Socialist Party and the ascent of the radical-left party, Syriza. Belgium was regularly without a government at all. In June 2016 it was Britain's turn to perplex fellow Europeans with its vote for Brexit, followed by uninterrupted political melodrama. The following year, Spain was thrown into turmoil over the illegal Catalonian independence referendum. Next to such convulsions, France in the run-up to 2017 looked like a model of institutional and party-political stability. After the chronic weaknesses of the Fourth Republic, de Gaulle's constitution for the new republic in 1958 guaranteed a strong central executive. Governments came and went at the ballot box. If anything, political culture in the preceding decades seemed to be characterized by *immobilisme*: a state of cautious conservatism, shaped by self-serving political parties and entrenched interests.

Despite such appearances, however, by the second decade of the twenty-first century, France was in reality in the midst of a cycle of deep political stagnation, disillusion and collective malaise. It was precisely the exhaustion of French society towards the end of this cycle, and the national depression that had by then taken hold, that left the country yearning to evict the old guard. In some ways, this disillusion reached back to the end of the *trente glorieuses*, the decades of rapid industrial expansion and shared prosperity that followed the post-war reconstruction and turned France into the world's fourth-biggest industrial power. But the origins of the more recent cycle can arguably be traced back more recently, to 1995, and the decision by Jacques Chirac and his prime minister, Alain Juppé, to abandon reform after paralyzing street protests. Over the following decade a number of signature events marked this malaise. After refusing economic reform (under Chirac that year), the French rejected immigration and the establishment in 2002 (by voting the far-right Jean-Marie Le Pen into the second round of the presidential election), and then Europe in 2005 (by voting against the draft European constitution in a referendum). It was the spreading sense of disillusion over this period that, in the end, made Macron's political siege possible.

Former mayor of Paris, and prime minister under the wily François Mitterrand, Jacques Chirac campaigned for his third attempt at the presidency, in 1995, on a promise to 'mend the social fracture', and put France back on track towards a future of collective prosperity. On entering the Elysée Palace, he inherited a restive country, with high unemployment, mounting debt, a disoriented electorate and a sense of political stagnation. Twelve years later, having decided not to run again for the presidency, the 74-year-old Chirac bequeathed to his successor Nicolas Sarkozy almost exactly what he found upon taking office: a restive country with high unemployment, mounting debt, a disoriented electorate and entrenched political stagnation. During Chirac's two terms (1995–2007) French unemployment averaged 10 per cent, GDP per head was overtaken by that of both Britain and Ireland, and public debt, at 66 per cent of GDP, grew faster than in any other European Union country.

Chirac was a professional schemer, old-school charmer and political chameleon, who had served in every government after that of Charles de Gaulle until he was elected president and formed his own. He was a master of political opportunism. At the presidential election in 1974, he ditched a Gaullist resistance hero, Jacques Chaban-Delmas, to back the rising star of the centre-right, Valéry Giscard d'Estaing, who went on to win. Seven years later, according to Giscard d'Estaing's memoirs, Chirac then swung against him and secretly backed François Mitterrand, whom he wrongly imagined would not last long in the presidency. Tall, imposing and gregarious, Chirac loved company. The first time I met him, at a champagne-filled New Year's reception for journalists beneath the chandeliers at the Elysée Palace in 2004, he was genial, relaxed and chatted contentedly for nearly an hour with his guests. At a later meeting with a small group of the foreign press, held around a table in a first-floor *salon*, he winked at the female correspondents. Out of favour with the Americans after his stand against the invasion of Saddam Hussein's Iraq in 2003, the president exposed his vision of the changing world order. He was in some ways prescient about shifting geo-strategic power. Fashionable French discussion at the time of a future multi-polar world, which the United

States took as a provocative strategic attempt to undermine the transatlantic alliance and challenge the pre-eminence of post-Soviet American power, was merely a 'self-evident' fact, Chirac said, in the face of rising China and India. America's 'uni-polar' moment, he declared, was over.

Genuine warmth and a flair for pressing the flesh made Chirac a formidable campaigner. For 30 consecutive years, after his first election as mayor of Paris, he lived in state palaces, swapping periods in the prime minister's mansion for spells across the Seine in the town hall. It was during his time as mayor of Paris that the party-financing scandals took place that led in 2004 to the conviction for political corruption of Alain Juppé, Chirac's right-hand man, who took the fall for his boss. Chirac's departure from the Elysée brought to an end his presidential immunity. He was subsequently convicted of the misuse of public funds when mayor of Paris in the 1990s and given a two-year suspended prison sentence.

Over a 40-year career in national politics, Chirac defied political classification. A descendant of Gaullism, he was the dynamic two-time prime minister (1974–6 and 1986–8) who, in his liberal second spell, demolished the Socialist nationalization programme of the early 1980s, carried out extensive privatization and – briefly – abolished the wealth tax, a charge on assets, including property, that was levied on top of income tax. Yet, as president, Chirac metamorphosed into an ardent defender of the status quo. Although he took courageous stands both at home and abroad, becoming the first French president to recognize the official responsibility of the French state for the deportation of Jews from Vichy France under Nazi occupation, and defying America over the war in Iraq, his domestic agenda shrank as the years went by. Chirac compared the dangers of liberalism to those of communism, increased the state's overall tax take and insisted that the strained French social system, which was piling up public debt, was 'perfectly adapted' to the modern era. The events that turned him into a cautious domestic leader began only shortly after his election as president.

Chirac had appointed the stiff and technocratic Juppé as prime minister, and by the autumn of 1995 the government was under growing pressure to tighten spending in order to meet the convergence targets of the Maastricht Treaty. The prime minister came up with what was known as the *plan Juppé*, designed to curb public spending, overhaul the social-security budget and stabilize public finances. It included planned cuts to family benefits and the health system, and a tightening up of public-sector pension rights. 'The time of real reform for France has come,' declared a crusading Juppé. But the French were to decide otherwise. An initial one-day strike by railwaymen, teachers, post office, electricity and other public-sector workers on 10 October swelled by the end of November into an all-out paralysis of public services. For three weeks, trains, buses and the Paris metro came to a virtual standstill. By December, despite an icy cold snap, as many as two million people had taken to the streets. It was the most sweeping public protest that France had witnessed since the student uprising of May 1968, and taught a generation of politicians to fear reform – or at least to acknowledge, as Macron did once in office, that 'The French don't like reform.' The mood was sinister, the scale of the strikes menacing. 'This is the end of the social-security system, the greatest act of pillage in the history of the republic,' declared Marc Blondel, a union leader.[4] In the end, as the revolt hardened, Chirac and Juppé backed down, shelving their planned reform of pensions altogether.

The lesson that the Gaullist president drew from the affair was that France was too fragile to be pushed out of its comfort zone. 'The truth is,' Chirac concluded, 'that we live in a profoundly conservative country and it is very difficult to change things.'[5] Franz-Olivier Giesbert, a writer who knew Chirac well, judged that the Gaullist leader, traumatized by street revolts, 'ended up convinced that France is not able to tolerate any major reform'.[6] After that crippling winter, Chirac's domestic ambitions shrivelled. A verb was born to capture the way in which a politician retreated into excessive caution: *se chiraquiser*. By 1997, amid ongoing economic and budgetary difficulties, Chirac made a disastrous decision to dissolve parliament in a bid to seek a clearer mandate. He lost his majority, Juppé lost his job, and the president spent five years 'cohabiting' with a Socialist-led government, which brought in the 35-hour working week. By 2005, Chirac seemed to have lost touch with the national mood. During a two-hour televised debate held at the presidential palace ahead of the European referendum, the French head of state sat on a stool, surrounded by some 80 young people. As the fearful outpourings from the audience multiplied, his brow creased. 'This is a feeling, I won't hide it from you,' he said, 'that I don't understand.'[7]

Although Chirac decided in his first year in office that the French were too conservative to tolerate change, he was persuaded 11 years later by his debonair new prime minister, Dominique de Villepin, to give it another go. The former foreign minister, with a mane of greying hair, who had earned worldwide renown for the stirring speech he made against the invasion of Iraq at the United Nations Security Council in New York in 2003, saw himself as on a domestic mission to tread boldly into hostile territory. He kept a bust of Napoleon in his office, wrote poetry in his spare time, and was a man more at home with discussions of destiny and grandeur than the management of labour-market policy. Eight months after being appointed to the job, De Villepin introduced a contentious flexible labour contract for the young, the *contrat première embauche* (CPE). Controversially, it carried a two-year trial period during which an employer could get rid of a new employee, far longer than that of a standard permanent French work contract. Students, and their families, were irate. In the face of massive demonstrations that drew at one point between one and three million people onto the streets of cities across France, De Villepin forced the bill through parliament, only for Chirac to then repeal it, even after it had been signed into law. A pattern seemed to have been set: the street objects; government backs down; *immobilisme* digs in. The resistance of French society to change seemed confirmed.

A different conclusion might have been drawn: that reforms which a candidate does not come clean about during an election campaign have little chance of going through once in office. Chirac's electoral promise in 1995 to heal social wounds collided directly with Juppé's rigid determination to force through his cuts just a few months later. Or it could be argued that both Juppé and De Villepin failed because each did not in his time prepare the ground, and consult enough up front, in order to build a political consensus. But this was not the version that took hold in the collective imagination. It was, rather, that the French, with their romantic affection for revolutionary rhetoric and theatrical protest, were resistant to reform. For politicians, it became received wisdom that governments that pushed too hard would be punished on the streets or at the ballot box. For voters, it seemed that politicians were not to be trusted; they were elected on one programme, only to put into place another, much harsher, once in office. In 2003, a year after Chirac was re-elected, in a second-round vote that was as much against Jean-Marie Le Pen as it was for the Gaullist, Nicolas Baverez, a lawyer and commentator, wrote in a landmark book that 'the government does not run the nation's politics but acts like a psychological support unit, as ready to display empathy with victims as it is reticent to remedy their situation'.[8]

Of course, France's trajectory between 1995 and 2017 was not a linear slide towards political disillusion and economic stagnation. Growth in the years under the Socialist government of Lionel Jospin (1997–2002) was remarkably healthy, and unemployment dipped from over 10 per cent to below 8 per cent. The government credited its introduction of the 35-hour working week, which it considered to be a means of sharing out jobs more fairly, although job creation was generated more by the rapid expansion of the global economy at the time. 'Frankly, it will have brought a lot of disorder to create relatively few jobs,' one Socialist minister in the Jospin government told me in 1999, even as the policy was being drawn up. Above all, the presidential election of 2007 offered a fleeting moment of hope for renewal, as two younger politicians – Nicolas Sarkozy on the right, and Ségolène Royal on the left – promised alternative visions of a more modernized

France. The victory of Sarkozy, at the age of 52, marked the election of the first president who had been born after the Second World War; the first Gaullist president never to have served in government under Charles de Gaulle himself; the first centre-right president since Pompidou not to have graduated from ENA; and the first president whose father (a Hungarian immigrant) was not French. He also seemed to have the outsider's drive to succeed. An aristocrat who fled communism to settle in France in the late 1940s, his father once told the young Sarkozy: 'With your surname, and the marks you get at school, you will never succeed in France.'[9] President Sarkozy promised a 'rupture' with past ways of governing, urged the French to 'work more to earn more', and set about a vigorous effort to energize the country.

Sarkozy certainly brought a new tone to the presidency, which shocked the purists and impressed his supporters in equal measure. After the staid Chirac years, he would set off in running gear from the Elysée Palace, an NYPD T-shirt on his chest and headphones in his ears. 'Is jogging a right-wing activity?' asked *Libération*. It was, at any rate, an 'undignified' one, replied Alain Finkielkraut, who argued that strolling was a more appropriate presidential pace. Sarkozy brought dynamism to policymaking too. In the autumn of 2007 he had what some observers called his 'Thatcher moment': a showdown with the unions, after he put an end to special pension privileges for train drivers, gas and electricity workers and others, which enabled them to retire early. For once, a French president stood firm in the face of a crippling nine-day strike, which brought Paris to a halt, and refused to cede ground. Sarkozy introduced a degree of autonomy for the country's universities, which were then governed centrally by the ministry in Paris. He succeeded in pushing up the legal retirement age from 60 to 62, no mean feat, even if it was not enough to balance the pension regime. He also introduced rules that made it easier to organize minimum services on the metro and railways during strikes, bringing an end to periodic paralysis. And, from 2008, Sarkozy was an energetic partner for Britain's Gordon Brown in dealing with the financial crisis. In a carefully pitched speech in Toulon, in September that year, he promised that 'whatever happens, the state will guarantee the continuity and the stability of the French banking and financial system'. It was a crucial moment, helping to contain the mounting sense of panic in France and buy his government negotiation time. For the next two years, Sarkozy's energies were diverted into helping manage the crisis and its after-effects in Europe.

Yet in the end the Sarkozy presidency did not manage to restore France's wilting faith in politics. This had a lot to do with presidential style. His touch may have been modern, but it was also seen as self-promoting and vulgar. From the start, when the newly elected president celebrated his victory at Fouquet's, a flashy restaurant on the Champs-Elysées, and then jetted off to the Mediterranean for a three-day holiday on a yacht belonging to the billionaire Vincent Bolloré, the tag 'bling' stuck to him. The French like their wealth to be discreet, tied up in elegant apartments or works of art. Their literature, from Molière and Balzac to Sartre, denounces the corrupting power of money, and ridicules the grasping *nouveau riche*. 'Elsewhere, material success is readily admired ... billionaires are applauded (and envied), bosses are acclaimed, self-made men celebrated,' wrote Alain Duhamel, a French political commentator. 'In France, not at all. Wealth embodies evil, money represents the devil.'[10] Sarkozy's taste for expensive watches, designer sunglasses and show-business friends spoke of vanity, ostentation and a crude materialism that sat uneasily with deep French ambivalence about money. By December of his first year in office, *Libération* ran a cover entitled 'Président bling-bling'. The label stuck.

Sarkozy had hoped to show the French that he was a young, contemporary president in touch with the lives of ordinary people and the modern family. He turned up to his inauguration in 2007 with his wife, Cécilia, and the five children they had from various marriages. Little did people know then how intimately they would soon be in touch with his domestic affairs. The couple's divorce five months later, the first for a sitting French head of state since Napoleon divorced Josephine in 1809, was splashed across magazine covers and chewed over on broadcast talk shows. 'Desperate housewife', was *Libération*'s verdict. *Paris Match* magazine devoted a 16-page cover story to the subject. Cécilia Sarkozy joined in, giving *Hello*-like interviews – 'I met someone else, I fell in love' – to the press. Next to the quiet discretion, and even quieter indiscretions, of the Chiracs, this American level of exhibition of a president's private life came as a shock to the French. All the more so when Sarkozy courted, and married, Carla Bruni, the Italian folk singer and former supermodel, in a very public romance shortly afterwards. 'Between Carla and me, it's serious,' he grinned, like a lovesick teenager, at a formal press conference in the *salle des fêtes* at the Elysée Palace. The coarse Sarkozy exterior masked an emotionally charged individual who had trouble keeping his feelings, whether anger or passion, to himself. In private, he could be hectoring and rude. It was in many ways his fatal flaw.

By the time Sarkozy came to the end of his term in office, the words that sprang to mind were: what a waste. He was by then regarded as a divisive figure, who set the French against each other, used abrasive language – *racaille* (yobs) to refer to troublemakers in the *banlieues*, or his cursing at a passer-by at an agricultural fair – and whose behaviour dismayed even his natural supporters. He had become such an object of dislike that the French seemed to have forgotten why they voted for him in the first place. A whirlwind in perpetual motion, he left the country irritated and exhausted. After he departed from office, a number of judicial investigations into his, and his ministers', behaviour in government were opened, which left a murky trail behind him. The tragedy of the Sarkozy presidency was that he seemed in the end to have been his own worst enemy. He fired off in so many directions that it left the French confused, dizzy and worn out. Sarkozy had many virtues, but channelling his energy was not one of them. A tax-cutting candidate, he ended up increasing the overall tax take in the economy. A politician who criticized the 35-hour week, he left it on the statute books. A president who wanted to free the French from their complex about wealth and success was ultimately regarded as a cliquey 'president of the rich'. A leader who promised to promote a French Condoleezza Rice finished his term with no ethnic-minority ministers in senior government positions, and turned to toxic identitarian talk about 'too many immigrants' in a chase for the far-right vote during his campaign for re-election in 2012. Through all of this, Sarkozy seemed too often unable to control his own impulses. If his political results had been more impressive, the French might have forgiven him these foibles. But his was a tale of showmanship over application, of haste over deliberation, of transparency over reserve. Yasmina Reza, the French playwright, put it well when she wrote of Sarkozy's restless desire to 'combat the slippage of time'.[11] In the end, he could not stop the clock. At the presidential election of 2012, the French did not so much vote for Hollande as against Sarkozy. He ended up defeating himself.

After Chirac's caution, and Sarkozy's excess, the French sought a compromise and opted in 2012 for a 'normal' president. This sounded fair enough. Hollande chose the term to define the sort of president he promised to be. To the French ear, it meant more than ordinary: it suggested something that conforms to the rule, the way things should be. After the 'look-at-me' term of Hollande's predecessor, Nicolas Sarkozy, the word 'normal' met a yearning for more modest government and a simpler form of politics. Yet Hollande soon discovered that he had cast himself as a normal president for what turned out to be highly abnormal times. The economy slid back into recession. His budget minister, Jérôme Cahuzac, who was appointed to crack down on tax evasion, resigned after it emerged that he had a secret bank account in Switzerland. The Greek sovereign-debt crisis unfolded, testing the eurozone's capacity for survival.

Hollande turned ambiguity into an art form. The Socialist leader was elected to bring an end to austerity in Europe, put youth first, bring down unemployment, introduce a top income-tax rate of 75 per cent, squeeze the rich and distribute purchasing power to the rest. He ended up beholden to eurozone budgetary discipline (although he managed to postpone a reduction in the deficit), presided over rising joblessness including for the young, increased taxes on a broad swathe of the middle class, and shelved the top tax rate when it was ruled unconstitutional. The heavy overall tax hikes Hollande put in place in his first year in office prompted his own finance minister, Pierre Moscovici, to declare that the country was suffering from a *ras-le-bol* (fed-upness) with taxes. They also helped to choke economic activity.

Two years after his election, Hollande conducted a U-turn, naming a new, more business-friendly government under the sensible centre-left Manuel Valls – who had himself run for the Socialist primary in 2011 with a brave programme of economic reform – which began to undo some of the damage. In the autumn after he was appointed prime minister, Valls declared that the government had 'lost time' and made 'poor choices' during Hollande's first two years in office.[12] Hollande had been the Socialists' secretary-general for 11 years. Yet the party, as Valls recognized, had never settled a raging internal debate that pitted those who favoured heavy public spending and redistribution to underpin economic growth, against advocates of supporting business to create wealth first. In office, Hollande tried the former, then swung to the latter, leaving voters confused, angry and short in the pocket. The price was both his popularity, and the credibility of governing parties. The tacit social bargain accepted by the French – by which they tolerated their technocratic elite, narrowly drawn from ENA, and which shuffled painlessly from government to the great institutions of state and on into state-run industries, as long as it delivered a better life for ordinary citizens – began to crumble. Confidence in the political class collapsed.

To make matters worse, Hollande's complicated love life crashed into the public eye, just as Sarkozy's had done, rendering his presidency anything but normal. In January 2014 *Closer*, a celebrity magazine, stunned the French by publishing claims of a liaison between Hollande and Julie Gayet, a French film actress. The magazine's seven-page report included photographs of a figure in a crash helmet on the back of a scooter, driven by a security guard, arriving at an apartment building just across the street from the Elysée Palace, and leaving the building the next morning. The president did not deny the allegations, but 'deplored the breach of respect for his private life'. 'If nothing else', confided a businessman at the time, 'it makes him look ridiculous.' The first lady, Valérie Trierweiler, a journalist at *Paris Match*, was taken to hospital with exhaustion. Their separation became official, and Hollande tried to banish all talk of scooters and love-nests. But in September that year Trierweiler published a tell-all account entitled, with bitter irony, *Merci pour ce moment*. It was an excruciating read. She described Hollande in office as increasingly crushing and distant. 'Does it take long to make yourself look so beautiful?' he asked her before a state dinner. 'Yes, a bit,' she replied. 'At the same time, we don't ask anything else of you,' he hit back. She came across as insecure and jealous; he was erratic and snobbish, mocking the 'toothless' poor. For the French, who traditionally considered the public interest to stop at the bedroom door, it was a political earthquake.

Like those of Sarkozy and Chirac before him, Hollande's presidency was not without achievements. The Socialist president legalized gay marriage, and took a bold decision to send French soldiers to beat back an incursion by Islamists in Mali. He was, bafflingly, funny and self-deprecating in private. After a state dinner for Queen Elizabeth at the Elysée Palace, on a warm evening on the terrace overlooking the gardens at night, the unpopular Hollande recounted his trip in the royal limousine up the Champs-Elysées before flag-waving crowds. 'The best thing about it was that people cheered,' he said, and then paused for effect: 'That doesn't happen to me often.' But Hollande, the 'normal' president, singularly failed to restore faith in politics. Never one to choose clarity over ambiguity if he could avoid it, he presided over a zigzagging economic policy, first raising taxes and vowing to punish the rich and put an end to austerity, then trying to lower taxes, curb public spending and support business instead. He had declared during the 2012 campaign that 'his real enemy' was finance; but he pretty much left the banking system alone. Workers at a closed blast furnace in Lorraine, which

Mr Hollande had promised on the campaign trail to save, erected a stone plaque marked 'Treason', which read 'Here lie Mr Hollande's promises of change'. By the time he decided not to run for re-election, in the autumn of 2016, Hollande's poll ratings were in single figures.

This was the cycle of political disenchantment and economic under-performance that reached its peak in the run-up to the 2017 presidential election. Emmanuel Macron was a keen observer of all these events. He was still a student at ENA when Le Pen senior made it into the presidential run-off against Chirac in 2002, carrying out a six-month internship at the French Embassy in Abuja, Nigeria. 'I absolutely didn't want to go to Brussels or Washington like everybody else,' Macron said, so he had asked to be sent 'somewhere very far away'. He ended up in the capital of a former British colony, deep in the country's interior, watching the French election results in consternation from afar. The shock outcome, he judged, ought to have heralded a period of deep introspection and political renewal. And yet 'nothing changed' in French politics after 2002, as politicians in Paris picked them- selves up, licked their wounds, and continued as before. It was as if the political class was in denial after a trauma, 'sleepwalking', as he described it, refusing to see what was rising up in front of their eyes, and incapable of learning any lessons.[13] The presence of Jean-Marie Le Pen in the 2002 presidential run-off should have jolted France out of complacency. Instead, parties put for- ward 'the same faces', made the same speeches and came up with the same policies as before, never daring to say or propose anything that might supply ammunition to the National Front. Macron was 'very affected, as all our generation were, by April 21st 2002', Adrien Taquet, a political consultant who devised the name En Marche, told me; 'What he didn't want for France was to find ourselves in 2017 with Sarkozy, Hollande and Le Pen.'[14]

One of the consequences of the 2002 vote was that reform in France increasingly proceeded by stealth, for fear of prompting a backlash, and Europe became a scapegoat for it. Governments on both the right and the left blamed the European Commission, or Germany, for policies implemented in France. Few French politicians had the courage to tell people that they needed to sort out the public finances for the sake of their own future, and sovereign independence. Such constraints were more often portrayed as the diktat of Berlin or Brussels, or financial markets. Rare was the political speech that made a positive case for Europe, or for reform at home. Little wonder that voters grew increasingly sceptical towards the EU. In 1992 the French had approved the Maastricht Treaty, which prefigured the creation of the single currency, by only the slimmest of margins. By the time of the referendum on the draft EU constitution in 2005, which the French rejected with a 55 per cent No vote, Europe was regarded as an elite liberal project that threatened ordinary workers. The 'Polish plumber' became the mythical emblem of the No campaign, a symbol of unfair competition from low-cost eastern members of the EU. In the referendum vote over 90 per cent of the far left and the far right voted No, as did 56 per cent of Socialist voters. In a warning sign of an emerging fracture, the industrial towns of northern France and nearly four-fifths of blue-collar workers voted No too. The referendum result was an astonishing outcome for a country that was co-founder of the European project, and whose land is scarred by the blood of battles and graveyards of the dead, the very reason the EU's architects worked so hard to devise the union. Yet once again, the political class seemed to retreat into cautious silence. If the EU was a source of anxiety, even rejection, for the French, better to keep quiet about it.

Successive crises in the following years, over sovereign debt, austerity and refugees, served to fortify the idea fanned by French populists that Europe had turned into a rigid rule-bound project, chiefly serving German economic interests. By 2011, Arnaud Montebourg, the sender of burgundy wine, was comparing Angela Merkel to Bismarck, accusing her of profiting from the ruin of others. Jean-Luc Mélenchon published a book in 2015 entitled *Le hareng de Bismarck: Le poison allemand (Bismarck's Herring: The German Poison)*, arguing that 'Germany is again a danger', and calling the EU its 'new empire'. On paper at least, polls suggested that the EU had become even less popular in France than in Britain. Marine Le Pen embraced the rising Euroscepticism with zeal. Rejoicing at the vote for Brexit in 2016, she called it a model of emancipation from the shackles of the 'European Soviet Union'.

Of course, looking back, France's No to Europe in the 2005 referendum was only partly a rejection of Europe. It was also another howl of rage at the failure of the political elite, and the hollowness of political parties. Unemployment had crept back up to 9 per cent, and was cited in exit polls as the single biggest reason for a No vote, according to TNS-Sofres. Exasperated by out-of-touch leadership in hard times, intoxicated by the chance to rebel, and encouraged by populist No campaigners, the French revolted. The vote, said Serge July, editor of *Libération*, was an 'electoral riot'. The French had many reasons to reject the constitution, but their underlying defiance was simple: times are hard, jobs are scarce, nothing changes, promises go unkept, we are fed up, and you – the political class – refuse to listen.

Macron observed the fall-out over the subsequent years. Increasingly drawn to political life, he analysed this 'divorce' between political discourse and action in an essay he published in the review *Esprit*, in the spring of 2011, when he was a banker at Rothschild's. The rise of the National Front, and the vote for the extremes, he argued, were also the symptom of this disconnection. French presidential elections, Macron suggested, had become a five-yearly 'spasm' in which candidates either promised everything, and then failed to deliver, or denounced the impossibility of doing anything within the system as it stood.[15] At all other times, meaningful public debate, either within parties or without, was largely absent. This undermined public faith in politics, prompted disillusion and distrust, and stored up trouble for the future. France had to reform for its own sake, he argued, not under orders from afar. 'I don't blame Germany,' Macron told me a month after becoming a minister. 'Our problem is ourselves.'[16] To conduct reform in disguise, to blame others for policies, or to put in place measures for which there was no electoral mandate, was to play into the hands of populists. 'The politician's word is exhausted,' he told me.[17]

In the years leading up to the 2017 election, in other words, France was in a state of unstable equilibrium. Long-simmering anxieties, and political distrust, were rising up. Political parties were tired. Small and sudden change had the potential to topple things to the ground. 'We have to prepare ourselves for upheavals the contours of which we cannot today apprehend,' Macron argued in *Révolution*.[18] A society deemed to be cripplingly conservative had worn itself out. A country that appeared immune to change in reality craved something new. 'You mustn't forget that the French have a revolutionary, and counter-revolutionary, temperament,' Christophe Prochasson, a historian, once told me. 'Belief in a better tomorrow has come to an end. There is a crisis of progress. The future no longer offers any perspective.'[19] It sounded like a warning of turbulence to come. 'Are we in 1789?' was the title on the front cover of *Le Point* magazine in 2013. 'We no longer know where we are heading,' wrote Pierre Nora, another historian, 'and we no longer know where we came from.'[20]

A country with a long disrupted history, marked by five monarchies and five constitutional republics since the Revolution, and invaded three times by its neighbour since 1870, had found constitutional stability. But the price seemed to be political inertia, and an inability to offer a credible sense of hope to a fatigued electorate, which was running out of patience.

Macron may have come late to Twitter, possess an unfashionable taste in music, and be described by friends as 'uncool' as a teenager. But he seemed to understand his era nonetheless. He saw that France had advanced through spasms throughout its history, and that technology was accelerating the pace of change and throwing up new possibilities for disruption. 'Macron understood that the history of France is one of rupture,' Sylvain Fort, his speechwriter, told me. 'France is a revolutionary country and only advances by breaking with the past.'[21] There was an arresting moment during Macron's inauguration ceremony, in the *salle des fêtes* at the Elysée Palace in May 2017, which opens onto the palace gardens. It felt like an intimate occasion, with only a few hundred people present in an immense reception room, including his parents, his wife's adult children, and other members of her family, who stood like guests at a cocktail party to watch the brief ceremony. When Laurent Fabius, the head of the constitutional council, conducted Macron's swearing-in, he quoted Chateaubriand: 'To be the man of his country, one must be the man of his time.' Macron saw that the time was right, that it might not last, and went for it. What he needed, however, was to anchor his personal ambitions in a collective, popular project. This was the second factor that enabled him to win power: the construction of a political movement out of nothing, capable of detonating the two-party system.

4

EN MARCHE TO THE ELYSÉE

Dans la vie il n'y a pas de solutions. Il y a des forces en marche: il faut les créer et les solutions suivent.
('In life, there are no solutions. There are forces on the move: create them, and solutions follow.')

Antoine de Saint-Exupéry, *Vol de nuit*

On successive Saturday mornings in the autumn of 2015, the lift to the young government minister's apartment was in constant use. In a series of secret meetings, plans were hatched to launch something, although none of the participants knew at the time quite what it would turn out to be. 'A club for reflection, or a think tank' was one idea, recalls a member of the group. 'An appeal for action', says another. The exact shape of the venture to come was a matter of debate. But what all members of the group shared with Emmanuel Macron, the minister in question, was a frustrated sense that there was a hidden majority in France in favour of reforming the country, but no way to unlock it.

Over a period of months, in clandestine gatherings at cafés in Paris, and via email threads and coded Telegram chat groups, a tiny band of metro-chic advisers in well-cut suits set to work on what finally emerged as En Marche. It was a tight-knit group, of young (and predominantly male) loyalists – later dubbed mockingly by the press *les Macron boys* – most of whom followed Macron from the ministry to the movement they created, and on into government or the Elysée Palace. At the operational nerve centre were two figures. One was Ismaël Emelien, then 28 years old and a figure who shies away from the public eye, recognizable by his big-framed glasses, five o'clock shadow, and taste for sleeveless puffer jackets. Originally from Grenoble, Emelien gravitated to the moderate centre-left of the Socialist Party while a student at Sciences Po, and helped out while still a teenager on Dominique Strauss-Kahn's campaign for the 2006 Socialist primary. He joined Macron's staff at the ministry in 2014, and became a close adviser. 'Emmanuel had the vision; Ismaël saw how to achieve it,' said Laurent Bigorgne, the director of the Institut Montaigne, and a participant in those early gatherings.[1]

The other was Julien Denormandie, a 35-year-old engineering graduate with the clean-cut, well-coiffed look of a member of the Parisian bourgeoisie. A former civil servant, he was an adviser to Pierre Moscovici at the Finance Ministry while Macron was working for Hollande at the presidency, and the pair were in regular contact. When Macron decided to quit the Elysée Palace, both Denormandie and Emelien were due to join him in developing a digital-learning start-up. Instead, Macron became a minister, while Denormandie became his deputy chief of staff, and later took over the organization of En Marche. Like the team they later recruited, both Denormandie and Emelien had the hyper-connected habits and informal codes of the social-media generation, zapping off messages to colleagues sprinkled with emoticons and irritating *franglais* – '*le pricing*' or '*le nudge*'. If Emelien was the strategic mind, Denormandie was the details man.

During the summer of 2015, the mood in the minister's office was one of frustration. Macron felt increasingly humiliated, and marginalized within government. He had lost his parliamentary battle with Manuel Valls, over the bill to deregulate Sunday trading. He was considered an agent of ultra-liberal capitalism by the left wing of the Socialist Party. But was he so out of touch with public opinion? In July the team organized a town-hall debate, open to the public and publicized on Macron's Facebook page. 'We had no idea whether we would have just 50 people, or more than that,' recalls one of the coordinators. After six hours, they had to close online registration. On a warm July mid-week evening during the school holidays, when many of the metropolitan types likely to be drawn to Macron had left Paris, more than 500 people turned up to ask questions about the future of France, and Europe. Microphone in hand, Macron told the audience that he was looking for ideas that could help to 'liberate' the country's energies. 'How do we invent a new model? How do we regain the initiative?' What the team took away from the town-hall meeting was not only that Macron had the power to draw a crowd, but that there was a divorce between the interests of the general public and those of the Paris elite. If France was to debate the underlying issues during the election campaign in 2017, the stale political establishment had to change.

But how? The young minister consulted widely. A number of different circles gravitated around him, their members sharing ideas over dinners at the ministry, or in his apartment. The flow of visitors included economists, Socialist-linked think-tankers, social democrats close to Michel Rocard, the former centre-left prime minister, as well as liberal policymakers and intellectuals. Views differed. Some suggested that Macron should stand for parliament in 2017. Others urged him to think of a presidential bid. 'He needed to give himself the means to have the possibility to run,' was how Bernard Spitz put it to me.[2] Macron listened, noted, all the while divulging nothing. In September 2015, I interviewed him for a column on progressive politics and digital disruption. With hindsight it is clear that Macron was already thinking then about how to transform his ideas into a new form of political action. 'The left has built its history around the extension of collective rights,' he told me. But 'the transformation of the economy risks bringing to an end this adventure of collective progress'. The challenge now, he said, is to 'build a form of neo-progressivism, structured around the idea of individual progress for all, in a way that combines agility with security ... We have to rethink the framework, and undertake an ideological renovation. It will happen. We need to show the way.'[3]

That month, he started to discuss the options with Emelien and Denormandie. One, pushed by his 91-year-old mentor, Henry Hermand, who had first met Macron when he was doing a civil-service internship at a *préfecture* outside Paris and sat at the top table at his wedding, was to create an association or publish a letter 'in defence' of the minister. Macron at the time was the object of irritation inside the Socialist Party, for declaring that young French people should 'want to become billionaires', or that the time when 'France could get better by working less' was over. Martine Aubry, the wily Socialist mayor of Lille, who had designed the 35-hour working week when labour minister, snapped that she was 'sick and tired' of Macron and his 'arrogance'. A member of the party's national bureau launched a petition calling for the minister to resign. Adept at charming an older generation, Macron held Hermand in high esteem, as well as affection. A prominent backer of moderate centre-left politics, and close to Michel Rocard, the elderly businessman had lent Macron money to buy his first flat in Paris. He also co-founded a newspaper, *Le 1*, which interviewed Macron on several occasions. That autumn, Hermand 'kept telling Macron that he had to start preparing to run for president in 2017', said Eric Fottorino, the editor of *Le 1*.[4] But the team was unpersuaded by Hermand's scheme. Alternative projects included a plan to set up a foundation, which Macron would leave the ministry to run. During the summer a proposal along these lines designed to help social entrepreneurs in fields such as digital learning was thrashed out with Bigorgne, a specialist in education. Another idea was for Macron to quit government to run, or set up, a think tank.

Emelien and Denormandie began to recruit various small groups to work on such ideas, under the radar. There were meetings in cafés near the ministry, or in each other's homes. Very few members of Macron's staff at the ministry knew what was going on. One who most certainly did was Alexis Kohler, a discreet fellow *énarque* with the look of an austere pastor, who ran Macron's staff and enjoys his trust, a privilege he went on to keep as the president's right-hand man at the Elysée. Outsiders were progressively brought into the loop. 'I got a call in October 2015 from Ismaël Emelien saying that Emmanuel Macron wants us to meet, but he didn't say why,' recalls Benjamin Griveaux, another former member of Strauss-Kahn's campaign team who was then working for a commercial-property firm, and went on to become the En Marche spokesman and then a junior government minister.[5] The discussion Griveaux attended, on a Saturday afternoon in Macron's office overlooking the Seine, was studious. If the country continued to tinker with the model that had served it well during the *trente glorieuses*, but which was ill adapted to the new economy, the group concluded, France was condemned to decline. 'Never did he say at that point "I'm going to be a candidate at the presidential election in 2017",' Griveaux told me. On another Saturday morning that month, a different group met over coffee in Macron's apartment to analyse how politics had become a lifelong profession and how this undermined public trust. Macron did what he always does: he listened to everybody, and made up his own mind. A think tank or a foundation, he concluded, would not be enough. 'We said to ourselves that we couldn't just be observers, and just have ideas, because the only thing that the political world understands is relations of power,' Emelien told me. 'We needed to give ourselves the means to really weigh in on the debate, to impose subjects. And for that we needed people behind us. That's how the idea emerged to create a political movement.'[6]

As detailed work into legal statutes and financing arrangements began, a few others were taken into their confidence. Among them was a trio of young friends who had been at business school near Paris together, Emmanuel Miquel, Cédric O and Stanislas Guerini, a couple of members of his ministerial staff, including Stéphane Séjourné, as well as others with specific expertise. Christian Dargnat, then director of BNP Paribas Asset Management, joined to work on fundraising. Adrien Taquet, who co-ran a communications company called Jésus et Gabriel, was tasked with branding and a name. Guillaume Liegey, the political consultant, worked on grass-roots participation. The team consisted of a dozen people, almost all of them men, many occupying full-time jobs and working for Macron after hours. There was no *éminence grise*, no heavyweight political veteran, no member much over the age of 40. Miquel had even been a student at Sciences Po in a class on 'general culture' taught part-time by Macron. The tight-knit nature of the group made sure that nothing leaked. Communication was transferred to Telegram's encrypted service. 'We were very careful,' recalled Bigorgne, 'because we didn't know if we were being listened to.'

From December 2015 onwards, things moved fast. The team needed to register the organization, which they hid behind an anodyne title – The Association for the Renewal of Political Life – and chose an address that would not raise eyebrows. Bigorgne, who lived in a suburb south of Paris, volunteered his address, and Véronique Bolhuis, his partner, was for a time made president of the association to bury the link deeper still. They also needed money. Dargnat quit his job in finance in December in order to take charge of fundraising full-time, along with Miquel, who worked in his spare time and weekends. Finally, and crucially, they also needed a name.

At a corner table at the bohemian-hip Hotel Amour, just south of the capital's once-sleazy Pigalle district, Emelien met up with Adrien Taquet, the brand consultant. Macron was keen to convey the '*élan* of movement', 'the idea of progress' and a 'sense of disruption', Taquet told me.[7] Starting with Macron's initials, and handwriting, Taquet came up with a few options, as well as that irritating exclamation mark the movement originally used. 'He's very decisive,' he said of Macron. 'Straight away, he wanted En Marche!' For Taquet, the name was an echo of the line from La Marseillaise, 'Marchons, marchons', as well as a nod to the Marche des Beurs, a long anti-racism walk that took place across France in 1983. Unbeknown to him at the time, En Marche also drew on a line from Antoine de Saint-Exupéry's novel *Vol de nuit*: *Dans la vie il n'y a pas de solutions. Il y a des forces en marche: il faut les créer et les solutions suivent* ('In life, there are no solutions. There are forces on the move: create them, and solutions follow.')[8] The reference was unintended, but captured perhaps best of all the spirit of what Macron was trying to do.

Four months of clandestine preparations followed. It was a hard slog involving late nights, low budgets and paranoid organization, sustained by the adrenalin of taking part in a project that many judged far-fetched, or downright delusional. Macron's gamble to go it alone was 'either lucid or mad', said Dargnat. All the while, the minister was at his job at the Finance Ministry, trying to get things moving again with a second *loi Macron*, designed to free up opportunities in the new economy, encourage start-ups and loosen the labour market. But it went nowhere. Increasingly exasperated by Macron, Manuel Valls emptied the economy minister's draft bill of all elements relating to labour reform, and then relegated Macron in a government reshuffle. Humiliated again, Macron realized that his space in government was shrinking fast. The timing was right for the launch.

When Emelien originally contacted Liegey in the autumn of 2015 to ask whether he wanted to help, the political consultant's first piece of advice was: 'get out of the office'.[9] This was the thrust of an article he had written in July that year, arguing that the modern political party had to behave like a start-up: respond to real problems, serve 'customers' meaningfully, search for new talent, and spend time getting to know what 'the market' wanted. It turned into a sort of checklist for the design of En Marche. Macron was a banker. He could not launch a credible party if it was perceived as merely a product of the Paris elite. They needed, rather, a grass-roots movement to give him popular legitimacy. To build one up, Liegey's agency came up with the idea of a 'Grande Marche', a giant information-gathering exercise across France, which was organized during the summer of 2016, to find out what people wanted from politics. The volunteers who emerged to run it, who liked to call themselves *marcheurs*, turned into the network that formed En Marche, and, ultimately, supplied it with candidates for parliament.

To see how it worked on the ground, I took the TGV high-speed train to Strasbourg in eastern France. The fine Alsatian city, with its half-timbered houses and tea salons, lies just on the French side of the Rhine, in the Franco-German borderlands. On a tree-lined square near the University of Strasbourg, the local coordinator for En Marche turned up for a session of door-to-door campaigning on a bicycle, his basket stuffed full of leaflets. Aged 38, and with an earnest demeanour, Bruno Studer was a high-school history and geography teacher in one of the city's tougher neighbourhoods. When Macron launched En Marche, Studer straight away set up a local support committee. At his lycée, he taught his pupils about the great speeches of history made in the National Assembly – one by Robert Badinter in favour of the abolition of the death penalty, another by Simone Veil pleading for the legalization of abortion – but he had never set foot in the building. In June 2017 he was elected to parliament as a deputy for En Marche.

Studer's story was repeated across France. Scores of political outsiders with no experience of campaigning, in all corners of the country, turned out to knock on doors for En Marche; and hundreds then went on to stand for parliament for the movement. At the start of 2017, Sandrine Le Feur was growing leeks and raising Highland sheep on her farm in northern Brittany. Bruno Bonnell, a jovial entrepreneur, was running a successful international robotics business in Lyon. The tall, gangly Hervé Berville was a Rwandan-born development economist. Jean-Marie Fiévet was working as a fireman in western France, a job he had held for 25 years. Six months later, all of them were elected to parliament. En Marche, in other words, was not just a vehicle for the election of Emmanuel Macron. It propelled political newcomers into the highest corridors of legislative power. Fully 45 per cent of the new deputies were women; 28 out of 577 were aged under 30. No fewer than 96 deputies aged over 70 sat in the outgoing parliament; in the new one there were only 13. In June 2017, at a shaded terrace café on the Place du Palais Bourbon, outside the National Assembly, such first-time deputies were to be found huddling over their welcome packs. Included among the helpful documents was a map of Paris.

The path from a high school in Strasbourg or a farm in Brittany to the National Assembly was no less improbable than that of an electoral debutant to the Elysée Palace. Neither would have been possible without the other. En Marche was primarily a vehicle for the ambitions of one man, and operated under his impulsion. This is why it managed to get national traction on the ground, where other citizens' movements failed. That Macron was able to win the presidency came down to the unusual articulation between an open grass-roots organization, whose members at least felt they had influence, and a tight-knit central team of 30-somethings who were really calling the shots, under the leadership of the man they called *le chef*. En Marche was a political start-up built as a hybrid: a forceful personality at the top, around whom all decisions ultimately turned, and a decentralized citizens' movement, trusted to devise events and mobilize support on the ground. Along the way, En Marche turned into a nationwide talent filter that netted its own future deputies. Within days of its launch, the movement had signed up 13,000 members. Within four months, the number reached 100,000, and it had overtaken the Socialist Party. By 2017 it had 310 deputies, or 54 per cent of the National Assembly.

On that warm spring day in Strasbourg in 2016, Bruno Studer explained how the movement took off locally. He created a Facebook page, became the movement's local representative, and took part with fellow volunteers in the 'Grande Marche', knocking on doors and gathering answers to the survey questions devised in Paris, their data sent directly from tablet computer to En Marche headquarters. That autumn, the history teacher organized a meeting in Strasbourg, and Macron arrived by train to present the first results of those surveys. By April 2017, with a limited budget and low-cost campaign, the movement had signed up 3,200 members in Bas-Rhin, the *département* surrounding Strasbourg, distributed 100,000 flyers and held 50 public meetings. In June, Studer beat his Republican opponent, and secured 60 per cent of the vote in a constituency held by the centre-right for 20 years.

'The most important factor was that they trusted us,' Studer said.[10] The message, and the programme, of En Marche was drawn up in Paris. But the local committees that sprang up in different neighbourhoods and villages used the internet platform built by the team at headquarters to plan and communicate themselves. The pro-European message Studer conveyed at public meetings carried particular symbolism in Alsace, land of conquest and bloodshed during two world wars between Germany and France. Studer's grandfathers, one a member of the French Resistance, the other forcibly enrolled by the Germans to fight for the Reich, ended up at war on opposite sides. Pro-European feeling in the city had deep roots, but remained fragile. Shortly before I visited, in the village of Monswiller just 50 kilometres away, over 1,000 locals had turned out to hear Marine Le Pen. They chanted what became her supporters' xenophobic battle cry, '*On est chez nous*' ('This is our home'). It mobilized Studer's En Marche volunteers all the more.

Perhaps the most surprising hallmark of En Marche local campaigns was the old-fashioned emphasis on knocking on doors, a technique almost never used in French election campaigns. The French consider their voting preferences to be private. Campaign posters are restricted to an official municipal billboard that mysteriously emerges from the town hall ahead of every election. Activists hand out leaflets to commuters at train stations or shoppers at weekend food markets. But in France, the forest of American-style lawn signs that spring up in election periods, or the British window posters, would be regarded as inappropriate, dangerous or vulgar. So when Macron announced that he was going on a Grande Marche to knock on doors, he was much mocked in Parisian political circles. Unlike in America or Britain, doorstep canvassing in France appeared to be borrowed from another era. 'Knocking on doors, how modern!' sneered Jean-Christophe Cambadélis, the first secretary of the Socialist Party, on French breakfast radio. A government minister and then colleague of Macron's posted a link on her Twitter account to a song by Jean-Jacques Goldman: '*Je marche seul*' ('I walk alone').

Yet Liegey, along with his two partners, Arthur Muller and Vincent Pons, borrowed heavily from insights garnered from their time as volunteers on Obama's 2008 Democratic campaign. All three were students at the time in Cambridge, Massachusetts – Liegey and Muller at Harvard's Kennedy School of Government, and Pons at MIT – and observed up close the way the campaign used algorithms to micro-target voters, whom volunteers then bombarded with personal doorstep visits or phone calls. The winning blend, Liegey told me, was 'tailored technology and human contact'.[11] Back in Paris, and within the constraints on data-gathering imposed by French data-privacy laws, the trio built their own predictive software, and tried it out on Socialist Party campaigns, first in the Paris region in 2010 and then for François Hollande in 2012. Similar to NationBuilder, the American electoral software package, the French model, built by Pons, crossed data from 67,000 polling stations in France with publicly available metadata on socio-economic background. Although privacy laws meant that they could not target individuals, they were able to use aggregated data to identify blocks of streets, according to an index measuring the likelihood that voters living there could be persuaded or mobilized to vote.

On the ground, En Marche door-knocking did feel laborious and thankless. 'Lots of people just tell us all politicians are rotten,' Sophie Zeugin, the local En Marche representative in Châteaudun told me with a sigh when I went to the town to watch her canvassing. Perched on a river bend in an unfashionable expanse of central France, Châteaudun is in many ways a typical French town. It boasts a fifteenth-century château, an unemployment rate of 10 per cent, a fine main square shaded by plane trees and a Turkish kebab restaurant. The town of 13,000 inhabitants also happened to have a record of voting in line with the rest of the country. In 2007 locals backed the winner, Nicolas Sarkozy, on the right. In 2012 they voted for the victor, François Hollande, on the left. But in 2017 the campaign felt too close to call. A local entrepreneur, Zeugin went out knocking on doors with a basket of leaflets hanging off her arm and multi-coloured

En Marche balloons in her hand, in an attempt to bring a festive note to her doorstep intrusions. The good folk of Châteaudun were scarcely more welcoming on the doorstep than those I had seen in Strasbourg. Yet what was striking was the movement's ability to harness local goodwill. Zeugin told me that it had been simple to set up her local committee with just a few clicks on the En Marche website, and she was busy organizing local meetings, even when no more than 25 people on average turned up. In cafés and meeting rooms across France, their T-shirts emblazoned with the En Marche logo, local volunteers became Macron's unpaid army. They were the cheerful faces manning the doors and managing the queues when Macron turned up to speak. This campaign, after all, had an exclamation mark! In the town of Conflans-Sainte-Honorine, which lies on a wooded bend of the Seine to the west of Paris, Mickaël Littiere told me that when he first held a meeting for his local En Marche committee in a bar near the river, only one person bothered to come along. In the run-up to the presidential election, there were three different En Marche committees in Conflans alone.

'Anybody could create a local committee, which was the base unit of the movement. And anybody could leave one and join another with just one click. This meant that we had 4,000 local committees, but no problems with them. We lost zero time and spent zero energy managing internal problems,' Emelien told me.[12] The key, he said, was to 'make them feel useful, and trusted. And we gave them responsibility, territorial autonomy and the freedom to organize.' At the same time, this was a political movement built by business-school graduates who knew the value of 'growth-hacking', using free membership (En Marche charged no fee to join) to secure a valuable database, for crowd-funding and campaigning. The starting point, Emelien said, was to 'give our members useful tasks. That is to say, to give them responsibility, to treat them as our only resource, our only asset, our only chance. So we completely turned the pyramid upside down. Everywhere else, party members are at the service of the level above. They serve their elected representative, who serves the local political baron, who serves the presidential candidate, who serves those who organize elections. For us, it was the other way round. We spent days and nights making ourselves useful to our members.' The message was: the members were the movement, the organizational force, the canvassers, the fundraisers.

Of course, this was not entirely true. En Marche was built in two distinct phases, each tightly managed by Macron and his team at headquarters in Paris. The Grande Marche of the summer of 2016 was, in effect, a pilot experiment. Volunteers used the giant survey to identify issues that voters in districts potentially sympathetic to Macron cared about. Questions included: If you had one thing to ask from politics what would it be? What do you think works well in France? What doesn't work? What worries you the most? What's your greatest hope? Answers were recorded on a customized smartphone app, connected to a digital platform, and analysed in Paris using third-party software. 'We really made an effort to make sure the app experience was both pleasant and efficient,' said Emelien. By the time it was over, 600 coordinators and 5,000 volunteers across France had knocked on 300,000 doors and gathered answers from 25,000 people. Over 1.5 million words were stored in a searchable database, organized thematically. The results confirmed what Macron's team had sensed: an exasperation with politics, disillusion with politicians and, said Griveaux, 'above all, a perception that the system was holding people back'. The second phase began after Macron declared his candidacy in November 2016, and turned into the election campaign proper. In each case, what made En Marche work was a form of local semi-autonomy combined with the tight grip of Macron and his team at the top. Above all, the exercise provided the former banker, seen as remote from ordinary people, with a locally rooted network, enabling Macron to claim to be at the forefront of an emerging citizens' movement.

So there was a cynical element to the design of En Marche, one that may store up some trouble for the future as grass-roots idealism collides with the hierarchical reality of government. But it was also a genuine attempt to draw people back into politics and repair disillusion. Plenty of French people volunteer to run associations, local football clubs and the like. But this civic enthusiasm is more usually matched by political apathy, or hostility. Politics in France had become a lifetime profession, and lost credibility as a result. By 2017 confidence in political parties had dropped to 11 per cent, according to a poll by CEVIPOF, a research institute at Sciences Po, lower even than that in the media, trade unions or banks. People trusted their local mayor, but not their lawmakers or their president. Over the decades, France seemed to have created a particularly problematic form of political gerontocracy, which failed to bring in fresh blood, and obliged the younger generation to wait its turn. 'We started from the observation that in France, politics had become a career,' Dargnat said.[13] 'You start at the age of 18 years as a member of a political party, then become a parliamentary assistant. If you become a senator, you keep going until you are 80. You can be in politics for 40 or 50 years. This was abnormal.'

Not only were French politicians removed from the real life of their constituents, but political parties had become sect-like and doctrinaire. 'The most chemically pure incarnation of what the French rejected in politics was parties,' Emelien told me. 'Because parties had, little by little, abandoned all the reasons for which they were invented. They no longer selected the best. They no longer trained their activists. They no longer threw up ideas. And, above all, they were exhausting themselves by focusing on the conquest of power without knowing what to do with it afterwards.' The upshot, he judged, was a succession of internal power struggles, ritualized but empty annual party conferences, and 'a totally disappointing customer experience'. As in many other Western democracies, party membership in France collapsed. After the Second World War, the French Communist Party was a genuinely popular movement, claiming 800,000 members, more than the British Labour Party at the time. By 2016 all France's mainstream parties were bleeding adherents, as voters turned away from traditional politics towards single-issue groups, volunteer movements and non-governmental associations. The French, like other Western Europeans, seemed more likely to sign up to defend land from development than they were to join a political party. Movements and causes drew supporters and activists; parties tended to put them off. By 2016, France's Republicans claimed around 230,000 paid-up members; the Socialists were down to just 85,000. 'What doesn't work is the system of parties, which are decision-making machines that are distant from people,' Macron told me in July 2016.[14] 'That's what feeds populism. We need to find far more direct forms of exchange with people.' In particular, he wanted to use new technology to connect with voters. 'It's a political approach that involves talking directly to people, both via technological platforms but also physically on the ground. We need to build both a digital network and a territorial offering that brings in new people.'

En Marche became the vehicle. Some 70 per cent of its volunteers had little or no history of political activism. En Marche representatives were able to use the techniques employed during the Grande Marche to campaign during the election. The principle of local autonomy was fairly well preserved. After a day out reporting in Châteaudun during the presidential campaign, I came across Lex Paulson, an American political scientist teaching in Paris, who had also served as a volunteer on Obama's campaign in Connecticut in 2008. He helped to train volunteers for En Marche, and had just spent a day with a team in the nearby city of Chartres. The crucial factor, he argued, was that the movement treated volunteers as 'ambassadors not robots'. This required headquarters to trust local campaigners, and not overly dictate to them. The volunteers I met selected the bits of the En Marche campaign kit they thought would go down well. When she went knocking on doors in Châteaudun, her basket of leaflets on her arm, Sophie Zeugin said that she didn't use a line that Macron favoured about the complexity of life. Voters didn't relate too well to that, she said. But they were interested in his promise to clean up politics, and clear out the old political class. Over in Chartres on the same day, the En Marche representative for the *département* of Eure-et-Loir, Guillaume Kasbarian, told me that the best way to convince voters was to sound as revolutionary as possible. 'There's an edge for the candidate who sounds the most *dégagiste*,' he said, referring to the promise to kick the old guard out: 'Voters don't want to hear about a woolly centrism.'[15] Trusting local reps to tailor the message improved efficiency, and helped to mobilize volunteers.

So the old-fashioned En Marche doorstep campaign brought a useful human dimension to the movement. It was a way of contradicting in voters' minds the idea both that politics was distant and removed from the electorate, and that Macron was just a product of the elite. 'Even in an age of social media, a face-to-face message can be ten times as effective,' Paulson argued. Macron's French campaign was not an exact remake of Obama's. Under the aforementioned French privacy laws, En Marche could collect email addresses and personal data only from those who signed up to the movement, and had to use metadata to target broad electoral districts, rather than individual voters. As a start-up, its structure was far flatter, and its headquarters smaller, than that of a traditional political party, let alone the American Democratic Party. 'We created something that was different, not just a replica in France of another model,' Emelien said. 'We took bits from all over the place, then invented certain things that were new.'

As it grew, En Marche took on many young volunteers, and moved to a nondescript office building on the rue de l'Abbé Groult, a narrow street in the 15th arrondissement of southern Paris. Policy experts came on board. A respected economist, Jean Pisani-Ferry, was brought in to coordinate the drawing up of a manifesto, lending the movement intellectual credibility. Despite the expansion, En Marche managed to retain the feel of a small start-up. At the ministry, Macron had enjoyed access to a dining room, with butlers, and a chauffeured car. En Marche was run on a shoestring, and an invitation to a lunchtime event would involve sandwiches in brown bags. The movement generated its share of chaos. Working groups on diplomatic affairs were 'a shambles', recalled one adviser, with 'too many bright young untutored diplomats incapable of imposing discipline'. On the whole, though, as a campaign organization, it worked.

En Marche also turned into a handy fundraising machine. It began with nothing. 'At first we had no offices at all,' Christian Dargnat recalled. 'We had no money. The first place we rented was tiny, and had no air conditioning, so we struggled with the heat that summer.' French financing rules, which base public subsidies for political parties on legislative results, keep the mainstream parties flush with cash and put newcomers at an acute disadvantage. The Socialist Party, with its headquarters in a grand nineteenth-century left-bank mansion on the rue de Solférino, just off the boulevard Saint-Germain, had a war chest to use. Macron had to raise individual donations, and take out a bank loan insured on his life. In 12 months, En Marche managed to raise over €10 million – pocket money by American standards but a record for France, where electoral-finance rules cap any individual donation at €7,500 a year, and preclude any single financier from bankrolling a presidential bid. Over 32,000 individual donors had contributed, a third of whom gave under €30 each.

In reality, though, En Marche relied heavily on contributions near the upper limit from members of the very French elite whom Macron was keen to distance himself from in public. With a fundraising team of just half a dozen – run by Dargnat and Miquel – the team leveraged every network it could, working its way through their collective address books, and holding dinners in private apartments in Paris, as well as in London and New York. 'I started with my friends, and then friends of friends; then I realized that I didn't have enough friends,' said Dargnat. Each event was designed to extract as close to the maximum limit as possible. Macron went to London – home to a big French expat community of financiers – six times alone. In total, some 60 to 70 such dinners were held. It wasn't difficult to find people to attend, but it was far harder to persuade them to part with a cheque. In the end, 70 per cent of the total funds donated to En Marche came from individuals willing to shell out sums close to the upper limit of 7,500 euros. En Marche ended up building a citizens' movement around a former banker, and a grass-roots election campaign on finance from the moneyed French elite.

Such was Macron: the insider's outsider, the leader of an insurgency against the establishment by one of its own. If the democratic purge of 2017 was revolutionary, it was conducted from inside the machine. En Marche was a product both of the elite and of civic participation, a mix that went on to generate its own tensions. This hybrid design helped to put both a novice in the presidency, and debutants in parliament, cleansing an entire political class. Neither would have happened without the other. A year after they set up local committees in their home towns, many En Marche representatives found themselves sitting on the benches of parliament. Shortly after the election, I found Bruno Bonnell, the 58-year-old tech entrepreneur from Lyon, admiring the view from his new office, overlooking the cobbled Place du Palais Bourbon. The first time he stepped into the National Assembly as an elected member of parliament, he shed a tear. Bruno Studer, the history teacher from Strasbourg, talked of the burden of 'responsibility' he felt as an elected MP. He hadn't yet been allocated an office, so we met for coffee at a terrace café behind parliament. The 39-year-old kept teaching at his lycée until mid-June despite the campaign. Having seen on the doorstep how vehemently voters distrusted politicians, Studer felt that it was up to his generation to restore confidence. Weeks later, deputies passed a law to clean up politics, put an end to employment of family members, and tighten up expenses rules.

Hervé Berville, who had joined the parliamentary foreign-affairs commission, recalled how much people had mocked En Marche early in the campaign. Born in Rwanda shortly before the genocide against the Tutsi ethnic group, to which he belonged, Berville was orphaned and adopted in 1994 by a French couple from Pluduno, a quiet village of dark-grey granite houses in inland Brittany. Working as a development economist in Nairobi in 2016, he set up a local committee in Kenya for En Marche and then returned to France to campaign for Macron, joining En Marche in Brittany, and going on to become the party's parliamentary candidate in his home region. 'For outsiders, it was risky, to put a black man in Brittany,' Berville told me: 'But I never had trouble.'[16] He knows that things could have turned out differently. In 1994 some 800,000 Tutsis were killed in Rwanda during the 100-day genocidal massacres. His mother had died at the age of 27. By the time he reached the same age, Berville was elected a member of the French National Assembly.

En Marche was in the end a curious hybrid, both flat and hierarchical, built from the bottom and run from the top. Macron's presidential bid would not have worked had the movement not taken hold, in cafés and meeting halls on the ground. He needed the popular legitimacy this conferred. At the same time, the reason it worked on the ground, and that activists believed that they were shaping the campaign themselves, was because of the self-belief, tight grip and charisma of the candidate. If Emmanuel Macron had not been present at the fundraising dinners, people would not have been persuaded to write out cheques. Victory in 2017 depended not only on identifying the political space, and building a party; it also required a particular sort of leader. 'You can construct a movement around common values, build a campaign, create a political narrative, raise enough funds to carry it out professionally,' Guillaume Liegey told me, recalling his American experience. 'But you still need a Barack Obama.' In the end, for all that the *marcheurs* on the ground felt that they were building this campaign, it was ultimately dominated by the figure of Macron himself.

5

Jupiter Rising

'I'm claustrophobic about life. I can't stand being shut in, I have to get out, that's why I can't have a normal life.'

Emmanuel Macron to Emmanuel Carrère, 2017

Emmanuel Macron has just been hit in the face with an egg. It is a perfect arc of a lob, thrown over the heads of his security guards, the hard shell landing with a splat on his forehead, disgorging glutinous yellow yolk into his hair and onto the fine cloth of his well-cut navy suit. Instantly, a bodyguard thrusts his arm over the candidate's head, and hustles him to the side. But Macron is unfazed. 'It's an egg!' he protests. 'It's nothing. Don't worry.' That evening, in a scene broadcast later in a television documentary, Macron looks at the video replay on his campaign director's phone, letting out a high-pitched giggle as he watches the egg land with uncanny precision smack onto his head. 'I took it right in the face! ... He threw it from far, did you see that? The guy was really lucky.'[1]

Macron is unflappable. Almost preternaturally so. He can be tough, exacting, authoritarian even. He knows what he wants, and what he needs to do to get it. He drives himself hard, and expects the same of his team. He sleeps little, and sends texts in the early hours. 'He is incredibly demanding of himself, and of others,' Adrien Taquet, the brand consultant, told me. 'It's very tiring working for him.'[2] But, say aides, he does not panic. And he almost never loses his temper. 'He has an Obama-like level of self-control,' said François Heisbourg, a security analyst from the Foundation for Strategic Research think tank who advised him on counter-intelligence policy during the campaign.[3] Among the rare times that Macron was known to swear during the election was when his football team, Olympique de Marseille, lost. 'Oh *merde*, for the second time, *putain!*' he was heard muttering after one such defeat, the scene caught on camera. 'I have never known anybody as serene,' said Laurent Bigorgne, who has been a friend for over a decade. 'Nothing – nothing – gets him annoyed.'[4] If anything, Bigorne said, Macron is 'sometimes almost expressionless. He's afraid of nothing. He has total self-control.' He does not even sweat, Emmanuel Carrère, the French novelist, noticed while accompanying him to the hot and humid Caribbean island of Saint Martin after a hurricane struck in September 2017.

'He has an absolute calm, an incredible sang-froid,' Benjamin Griveaux, Macron's campaign spokesman, told me.[5] When his friends talk about him this way, it sounds improbable, excessive, robotic almost. Yet I saw it myself, when I accompanied the then minister in the autumn of 2015, aboard a small government Falcon jet back from RAF Northolt in London to a French military base near Paris, in order to interview him while in transit. As we approached the French capital, we flew into a violent storm. Sitting opposite him across a table, I clenched the seat handles. Members of his staff on board exchanged nervous glances. Lightning flashed through the porthole windows; the plane began to shudder and lurch, on its way to a bumpy landing. He did not flinch once. 'I'm not made to lead in calm weather; my predecessor was,' Macron said after reaching the presidency two years later, 'but I'm made for storms.'[6]

This inner poise made him an unusually calm and self-assured campaign manager. But did Macron have what it would take to seduce voters? What was not clear before the presidential election campaign was whether the former investment banker, *énarque*, adviser to the most unpopular president in modern French history, friend to the Parisian financial elite, defender of globalization, and pro-European to boot, would make a good sleeves-rolled-up, on-the-stump campaigner. 'I remember a conversation quite early on, when I was urging him to run for the presidency, and sensed his anxiety,' a friend of his told me. 'It wasn't about whether he would be a good president. His anxiety was about whether he could be a good candidate.' In private, Macron deployed his legendary charm. French ministers, who are treated like minor royalty and fussed over by butlers and chauffeurs, often adopt a demeanour of entitlement while in government, mistaking the trappings of political office for personal self-importance. There was none of that with Macron. In his office overlooking the Seine, in the modernist Finance Ministry, the minister would leave his suit jacket on the back of the chair, and strike a friendly conversational tone that steered clear of the overly chummy. 'On form?' he would ask cheerfully, before sitting down on the deep black-leather sofa to give questions his full attention, both mobile phones lying unattended beside him. The technocrat, in other words, had demonstrated a private capacity for political seduction. But could he win over the public?

In some ways Macron was a disappointing performer. He turned out at first to be a stilted public speaker, bewilderingly so for someone who had spent his teenage years on the stage. His speeches often lacked lyricism or rhythm. The first time he held a rally after the launch of En Marche, at the Maison de la Mutualité in the 5th arrondissement of Paris, Macron emerged on stage, and paced about, struggling to project his slightly metallic voice. His final line carried promise: 'This movement, nothing will stop it. Because this movement, it's the movement of hope, that this country needs. This movement, we will carry it together, until 2017 and until victory!' But, from where I was sitting, his voice lacked resonance or range. If this was a politician hoping to become a Barack Obama *à la française*, he had none of the American politician's cadence or crescendos, let alone his musical notes.

Over time, Macron hired a voice coach, deepened his pitch and improved his performance. His rallies, warmed up with the booming bass of the track 'Walk In', and packed with supporters who had queued in the street to get a place, carried an authentic zeal and fervour. Yet, even so, Macron's speeches were too long-winded, as Brigitte Macron kept telling him.[7] He was rarely conversational in tone, shied away from the particular, and tended to submerge his audience with theoretical abstractions. The end of his rallies often left the audience dissatisfied, his words short on intimacy and emotion, dramatic build-up or dénouement. The great advantage of campaigning in France is that, when short of a good final note, there is always the cry of 'Vive la République! Vive la France!' followed by a rendition of La Marseillaise, a national anthem made for political campaigning. Yet the final lines of a Macron speech often fell flat, as they did at his rally in Reims: 'Because the real patriots are here. They love France. Because real patriots look at the past and the future, and reconcile them!'[8] In Dijon he ended his speech: 'Yes, my friends, during these 30 days, be real patriots. You are defending France, you are defending a project, an ambitious project, a project of reconciliation, a generous project. You are patriots and progressives. Fight each hour and each day!'[9] And in Besançon: 'My friends, right to the last hour, I want your mobilization, your energy, because we are going to win!'[10] Macron, who could recite long passages from Molière by heart, did not do folksy. He spoke of his grandmother, but seldom mentioned an encounter with ordinary people on the campaign trail. The closest he got to a personal anecdote was the tale of an incident that concerned a philosopher.

Even his first televised debate, on 20 March 2017, was not an unequivocal success. Macron put in a competent performance, which kept him in the race. But he lacked the killer one-liner of the sort that Jean-Luc Mélenchon was able to deliver with quick-witted ease. At one point, François Fillon argued that labour relations should be decentralized to company level, to which the far-left firebrand retorted: 'I'm not in favour of one labour code per firm, just as I am not in favour of one highway code per road.' Macron's intellectualism, his long elaborate sentences and splendid abstractions, seemed to hamper his ability to make a mark. 'You've spoken for seven minutes, and I have no idea what you said,' Marine Le Pen snapped at him, in one of her feistier moments. 'Every time you talk, you say a bit of this, a bit of that, and never decide.'

Yet, as curiosity about Macron began to swell, and the queues to get in to see him started to snake down the roads ahead of his public appearances, it became clear that something was nonetheless happening. And this something had less to do with his performance, a work of political theatre, and more to do with the symbolism of what he was trying to achieve. If Macron had charismatic leadership, or the ability to inspire and lead others, it was through his capacity to incarnate hope and change. That he managed to climb steadily in the polls for months before he finally unveiled a manifesto, in March 2017, testified to the fact that this was a campaign constructed not according to a checklist of policies but around himself. Macron's programme was Macron. In this sense, the personal qualities that he brought to bear on the campaign were also fundamental to its success. Three stand out: his ability to cast himself as a disruptive insurgent that matched the anti-establishment mood; the authentic message of optimism he sought to embody; and his ability to set a broad objective and go about achieving it in a disciplined, orderly fashion.

On the first point, Macron transformed factors that might in ordinary times have disqualified his candidacy into markers of insurrectionary change. In the early months after the launch of En Marche, it had looked as if the candidate might attract only rootless liberal types. At his first rally, in the Latin quarter of Paris in July 2016, a trial run for the not-yet candidate, the hall was packed with the sort of well-heeled, young, mostly male, metropolitan crowd who might have stepped out of business school, or a tech start-up. It reminded me of the improbably well-dressed French students who queued up the winding staircase at the LSE in London to hear the minister speak while on a visit in the autumn of 2015, an early sign that Macron was stirring interest. If this was to be his support base, though, it looked desperately narrow: a conversation among like-minded professional types, not a pitch to France's broad middle.

Yet, as the campaign wore on, Macron managed to cast his net wider. He did this partly by using a political lexicon – 'revolution', 'emancipation' – that spoke directly to a far broader swathe of people. The language he employed was designed to tap into the *dégagiste* mood, urging voters to sweep the old political class aside: 'You will conquer,' he told them, 'This is your project.' On a bright wintry day in February 2017, I followed the candidate on the campaign trail in the *département* of Mayenne. This is an expansive stretch of rolling farmland, marked by villages without cafés and patchy mobile reception, that lies between Le Mans and Rennes in western France. The En Marche campaign then still had an improvised low-cost feel to it. To the surprise of fellow passengers, Macron travelled second class on the TGV from the Gare Montparnasse in Paris. The campaign team had no budget to lay on the logistical services – a press bus, sandwiches – that the well-financed parties provided for a full day on the road during an election campaign. Upon arrival by train in the city of Le Mans, we hired a car at the station, and tried to keep up with the candidate as he raced in his campaign car from village to village down narrow country lanes. At each stop, a small gathering of locals had got wind of Macron's visit, and were waiting for him to arrive. In a muddy farmyard near the village of Gennes-sur-Glaize, I came across Patrick Pervis, a bearded 63-year-old of generous girth who described himself as a *paysan* (peasant farmer). 'All the other candidates live off politics,' he told me, sinking his hands into his jacket pockets: 'But Macron hasn't been in politics, he hasn't had his nose in the trough.' While Macron trod his way through puddles and mud-splattered dairy pens, in his city shoes and Paris suit under a navy wool overcoat, Pervis displayed an arresting solidarity with the former banker. 'Macron, like us, knows the world of work.'

Later that afternoon, we arrived in Angers, a cathedral town on the river Maine and the medieval seat of the Plantagenet dynasty. Macron was due to hold an evening rally there, and long before he emerged onstage hundreds of supporters lined up on the pavement outside the convention centre, wrapped up in winter coats and scarves, hoping for a seat. The team had booked an auditorium for 1,200. In the end, nearly twice that number turned up. The atmosphere was electric. As Macron arrived on the pavement, volunteers dressed in En Marche T-shirts had physically to hold people back. When the auditorium was full, an overflow crowd of enthusiasts, the grey-haired as well as the young, sat on the floor in the draughty entrance hall, their coats buttoned up, to watch a broadcast of the speech on a screen. A retired tax inspector, who usually voted Socialist, told me that she was drawn to Macron because he was 'young and brilliant' but above all 'different'. She had 'had enough of dishonest politicians' and he, unlike them, had 'not been at it for years'. Voters, it seemed, were willing to make a distinction between a technocratic member of the establishment (good) and a political hack (bad). In other words, it was electoral party politics, not the quality of the country's administrators, that was seen as rotten. The same point emerged when I went to watch Macron speak at a small event for start-ups in the *banlieues*, Paris's high-rise suburbs, which seemed unpromising territory for the former investment banker. There too, participants appeared unbothered by his deep establishment ties. Macron was an outsider. He was 'not one of them', and had cultivated a reputation for insubordination that went down as both courageous and novel. 'In France we never try new things, it's always the same faces,' Yacine Kara, an entrepreneur of Algerian origin, said to me. 'His political inexperience is positive. He's taking a risk, like us.'

So Macron managed to turn political inexperience into an asset, wrapping it in the language of popular insurrection, and in doing so broadened his vote. In the end, his first-round score was indeed strongest among city dwellers, and those with university degrees. Macron did not capture the youth vote, which went to the extremes, to both Mélenchon and Le Pen. Yet he scored well in all age groups over 25 years. Macron gained as much backing from public-sector workers as did Mélenchon, and two points more than Mélenchon from those with no formal qualifications.[11] He scored twice as much of the unemployed vote as Benoît Hamon, the Socialist candidate, and two points more of the rural vote than François Fillon. En Marche deputies were elected even in remote parts of *la France profonde*, including in the *départements* of la Corrèze and la Creuse.

In the end, unlike Mélenchon and Le Pen, Macron represented a safe variety of insurgent. New to politics, untested and young, he was different in those respects. But he did not represent much of a risk. A former Sarkozy voter I met one February weekend buying waxy lemons in a fruit market in the naval port of Toulon, under an azure sky, told me that he was backing Macron because he is 'from the new generation, but he's also been a minister; he knows what he's doing'. That seemed to sum it up. Macron's appeal as a radical insurrectionist who would crush the old guard met the aspiration for renewal, but was softened by a reassuring familiar feel. You could vote for him as a form of protest against the establishment, with the comfort of knowing that he understood how to work the machine. Laurent Bouvet, a political scientist, called this the 'taking of power by the technocracy': the frustrated high-flying civil servants, who had complained for years that politicians failed to reform France as other countries had done, finally had found one of their own.[12] Macron, Bouvet said, was the first of them to say: 'we can't just complain, we have to get on and do it'. Once an adviser to the prince, Macron decided to become the prince himself. For a country that veered between rebellion and regret, revolution and counter-revolution, Macron succeeded in embodying both change and continuity. His was a political insurgency without pitchforks or pikes: a response to the urge for revolt that did not frighten the French.

Macron's skill at reinventing himself to fit the *dégagiste* mood was matched by the second factor: a gift for conveying an optimism that had long eluded France. En Marche was launched at a time of deep French malaise. The country had been under a state of emergency since the bloody terrorist attacks in Paris in November 2015. The year 2016 brought more gruesome bloodshed. Two police employees were stabbed to death in their home by a jihadist. A lorry was driven into festive crowds in Nice on

Bastille Day. Terrorists slit the throat of an 85-year-old priest during mass in Normandy. This blackened an already sombre mood. Unemployment was at 10 per cent, and still climbing. Between March and July students and trade unions were on the streets almost weekly, protesting against new labour laws. Nativists of the far right and class warriors of the far left alike were building their politics on division and distrust. Political faces tended to be stern, frowns fixed and adjectives gloomy. Manuel Valls, the prime minister, who had warned the French that they had to learn to live with terrorism, seemed to wear a perma-scowl.

Up to a point, of course, melancholy is treated by the French as a badge of national identity. 'Optimism,' says a disabused Candide in Voltaire's novel, 'is the madness of insisting that all is well when we are miserable.' The strange beauty of sadness has been a constant of the country's literature. The French Romantics regarded miserabilism as a form of pleasure. 'Melancholy,' wrote Victor Hugo, 'is the happiness of being sad.' In the twentieth century, the left-bank literary clique led by Jean-Paul Sartre and Simone de Beauvoir, which gravitated to the cafés of Saint-Germain-des-Près, adopted *ennui* as a way of life as well as a philosophy. When Sartre handed the original manuscript of *Nausea* to Gallimard, his publisher, he gave the novel the title *Melancholia*. Monique Canto-Sperber, a philosopher at the elite Ecole Normale Supérieure, once told me that this outlook was due to French philosophical training and the art of critique. 'The rationalist tradition makes us sceptical; we exist through criticism,' she said: 'We treat those too full of hope as naive.' Michel Houellebecq, the Goncourt prize-winning novelist, populated such nihilist works as *Whatever* or *Atomised* with characters who invariably lead empty, often sordid and always disillusioned lives. 'In the end,' writes Houellebecq in *The Elementary Particles*, 'there's just the cold, the silence and the loneliness. In the end, there's only death.' The point is handed down through the generations. All French pupils are examined on a compulsory philosophy paper for the school-leaving *baccalauréat*, with such essay questions as 'Is man condemned to self-delusion?' Optimism, in Europe's most self-consciously intellectual country, is for the naive; sophisticates know better.

Yet France by 2016 was in a state of depression that went deeper than this. For over a decade, French intellectuals and academics had been dissecting the causes of what was known as *'le mal français'*: a fracturing of society, a collapse in economic competitiveness, an ossification of political life, a decline of diplomatic influence, a loss of cultural panache. Books with titles such as *Illusions gauloises* (*Gallic Illusions*), *Le suicide français* (*The French Suicide*) and *L'identité malheureuse* (*The Unhappy Identity*) became bestsellers. Commentators described France, variously, as in a state of economic decay, moral decline and political desolation. Declinism became something of an academic speciality. After *Le malheur français* by Jacques Julliard came *Comprendre le malheur français* by Marcel Gauchet. In a book published in 2003 the commentator Nicolas Baverez wrote of the 'atomisation of French society', the 'spread of social nihilism', and the 'anaemia' of French democracy.[13] In foreign policy, he argued trenchantly, the French had concealed the deterioration of their military capacity, misread the consequences of the fall of the Berlin Wall, and clung to a sense of global importance long diminished. 'There is effectively something metaphysical in the sentiment of decline which is engulfing the old world in general, and France in particular,' commented the writer Franz-Olivier Giesbert.[14] It was a time of disorientation for much of the West, faced with the rise of China and other emerging powers, the transformations brought by the digital economy and the revival of identity politics. But the French, with their universalist aspiration, seemed to feel it with almost unique pain. In *Adieu à la France qui s'en va* (*Goodbye to the France that has Gone*), Jean-Marie Rouart wrote lyrically of the loss of France's soul.[15] Pessimism, concluded Sudhir Hazareesingh, in his history of French thought, 'broadened out from a confined sense of anxiety to become one of the entrenched features of the contemporary French mindset'.[16] The country that brought the world the Enlightenment seemed trapped in the darkness of its own collective depression.

Macron's optimism came as a shocking remedy, a sharp tonic. Bruno Bonnell, the robotics entrepreneur who became a local En Marche representative in Lyon, compared Macron to a bereavement counsellor. 'We kept calling it a crisis,' he told me.[17] 'But in reality we were grieving for a former France.' The Socialists, he suggested, were still in denial. Mélenchon and Le Pen represented anger against the new world. Macron offered the French acceptance. 'He said bluntly: this is the world, we have to accept the reality, and then rebuild.' As minister, Macron had set the tone, linking himself to tech start-ups, a world defined by confidence and risk. 'The Spring of Optimism' was the title of a speech he gave at the Finance Ministry just weeks before he launched En Marche. 'What our country needs,' he declared, 'is to rediscover a taste for the future, rather than a morbid fascination for an uncertain past.' Macron blamed the country's obsession with post-modernism and structuralism for its cynicism and nihilism. During the campaign his speeches were resolutely upbeat, infused with positive semantics: 'optimism', 'confidence', 'ambition' and 'hope', along with a denunciation of 'miserabilist discourse' and those who inflamed the country's 'sad passions'. En Marche volunteers carried cheery balloons. The movement even came with an exclamation mark, which felt jaunty before it became tiresome, and later was often dropped. Macron's tone was unfashionably courteous. At rallies, he told his supporters not to boo or whistle at his opponents. This was positive politics done politely. Cécile Alduy, a professor of French at Stanford University, compared Macron to a preacher or tele-evangelist, an 'apostle of goodwill'. Against the odds, perhaps exhausted by their own depression, voters seemed to connect to this. 'It's the first time,' said the retired tax inspector I met in Angers, 'that a candidate is offering something positive.'

Of course, plenty of politicians promise what Sarah Palin called 'that hopey changey stuff'. On the centre-right, Alain Juppé had tried to campaign for the primary on the back of his plea for a 'happy identity' for France. Macron's breezy approach could have been lifted straight from the playbook of upbeat former campaigns, in France (Valéry Giscard d'Estaing in 1974; Mitterrand in 1981) or abroad (Bill Clinton in 1992; Tony Blair in 1997). Or even from the scripts of *The West Wing* television series, which several of his young advisers watched over and over again. Macron's declarations, that he 'believed in hope' or promised 'a new future', were neither novel nor eloquent. Even Hollande, after all, had vowed to 're-enchant the French dream'. The reason that such a message worked in Macron's case was that it felt authentic. It matched the persona of the candidate, and the nature of his political adventure. En Marche was the incarnation of optimism. I have taken my own risk, Macron seemed to say to voters; why not now take a bet on me? And the more he climbed in the polls, the less absurd or naive or quaint his adventure appeared. Macron gambled on his voters' better nature. Against the odds, he found a way to persuade a morose people, or at least enough of them, fatigued by the prevailing defeatist national mood, to believe in their country again. By the end of 2017, the share of French people polled by Harris Interactive who described themselves as optimistic about the coming year jumped to 59 per cent, ten points more than at the end of the year of Hollande's election, 2012. For the under-35s, the figure was a massive 75 per cent. The French seemed to have 'resigned themselves to optimism', said a commentator on RTL radio, as if it required a peculiar effort. Michel Houellebecq, better known for his own *nihilisme*, put it this way: Macron, he said, represented a form of 'group therapy' for the nation, a sort of collective self-medicated optimism.

No amount of defiant optimism or revolutionary rhetoric, however, could have carried Macron to the presidency without a third personal quality: his capacity to see the big picture and work out how to get where he wanted. For all the expertise gathered, and the loyal advisers assembled, Macron was ultimately his own campaign manager. Ideas were discussed; working groups convened; thematic papers prepared and debated. But almost none of the

A Picardy childhood: born near the battlefields of the Somme, Emmanuel Macron (left and centre below at La Providence) says he preferred reading and playing the piano to *boums* with his classmates.

NOM : MACRON

Prénoms : Emmanuel Jean-Michel Frédéric

Né le 21/12/77 à Amiens

Nationalité Français

Profession des Parents : médecins hospitaliers.

Adresse des Parents :

Tél. : _____ Code postal : _____ Ville : _____

The haircut: fellow students recall Macron's dishevelled look, recorded here on his Sciences Po card, as much as his stellar academic performance.

Au naturel: Emmanuel and Brigitte Macron posing for the cameras in the dunes at Le Touquet during the 2017 election campaign.

The godfathers: Macron as a young *inspecteur des finances* with Jacques Attali (left), one of the many sponsors who opened doors for him in Paris.

The gambler: Macron's decision to back François Hollande (left) landed him a plum job at the Elysée Palace and then a post in government. Hollande later said his young adviser 'betrayed' him.

The Grande Marche: the summer of door-knocking in 2016 seemed quaint and old-fashioned at the time, but turned into a useful rehearsal for the election campaign.

Full house: within four months of its launch En Marche counted more members than the Socialist Party; within a year Macron was filling venues like this one in Paris.

The dynastic challenge: in 2017 the National Front's Marine Le Pen (left) drew more voters than her father had in 2002. But a disastrous debate performance brought her future leadership into question, and turned attention to her hard-line niece, Marion Maréchal-Le Pen (right).

That blue felt-tip pen: Macron describes himself as a details man, who likes to take notes at meetings and rework his speeches in longhand (here at En Marche headquarters during the election campaign).

A student of symbols: Macron's solitary walk across the Cour Napoléon of the Louvre on election night recalled the choreography of Mitterrand's walk to the Panthéon in 1981.

Les Macron boys: the young and (mostly) male campaign team arrives at the Elysée Palace, among them Griveaux (second from left), Ndiaye (third from left, with Emelien partly hidden), Richard Ferrand (fourth from left), Girier (centre), Denormandie (fourth from right), Séjourné (second from right) and Fort (right).

Waiting for Putin: two weeks after his inauguration, Macron invited the Russian leader to the Palace of Versailles, earning himself the nickname Sun King to add to that of Jupiter.

A strange couple: Macron followed up his early knuckle-crunching handshake with an invitation to Donald Trump to attend the Bastille Day parade, prompting the American president to call him 'a great guy … loves holding my hand'.

In search of magic: Macron's difficult quest for a new Franco-German bargain with Merkel (left) will test his ability to act as joint leader of the new European order.

Eulogy for a rock star: Macron's speech outside the Madeleine church in Paris on the day of Johnny Hallyday's funeral was in some ways his 'Diana moment', an attempt to connect with popular French emotion.

movement's members had any more direct experience of a presidential campaign than Macron himself. Which is to say almost none at all. En Marche did not outsource the campaign to a professional hack or strategist. The consultancy they had used for the Grande Marche was unavailable due to an exclusivity contract with the Socialist Party. The campaign's behind-the-scenes director really was also its public face: Macron himself. In the spring of 2016, shortly after the launch of En Marche, the minister summoned his inner circle for a strategy meeting. At the time, it was widely assumed that Hollande would stand for re-election, and that Sarkozy or Juppé would be the Republican nominee. For ten minutes Macron outlined his baseline scenario for the rest of the year: Hollande, he judged, would not be able to run again, the party primaries would polarize the presidential nomination on the mainstream left and right, and this would open up an unusual space for him. 'I thought that either he was a genius,' said a person present, 'or that he had been smoking something.'

As the campaign unfolded, nobody at headquarters in Paris had any doubt as to who was in charge. Macron had no real campaign director. In theory, the 32-year-old Jean-Marie Girier, who had worked on Hollande's 2012 campaign, occupied the job. But his role was more organizational than strategic. For all that the grass-roots En Marche volunteers thought they were shaping this campaign from the ground up, the cajoling, the remonstrating, the setting of a strategic line ultimately came from Macron. The 39-year-old addressed his staff during the campaign as 'les enfants' (children); they called him le chef or le boss. He set the pace. Volunteers worked, unpaid, late into the night. Pinned to the wall behind the cramped kitchen sink at campaign HQ in Paris, next to a sign urging les helpers to wash up their dirty coffee cups, was a stern black-and-white photo of le boss, as if they needed a reminder. 'Everyone is tired ... but nothing is guaranteed,' Macron told his assembled team at campaign headquarters sternly, two weeks before the first round. 'Everybody needs to know that for the next fortnight they can sleep or eat,' he warned them, 'but the rest of the time they do nothing but this.'[18]

His attention to detail verged on the obsessional. Should he wear the navy-blue suit? What was the plan if there were any empty seats at the next rally? He redrafted and corrected printouts of his speeches by hand with a felt-tip pen, and took handwritten notes at his own meetings, as he continues to do as president, even at summits of European heads of state and government in Brussels. 'I have always been someone who wants to explore things down to the last detail so that I can understand them,' he told *Der Spiegel*.[19] It sounded suspiciously self-congratulatory. But I saw it one evening in the autumn of 2015, at a working dinner for entrepreneurs at the Finance Ministry hosted by Macron when he was in government. Blue felt pen and small sheets of paper in hand – to the amusement of the digital-native tech types present – he spent the evening moving from table to table, listening, jotting down notes, and asking guests how to make thing simpler for their start-ups to grow, invest and hire.

Surely there was dissent, or push back, against this hyper-personalized management style? Macron was 'not afraid of debate or being contradicted', claimed one aide. Ideas would be batted back and forth. In some ways he needed constant feedback. 'Was it OK? Did I say anything stupid?' he would ask after a television debate, or a public rally. 'He is smart, and smart enough to know what he doesn't know,' François Heisbourg, the security analyst, told me. 'He is a sponge, learns fast and remembers everything.'

Ultimately though, at En Marche HQ, as later at the Elysée Palace, all decisions were his, and Macron did not hesitate to take them. The campaign could not have worked without the backing of a citizens' movement, but was in reality run by a very small team and their boss. 'Macron has the charm of Obama, but unlike Obama he is decisive,' said Heisbourg. 'He takes decisions in his own time, and therefore benefits from a surprise effect, which can come across as very secretive. He absorbs things, mulls them over, thinks about it, doesn't tell anybody. Then suddenly there's a result.' Philippe Besson, a French novelist who followed Macron during the campaign, made this observation: 'he listens a lot, asks for comments, suggestions, yet he rarely deviates from his initial intent or his intuition.'[20] In the end, 'he decides alone'.

'He constructed his campaign without looking for a second at what the others were doing,' Benjamin Griveaux told me. 'He said: "I know where I'm going. The others can do what they want, with the calendar they like and the diary they like. I know exactly where I want to go."' Surely he had doubts, uncertainties about his decisions, or his ability to get it right? His campaign team insists not. Perhaps it is that self-control again, that ability to keep his fears and fragilities deep inside. For those who were working with him, biting their nails at every dip in the polls, or hacking attempt, the only member of the team who seemed to believe it was possible all the way through, and stay focused, was Macron. When preliminary charges were brought against Fillon during the campaign, recalled Griveaux, 'We were the ones to say: if Fillon is no longer the candidate, we'll have to change things.' Macron disagreed. 'He said: Fillon will go all the way and told us just to keep concentrating on what we were doing.' Such inner drive resembles the psychology of a professional sportsman, a point made by Macron's tennis coach, Patrice Kuchna. Once himself ranked 125th in the world, Kuchna said that his pupil has a 'rare' mental solidity in his game, describing the player as 'hyper-determined, rigorous and disciplined'. Kuchna coached Macron at the club in Le Touquet, even squeezing in a quick session on the eve of the second round of the presidential election, when the candidate crept out of his house via the back garden to avoid the paparazzi, climbing over a neighbour's wall to join his coach on the nearby courts.

Inevitably, this single-mindedness also had its casualties. Macron had no qualms about forging political alliances when they suited him, and dropping them when they did not. As candidate, Macron happily took on board François Bayrou when he needed him; and, as president, readily let him go when a preliminary inquiry was opened into the misuse of public funds by Bayrou's party at the European Parliament. Macron showed little mercy towards Manuel Valls, refusing to let him stand as a legislative candidate for En Marche – although he did not field a rival candidate against the former prime minister in his constituency, and he was able to keep his seat. Some of those who worked closely with Macron on the campaign were then passed over for jobs in government, and technocrats were preferred to economists for top posts at the Elysée Palace. 'Macron has an instrumental approach towards people,' one campaign adviser told me. 'Does he use people? Yes,' said another former aide who failed to get a job after the election. 'But it's part of the game. He's ruthless when he needs to be.'

As much as En Marche was built up from the ground, the presidential campaign of 2017 was in the end hyper-personalized, and centred on Macron himself. And this worked because of the way the candidate exploited the constitution of the Fifth Republic. De Gaulle devised an unusually strong presidency, and introduced direct elections to it four years later, precisely in order to remove power from the hands of political parties, which he blamed for the 'disastrous' manoeuvrings of the unstable Fourth Republic. A directly elected president would – like *le général* – embody the nation, and rise grandly above the grubby business of party politics. The French presidential election would therefore act as a 'meeting between a man and a people'. Over the previous decade, the introduction of primaries had added a filter not foreseen by the constitution, the party machine. Macron's gambit was that the visibility such primaries gave to political parties masked an opportunity, written into de Gaulle's original version: the direct unfiltered link between a leader and his fellow citizens. 'The Fifth Republic constitution was open to this sort of adventure,' said Sylvain Fort. 'It offers the possibility of winning everything in one go.'[21] Macron's was a political assault on political parties based on a return to the original source of legitimacy of a modern French president, introduced by de Gaulle after a referendum in 1962: the direct mandate of the people. In the end, Macron toppled the party system, but reinforced its institutions.

The danger of this strategy of hyper-presidentialization, of course, was that it would personalize the campaign to narcissistic excess. In an astonishing interview with *Le 1* newspaper in 2015, Macron had argued that the French had never really wanted to kill their king. At a time when he was still the economy minister, better known for discussing bond yields and market deregulation, Macron spoke of the 'emptiness' at the heart of the French Republic caused by the 'absence of the king'. The post-revolutionary Terror, he suggested, had created an 'emotional, imaginary collective void', which the French had tried to fill over the centuries with other monarchical figures (Napoleon, de Gaulle).[22] It was a presumptuous analysis for a sitting politician who might have harboured presidential ambitions of his own. Macron went on to alarm those who suspected him of grandiosity by developing the idea of a 'Jupiterian' presidency, in an interview with *Challenges* in the autumn of 2016. France's highest office of state, he suggested, like the Roman king of the gods, should be invested with a certain aura.[23] The concept of a 'normal' presidency, he argued, in a thinly disguised dig at Hollande, 'destabilized' the French, and made them feel insecure and leaderless. The French presidency was not merely an executive authority, he judged, but an embodiment of the nation, and so any pretender to the office had to believe he was in some way special. It was the form of charismatic authority that Max Weber identified: a leader 'treated as endowed with supernatural, superhuman, or at least specifically exceptional powers or qualities'.[24] 'Politics,' said Macron, 'is mystical.'[25]

At times during the campaign, the boy from the school called La Providence seemed to believe not just in the mysticism of politics, but in his own special powers. After a long speech at his first big rally as candidate, in a hangar-like conference centre on the southern edge of Paris in December 2016, Macron lost it. He began to yell, his voice became strained, and he flung his arms out wide in a Christ-like pose, face up and eyes shut. It was a moment of pretentious absurdity. Watching it on television later, he exclaimed: 'Shit, I look like a madman.'[26] Throughout the campaign Macron seemed to tread a perilous line between a desire to cloak himself in a sense of mystique and a risk of appearing preposterously self-aggrandizing. A month after launching En Marche he made a trip to Orléans, to pay tribute to Joan of Arc, the fifteenth-century folk heroine and symbol of French redemption. For years the National Front had monopolized her memory, and Macron, keen to embrace France's pre-republican history, sought to reclaim her. His speech that day, though, steered treacherously close to the ridiculous, with its parallel to his own missionary ambitions. 'Joan was a nobody. But she carried on her shoulders the will to progress and justice of an entire people. She was a crazy dream,' Macron declared. 'But she ended up imposing herself as something obvious.'

Such moments were a caricaturist's dream during the campaign. Plantu, *Le Monde*'s front-page cartoonist, depicted the candidate as a smug little Messiah. Macron was much mocked for his haughty manner, fuelled by his background as an investment banker, as well as an unfortunate history of making dismissive comments that caused offence. This made him an easy object of ridicule for his political opponents, who sought to underline his remoteness and disdain. At one point a fake video circulated on social media suggesting that Macron used a wet wipe after shaking workers' hands (the hand-wiping moment was in fact captured after he had been out on a small boat fishing for eel). The most sombre manifestation of this attempt to portray him as the arrogant banker was a caricature published during the campaign by the Republicans on Twitter, which depicted Macron as a hook-nosed, top-hatted banker. The echo of the anti-Semitic imagery of the 1930s was as crude as it was abject. The party retracted it.

Was Macron really as haughty towards ordinary people as he was portrayed? Three months after the launch of En Marche, in June 2016, I went to watch him in action at a shopping centre in the Saint-Lazare railway station, in the 9th arrondissement of Paris. This is not just a place for the pin-striped crowd. Commuter trains arrive here from the *banlieues* of north-west and western Paris, transporting 360,000 passengers in and out of the capital every day, most of them employees in services, offices and shops. To the surprise of passers-by in the station's indoor commercial centre, in walked Macron on the first day of the sales, past a children's clothing shop and cosmetic store, a small cluster of aides and television cameras trotting along behind him. Outside a lingerie shop, the minister hesitated. It was not on the schedule. But the store manager had spotted him, and insisted. So Macron found himself greeting astonished shoppers as they leafed through piles of underwear and lace-trimmed bras. By the time he made it out, a crowd had gathered, some eager for selfies, others for a chance to unload their discontent. He lingered and listened. 'It's rare to see a minister stop to talk to people like us,' said one astonished woman.

The first thing I noticed that morning was how tactile Macron is with strangers. He not only offers his right hand, but swiftly follows it with his left in a two-hand embrace. Then there is his willingness to engage with his critics, as if he has all the time in the world. This is not common with government ministers, most of whom pause for selfies, and move on. Macron stopped, listened, and argued his case. One woman stepped up to offload her grievances. 'It's not right that we work, and find it harder at the end of the month than those who don't,' she told him. 'We have to pay for school lunches, when the ones who don't work don't.' A young man of African origin wanted Macron to know how hard it was to get credit on a temporary work contract. 'That's why we need to make permanent contracts more fluid,' the minister ventured. 'Then they will hire people on permanent contracts.' One young man who stopped to listen to the minister told me that Macron was 'a fighter. He knows what he wants, and he wants to make a difference.' A woman who fell into conversation with him apologized that she had to go, or would be late for work. 'Tell them it's because of me!' Macron advised her. By 9.50 a.m., after more than an hour, his aides became agitated. He was due in a cabinet meeting at the Elysée at 10 a.m. But the minister showed no sign of wanting to leave. He posed for a few more selfies, and found more hands to shake on his way towards the street. At 9.55 a.m. he slid into his car, winked through the half-open window, and was off.

The political class in Paris continued, by and large, to dismiss Macron as aloof and out of touch, or to underestimate his chances. 'You aren't really old enough,' Bayrou told him in a smart Paris restaurant, even as the pair met during the campaign to draw up an alliance. Yet the long queues that formed in the streets ahead of his public rallies came over the weeks to define the insurgent campaign. Other candidates had to bus in supporters in coaches. Voters turned up by themselves to see the En Marche candidate: in Quimper in Brittany, in Lille in the north, in Albi in the south-west. They hadn't just come to support En Marche but to see Macron himself. At the time, I made a note to ask people at his rallies what they made of the candidate's programme (he hadn't got one). Policies didn't seem to be the point. At a rally in the Mediterranean port of Toulon, I came across Jean-Luc, a lycée maths teacher, who told me that he had never been to a political rally before, but was drawn to the sense of 'renewal, youth, and new generation' about Macron. The candidate's appeal, he said, 'is more the personality than the programme'. Also at the rally was Robert, a retired salesman who lived in a village in the hills of Provence; he had driven down to the port city specially to see Macron. 'He represents a different way of doing politics,' he told me, 'and it's time for politics in this country to change.'

Watching Macron hold his nerve throughout the campaign, I found myself often wondering what lay behind this polished, focused exterior. When the novelist Emmanuel Carrère asked him, once he was in the presidency, to identify a flaw in his character, Macron put it this way: 'I'm claustrophobic about life. I can't stand being shut in, I have to get out, that's why I can't have a normal life. Deep down, my flaw is no doubt that I don't love normal life.' Which was an interesting answer, because in Macron's case this is not really a flaw at all. A yearning to break out, head somewhere else and do things differently makes him sound like a wayward, tortured artist. Yet Macron seems to know exactly what he is doing, and where he is going. If he seeks a life that is not normal, it is because he seems to have the unfathomable self-belief and conviction that it will be a great one. 'He has always been different, and that difference he has always accepted. He lives with it,' said Antoine Marguet, the fellow pupil from Amiens. 'And this accepting of his difference, I think, could help him in the completely mad, completely hysterical, office which is the French presidency ... He will be armed, as few presidents are, to live something that is, I would say, an ordeal. That is perhaps what François Hollande didn't understand.'[27]

Indeed, by the end of the campaign, Macron the technocrat, the calculating banker, the man of uncommon self-control, came to offer a personal as well as a political narrative. This was a parallel story of triumph over adversity, centred on something he talks about only with reluctance: his unconventional marriage. Just as he and Brigitte Auzière had endured the social scandal among the Amiens *bourgeoisie* for many years before their marriage, so his public office made their marriage the subject of perpetual fascination and disbelief. Was it really possible to be married out of love to a woman 24 years older? 'But you know he's really gay,' people would say for months in Paris, long before the campaign started. Rumours were spread, and retold. I was myself the subject of several attempts by a French financier to persuade me that it was true, and proof of his duplicity. Yet Macron seemed to have armed himself against all such attacks. The couple had lived with the crushing force of bourgeois social censure, and deep family disapproval, for years. 'We've had our share of adversity,' Brigitte Macron told Emmanuel Carrère. 'To live a love like ours, we've had to harden ourselves against malicious remarks, mockery and gossip.'[28]

At one point during the campaign, rumours that Macron's marriage was a cover for a secret gay life became insistent. His press attaché, Sibeth Ndiaye, told him that even her Afro hair stylist had told her Macron could never become president because he was gay. The candidate decided to punch back, puncturing the gossip with humour. At the time, the tech-savvy Jean-Luc Mélenchon was beaming a live hologram-like image of himself into remote meeting halls as a way of holding simultaneous rallies in different places. Before a gathering of En Marche activists in

Paris, Macron took to the stage and joked that, if he was leading a double life, it was because his 'hologram has suddenly escaped'. The rumours were odious on two counts, he told *TÊTU*, a gay magazine: the homophobia behind the assumption that a gay man could not be elected president, and the misogyny underlying the idea that a man who lives with a woman 24 years older than him could only be 'either gay or a closet gigolo'. Macron paused, and then added: 'I've lived this from the start … I know how heavy the looks of others can feel.' Carrère followed the president and his wife for a week during his first year in office and described how 'Their eyes seek each other out, find each other'. It was obvious to him 'that you can't fake this sort of thing – not for that long, not all the time'.

Macron accepted that he had to put his private life on display during the campaign. Photographs of him and Brigitte were splashed on numerous front covers of *Paris Match* magazine, whose well-leafed copies lie about in doctors' waiting rooms and hairdressers across the country. It was part of the political game, and Macron embraced it with transactional sangfroid when he had to, recruiting a celebrity agent to control the sale of photographs, and commenting dryly that 'I sell. Like washing powder. Nothing more.'[29] That comment seemed to capture something important about Macron. Behind the earnest demeanour and private charm, he can be calculating and cynical when he needs to be. But Macron does not dwell on his relationship with his wife unless pushed. In the first draft of his book, *Révolution*, he scarcely mentioned her, or his family. Macron 'suffered', said Philippe Besson, who read an earlier draft, when he agreed to revise the manuscript in order to inject some personal detail and a modicum of emotion.

In reality, the period of ten years leading up to the Macrons' marriage in 2007 is little chronicled. So is the couple's choice not to have any biological children of their own, a risk that Macron's mother raised angrily with Brigitte Auzière after learning of their liaison: 'You don't realize,' she told Brigitte, 'you already have your life; he won't have children.' During a

2017 campaign visit to a primary school, a pupil asked Macron whether he missed being a father. He replied calmly that it was a 'choice' they had made, to focus on bringing up Brigitte's three children, and that lots of families look different these days. After Macron left Amiens to study in Paris, commuting up to Amiens or Le Touquet at the weekend, Brigitte Auzière was extracting herself from her marriage to André-Louis. 'I know that I hurt my children, and that's the thing I most reproach myself for,' she told *ELLE* magazine. That time is now behind them. But the experience seems to have hardened an outer shell, which seldom cracks. During the election campaign, there was a rare moment when Macron let his heart speak. It was his reply to a cruel sideswipe by Jean-Marie Le Pen, who had declared that Macron could not claim to talk about the future because he had no children of his own. 'Monsieur Le Pen,' Macron replied serenely, speaking onstage at a rally, 'I have children and grand-children of the heart.'

For many French women, his relationship even seemed to serve as an antidote to the patriarchal social and political codes that had long made it acceptable for male French politicians to be accompanied by women half their age, but not the other way round. Brigitte became a sort of 'heroine for feminists', suggested Pascal Bruckner, a French writer, a 'symbol of the revenge of the cougars'.[30] Provincial not *parisienne*, bourgeois yet anti-conformist, with an undisguised taste for luxury brands, Brigitte Macron was a different sort of modern French woman. 'Of course, we have breakfast together, me with my wrinkles, him with his fresh face, but that's how it is,' she joked. 'She gives him an unfiltered view, a total liberty of expression,' an aide told me. Their relationship, wrote the novelist Philippe Besson, was constructed against hostility, and in solitude: 'Having triumphed in such an adventure ... they have become invincible,' he wrote, 'armed with a force that those who have known only facility and comfort can neither imagine nor comprehend.'

If fortune favoured the schoolboy from La Providence, Macron's path to the presidency was also forged by the risks he took, as well as his ability to stay the course and withstand the violence of public electoral life. The campaign revealed a sangfroid that few had understood. Two years in the shadow of Hollande had taught Macron about the workings, and failings, of the presidency. Two years in government offered him lessons about the brutality and humiliations of politics. A transgressive personality, an insolent ambition, a calculating visionary mind – and a big splash of luck – propelled Macron to the highest office. Macron accepted his 'dose of narcissism' in embarking on this adventure. But at some level he seemed to live the campaign as an obligation, part of a mission. 'This campaign has transformed me,' he commented, while on a final election stop in the south-west. 'I have picked up the anger, the bitterness and the immense expectations of the country. I have the inner feeling that, faced with nihilism and moral collapse, we need to restore the efficiency of public action. We're on the edge of the precipice.'[31] Having conquered the highest office, Macron's task in power would be to pull France back from the brink.

PART TWO

POWER

6

Macronism

'France is an intellectual country ... This isn't Texas.'

Adviser to President Macron, November 2017

Decrypting Macronese is a high art. Like sinologists after the nineteenth National Congress of the Chinese Communist Party in 2017 decoding Xi Jinping's 'Thought on Socialism with Chinese Characteristics for a New Era', French commentators sit down after a long and often convoluted speech by President Macron to try to work out what he really means. What is his guiding ideology? What is his thinking all about?

Perhaps the best place to start is his phrase of choice: *en même temps* ('at the same time'). As candidate, Macron was much mocked for this rhetorical habit. It crops up in prepared speeches at rallies, or in spontaneous conversation. No Macronian sentence, it seems, can start with one point without swinging to another halfway through, thanks to this lexical hinge. During the campaign, Macron managed to pull off the unusual political feat of acting as his own contradictor. Every idea could be objected to, and he managed to voice both sides of an argument in a single breath, anticipating rebuttal before it was articulated. After a while, when he uttered the phrase, the crease of a smile would emerge at the corner of his mouth as he recognized the habit. It reflected, say his detractors, a 'culture of ambiguity, a rhetorical strategy ... a concern to avoid deciding in order not to displease anybody'.[1] Macronese seemed to be about evasive ambiguity, or an inability to make up his mind, which left listeners perplexed and opponents delighted. Macron – said Benoît Hamon, the

Socialist Party's presidential candidate during the campaign – is '*du bla bla bla*'.

Macron's politics are on the left, and at the same time on the right. He is in favour of reducing public spending, and, at the same time, he promotes a big public investment programme. He supports free trade and globalization, and at the same time seeks to 'protect' Europe and its citizens from competition. He has called the wearing of the 'burkini', the body-covering swim-suit that stirred up a furious debate in France over religious freedom, 'a problem', and at the same time is against banning it. When I watched him give a speech in Toulon, a naval port on the Mediterranean coast, Macron used the phrase *en même temps* 29 times. At another rally in Paris, his own supporters began to chant the phrase, turning it into a chorus of approval. It made Macron the object of merciless satire. The opening lines of one YouTube parody, a mash-up of clips of him speaking, went: 'On the left, on the right, but at the same time/Before you, behind you, but at the same time/In the middle, then on the left, and on the other hand/Yes, no, but at the same time.'

Ideal in an era of soundbites for partial quotation for political ends, it was also a habit that got him into trouble. During the election campaign, after Macron declared in a speech in Lyon that 'there is no French culture', the *bien-pensant* left and nationalist right rose up in unison, aghast. 'Far too hard to defend Molière, Victor Hugo, Proust,' sniffed François Fillon. 'Far easier to mix up all cultures in a melting pot of French identity.' Macron had in fact gone on in the same phrase to state that, at the same time, 'there is a culture in France, and it is diverse'. He was not belittling French literary greats, he later explained, and the French 'should be proud of their heritage', but he was 'against a conception of culture as an identity that excludes'.[2] Few bothered to listen to his sentence to the end. Macron's rhetorical reflex was also a gift to those who traded on simplistic binary messages. Those on the political fringes seemed to know what they wanted. For Marine Le Pen, it was 'no to Brussels; yes to France'. For Mélenchon, 'quit NATO; end "war" on Russia'. During a televised debate in 2017 among all 11 official presidential candidates, Macron interjected at one stage: 'I agree with you on that last point.' As Le Pen let out a howl of laughter, François Asselineau, a Eurosceptic candidate, shot back at Macron, 'Yes, you always agree with everybody.'

What is behind this verbal twitch? To say that Macron embodies contradictions is not quite good enough. A closer look at his accumulated public writings, speeches and interviews over the years, which reach back to 2000, suggests a structure to Macron's way of thinking, and a logic behind it. Jacques Delpla, the economist at the Toulouse School of Economics who served with Macron on the Attali Commission, told me that the key to understanding Macron is to know that 'he doesn't come to politics through the structures of power, but through ideas'.[3] And not humdrum ideas. Macron turned to politics from philosophical thought, and to political philosophy from metaphysics. This background is crucial to making sense of the way he conceives public policy and political action. 'Macron has an intellectual framework that is out of the ordinary,' Pascal Lamy, the former head of the World Trade Organization, told me. 'He has a philosophical foundation that is very stable, and very thought-through.'[4]

The main early intellectual influence on Macron was Paul Ricoeur, the French philosopher, whom he met while studying philosophy at the University of Nanterre. The young student's decision to enrol for this degree, in parallel with his studies at Sciences Po, was unusual for a French high-flyer, above all one who was preparing to take the entrance exam to ENA, which trains the future administrative elite. Macron chose to combine his time among the cafés and bookstores of the Paris left bank, around the Sciences Po site on the rue Saint-Guillaume, with trips on the distinctly unglamorous RER suburban railway out to Nanterre. A block-like concrete campus beside the railway tracks in an unfashionable district west of Paris, Nanterre was the birthplace of the 1968 student rebellion, before it spread to the Sorbonne. Ricoeur had been a member of the philosophy faculty during the May uprising, ignominiously ending up later with a rubbish bin on his head. (This was the anecdote Macron tried to tell his baffled supporters at a campaign rally.) At a time when Marxism and structuralism were the defining currents of French academic thought in the social-science departments of university campuses, Ricoeur was against philosophical dogmatism, arguing that it was necessary to 'grant equal rights to rival interpretations', and that philosophical thought rested on the uncomfortable contemplation of these. 'He is the exponent of the "both-and", and the opponent of the "either-or". Thus he finds instruction not only in both Kant and Hegel but also in both Plato and Aristotle, Augustine and Benedict de Spinoza, and Karl Marx and Freud,' wrote Bernard Dauenhauer, a Ricoeurian scholar. 'In short, in all his works, Ricoeur looks for "connectors to think together two antinomic poles".'[5] This is pure Macron. The president's syntax and approach to public policy, argues François Dosse, a French historian, can be traced directly back to Ricoeur.[6]

When Macron first met the French philosopher, the young student had been flirting with the political ideas of Jean-Pierre Chevènement, a maverick left-wing nationalist who had broken away from the Socialist Party.[7] Macron had chosen to write a master's thesis on Hegel and the public interest, as well as a dissertation on 'Political Fact and Machiavelli's Representation of History', and was following a class taught at Nanterre by the Marxist philosopher Etienne Balibar. Ricoeur, Macron said, 're-educated me'.[8] A social democrat, with a gentle courteous manner and proclaimed Protestant faith, Ricoeur was linked to a group of thinkers seeking to define a middle way between liberalism and Marxism, and was close to Michel Rocard, a moderate centre-left Socialist former prime minister. From Ricoeur's philosophical thought Macron absorbed a conviction that society should work collectively towards 'the common good' as well as, crucially, a belief in the constant need to confront ideas with reality, and to create a permanent tension between competing ideas themselves.

Fully 64 years separated the pair, and they formed an unlikely bond, Ricoeur becoming for the young student the first of many mentors who were decades older than himself. Ricoeur took on Macron as an editorial assistant for his work, *La mémoire*, *l'histoire, l'oubli,* on the recommendation of François Dosse, who had the young student in his class at Sciences Po.[9] Macron spent long hours with the philosophy professor, travelling out on the train to his home in an intellectual community in Châtenay-Malabry, in the southern suburbs of Paris, helping to check his references and notes, and offering annotated thoughts to the great master. Macron was a prodigious, and presumptuous, supplier of advice. Some of the notes he made on Ricoeur's manuscript, unearthed in the archives by *Le Monde,* betray an astounding self-confidence, given Macron's tender age and his own confession that he was 'completely incompetent' to offer such advice.[10] 'Define more precisely the concept of chronosophy', read one of Macron's notes.[11] 'Redo', reads another injunction. 'Specify from the start that you are presenting hypotheses.'

Ricoeur's politics may in reality have been more radical than Macron's, but he helped to shape both the young student's thinking and, later, his decision to go into politics. The French philosopher, Macron told *Le 1* in July 2015, taught him that 'any element thrown into public debate can be critiqued', and that the discipline of political philosophy involved a perpetual re-examination of theory in the light of experience, inflicting a necessary intellectual discomfort. Ricoeur's life work, Macron said, was 'the alternative path of 1968': a refusal to retreat into dogma and certainty, a responsibility to confront ideas with practice, and an acceptance of the intellectual instability that this implied.[12] Ideology, argued Macron, was 'a work of translation' between philosophy and politics: 'it is never perfect', and always subject to improvement and adjustment. Ricoeur, who had spent five years in Nazi detention camps and also shaped the young Macron's thinking about history and memory, trained him to think 'in a constant back-and-forth between theory and reality … It is in this permanent but fertile disequilibrium that thought can be built and political transformation can be carried out.'[13]

As much as he admired Ricoeur's mind, Macron knew that he did not have the temperament to stay in academia. 'I didn't want to have the same sort of life as him,' he said. A university career 'lacked a form of action, of participation in public action'.[14] Macron knew that he did not have the patience to spend his life as an academic, like Ricoeur, but wanted to roll up his sleeves and do things. It was Ricoeur, he told *Le 1*, who ultimately 'pushed me into politics because he hadn't done so himself'. Macron as policymaker picked up where Ricoeur as a political philosopher left off. Well before he went into politics, Macron began to think about the nature of political action, shaped by Ricoeur's scholarship. 'Contemporary political action requires permanent deliberation ... which enables decisions to be adjusted, reoriented, adapted to reality,' Macron argued in an article in 2012, while still at Rothschild's bank.[15]

Is it possible that, behind the opaque abstractions of Macronese, what passes for ambiguity is in fact a political translation of Ricoeurian philosophical thought? 'To want at once to liberate work and to protect the most precarious, this manner of introducing a sustained tension between two apparently incompatible formulations, is really very *ricoeurien*,' said Olivier Abel, professor of philosophy and ethics at the Protestant Institute of Theology in Montpellier.[16] Put in this context, some of the policies that Macron advocates may be less an exercise in evasiveness, or the quest for a woolly consensus, than a pragmatic attempt to put ideas into place within the constraints imposed on public policy. In a telling comparison, Macron once contrasted the job of the politician with that of the novelist. An author, he said, has to stop at some point, however imperfect the literary work. But 'in political life, dissatisfaction is remedied, or at least fought, through action,' he said. 'For as long as you are not totally satisfied, you remain active and keep going.'[17]

Could Macron's quest to reconcile apparently contradictory forces help make sense of what sometimes appears to be an ambiguous approach to fundamental policy issues: the trade-off between liberalism and regulation, between markets and protection? Might it, in a delightfully intellectual French way, help to explain the contradictions in his abstract formulations? Macron argued fervently during the campaign that he could not stop the forces of globalization, and that any politician who promised to do so was dishonest. Yet, once elected, those fellow Europeans who had concluded that he was a pure market liberal discovered to their consternation his insistence on a 'Europe that protects'. Maybe, some Northern Europeans wondered, the new French president was not as liberal as he professed to be.

To understand Macron's approach, it is perhaps more helpful to see it as an attempt to find a policy structure that serves apparently competing objectives, rather than as the expression of an ideology. It is a mistake, for instance, to try to cast Macron as a pure liberal in the English-speaking economic tradition, which the French call 'Anglo-Saxon'. When I asked him once whether he defined himself as liberal, he replied that he was 'liberal in a Nordic sense'. In Macron's book, he put it this way: 'If by liberalism one means confidence in mankind, I accept being categorized as liberal.'[18] That Macron calls himself a liberal at all is courageous in France. Jacques Chirac once described liberalism as a greater threat to Europe than communism. Ségolène Royal, the defeated Socialist presidential candidate, declared that 'to be liberal and socialist is totally incompatible'. In France, a state before it was a nation, *l'Etat* is dignified by capital letter and a special place in the collective imagination. The great French theorists of liberal thought, among them Jean-Baptiste Say, Frédéric Bastiat or Benjamin Constant, have been marginalized in the French mind by a history of 'permanent interventionism' that reaches from pre-revolutionary to republican France.[19] Over the past two decades, the ultimate political insult in France, and optimum way to shut down an argument, has been to label somebody not just liberal but *ultra-libéral*. When Alain Madelin ran for the French presidency as a liberal in 2002, he scored 3.9 per cent. Nobody tried again.

Macron may defend globalization and an open trading regime, but he is not an advocate for unbridled laissez-faire. Mathieu Laine, the liberal analyst, put it this way: 'he is not the product of a liberal intellectual tradition. His roots are on the progressive centre-left that reconciled itself to the market economy.'[20] Macron

is above all the intellectual inheritor of a social-democratic tradition, said Laine, whose ideas were then 'rubbed up against the
reality of the world of business' during his time as a banker, as
well as 'a deep understanding of the coming economic transformation', lending them a pragmatic social-liberal flavour. The
president's starting point is not liberalism as an ideology, but a
mix of rationalist Enlightenment belief about the perfectibility of
man and the need to liberate individual capacities along with raw
empirical observation. During his campaign, Macron insisted
repeatedly on the need to 'liberate energies' and 'give individuals
the tools to succeed'. As Laurent Bigorgne and his co-authors
point out, his belief in the capacity of individuals to 'realize their
talents' and 'choose their lives' carries a distinct echo of Ricoeur's
concept of the 'capable man'.[21]

This thinking also borrows much from Amartya Sen, the
Indian economist, and his work on empowerment. He conceived
of anti-poverty policy in terms of improving an individual's 'capabilities' to realize his full potential.[22] Macron acknowledges
that his reading of Sen 'structured a lot of my thinking on social
justice'.[23] His desire to put liberty back into the equation when
devising social policy in France, which on the left has long been
dominated by the quest for equal outcomes, is at the heart of
this philosophy. In this, Macron also draws on the work on
social justice by the American philosopher John Rawls, as well as
Ronald Dworkin, who are relatively little studied in France but
both of whom he has listened to in public lectures and found 'very
inspiring'.[24] Already, as a student at Sciences Po, Macron was
drawn to a form of social-democratic thinking that was based
on individual rights, 'not just the infinite extension of collective
rights', said Marc Ferracci.[25] Macron refutes the view that liberty
and equality are incompatible. It is egalitarianism, not equality
of opportunity, that he rejects. 'Our duty,' declared Macron in
his speech to a joint sitting of the two houses of parliament in
Versailles, 'is to emancipate our citizens.'[26]

At the same time, as it were, Macron watched what had
happened to France over two decades, and drew his own pragmatic

conclusions. If high taxes and high spending were the answer to poverty and joblessness, then France would have eliminated both (which it hasn't). If workable ideas could be borrowed from the right, there was no ideological reason to reject them (so he didn't). 'My predecessor taxed wealthy, successful people at a higher rate than ever before. And what happened? They left. And what came of it? Did unemployment drop? No.'[27] 'For a century and a half, the left and the right in France have tried to apply an ideology to reality,' Benjamin Griveaux, a co-founder of En Marche, told me. 'Our approach was the exact opposite. In our intellectual method, we were not very Socratic and more Anglo-Saxon, more pragmatic.'[28] It is in this sense that Macron's no-taboos approach to policy in France is radical.

Traditionally, the state has applied home-grown theory taught to successive cadres of mandarins. Macron's method is pragmatic, his inspiration eclectic. And his technique required a clear-out of old-school politicians, reminiscent of the call by the nineteenth-century political theorist Saint-Simon. Indeed, there is very much something of a Saint-Simonian about Macron, in his faith in technical competence and meritocracy, as well as his determination to sweep aside the class of rent-seeking career politicians and replace them with technocrats. In office, he put technical experts in government, among them Jean-Michel Blanquer (education) and Dr Agnès Buzyn (health), and has surrounded himself with technocrats at the Elysée, the nerve centre of his highly centralised administration, under the tight grip of his chief of staff and old ally, Alexis Kohler. Macron's problem-solving approach to policy is both top-down and non-ideological. His quest to transcend the political divide between left and right, in other words, is also built on a Saint-Simonian belief in applying rational, scientific analysis to problems. 'We need a state that says: I'm not going to lead your life for you, I'm not there to replace what you do,' Macron told me in July 2017. 'Some will do well, others less so. But I will protect you from the great accidents of life and I will help give you the capacity to succeed.' His project is about the possibility of individual emancipation, backed by the protection offered by the state.

'I believe in the market economy, the open world,' Macron told me in the same interview. 'But we need to rethink regulation so as to deal with the excesses of global capitalism.'[29] Rightly or wrongly, he judges such excesses to be behind Britain's vote for Brexit in June 2016. Voters, he argues, need to feel that they are not out there alone faced with the threat of machines or open borders. Otherwise they will gravitate to the likes of Le Pen in France, or Trump in America. What Macron seeks instead is an alternative, benign way for the state to offer reassurance: a framework of protection that breeds the confidence people need in order to feel that they can accept or adapt to change. Only then, he judges, will they accept the rules of competition and liberalization. 'He believes that if you want to keep a society open, you have to protect it,' one of his advisers said. Unless governments can provide a framework of protection for their citizens, along with opportunities within it, Macron argues, political extremism will win the day.

To Anglo-Saxon ears, this mix of market economics and social protection carries distinct echoes of Bill Clinton and Tony Blair. When I asked Macron about this, he dismissed the idea that Third Way politics or New Labour were an influence, let alone a model.[30] He has read Anthony Giddens, and has known Peter Mandelson and Alastair Campbell for a number of years, though he has met Blair only a few times. Macron sees the Third Way, rather, as a political response to a particular moment in British history, and the rejection of neo-liberalism after the Thatcher years. 'The Third Way, as conceived by Giddens, was justified in a country that emerged from 20 years of Thatcherism and that was hyper market-friendly,' Macron told me. 'France's challenge is different: one of an over-dominant state that needs to become more efficient, and to prevent rather than cure.'[31] In this sense, Macron insists, his ambition is very different in its philosophy. If anything, his model, as laid out in a speech at Davos in 2018, leans towards more protection and state control. The Third Way, Macron told me, 'revealed its limits in the absence of, or weak, regulation of the market'. His university friend Marc Ferracci put it bluntly during the 2017 campaign: 'Blair has never been a particular object of fascination for him.'

Certainly, Macron's grandiose presidential style is a world away from the call-me-Tony, shirt-sleeves manner of Blair's early prime ministership. Macron does not do Blair-style speechifying, with homespun anecdotes and sentences without verbs. He never sought to win power by reforming a party from within, nor to define his politics in relation to the left and the right. Perhaps Macron is also keen not to associate himself with the toxic politician that Blair, post-Iraq, became. Yet Blair and Gerhard Schröder, who developed his own version of the Neue Mitte, were in office while Macron and his friend Ferracci were students, and there was much discussion at the time about the new moderate form of social democracy that they represented. Back in 1989, Giddens identified Europe, global warming and regional devolution as matters about which it was unhelpful to think in terms of left and right, just as Macron finds it unhelpful today.[32] Third Way talk about rights and responsibilities, pragmatism and flexibility, and the redefining of opportunity in terms of skills and innovation, share a lot with the way Macron frames contemporary French public policy. It is hard not to be struck by the intellectual convergence between Macron's approach and, if not Blair's, then at least that of Gordon Brown, his successor as prime minister, and his particular focus on early education. When Brown in 2008 addressed the Labour Party conference and argued that 'the modern role of government is not to provide everything, but it must be to enable everyone', or when he called for 'a settlement where both markets and government are seen to be the servants of the people, and never their masters', the similarities cry out. It is interesting to note that Gordon Brown remains to this day close to Amartya Sen, the Indian economist, whose influence Macron readily acknowledges.

The underlying political reference points that Macron does acknowledge are, rather, what is known in France as the *deuxième gauche*, or the second left. This is a current of thought traced back notably to Michel Rocard, the chain-smoking, thrice-married, Protestant prime minister under President François Mitterrand between 1988 and 1991. Rocard's ambition to create a moderate centre-left set him for years on a collision course with Mitterrand, who was wedded to more of an anti-capitalist doctrine, and allied the Socialists to the Communist Party with his *programme commun*, a joint programme signed back in 1972. Rocard rejected the economic nationalization espoused by Mitterrand, and struggled for years against his party's Marxist-leaning wing, advocating instead a pragmatic centre-left based on a mix of market economics and efficient public services. The cynical, sphinx-like Mitterrand won that battle, becoming president twice and in the process sinking Rocard, who said that he was kicked out of the Hotel Matignon 'like a domestic servant'.

Rocard's minority current within the French left survived such indignities. The tall, bearded Edouard Philippe, a writer of political thrillers whom Macron made his prime minister, was once a young disciple of Rocard's, before Philippe moved to the centre-right. So was Macron, more than a decade after Rocard left the prime minister's office. 'Michel Rocard, like Mendès-France, thought about justice and social progress in a way that did not exclude liberty. That was the absolute error made by part of the French left, which thought about justice only in terms of equality,' Griveaux told me.[33] Rocard's free-thinking, disruptive approach to politics, his ability 'to say that we should do things differently, think about the world differently', said Griveaux, was a lasting influence on Macron. The former prime minister's support for private enterprise and risk, and his interest in grass-roots politics, chime with Macron's views today. So does Rocard's approach to anti-poverty, which stressed investment in education rather than a narrow focus on redistribution. Indeed, Macron's link to Rocard was one of friendship as well as admiration. They met shortly after Macron graduated from ENA, and Rocard was a guest at Macron's wedding. When the former prime minister died in July 2016, Macron described him as 'one of the great figures of the 20th century'. At a ceremony shortly after Rocard's death to award the *légion d'honneur* to Bernard Spitz, a former adviser to Rocard, it was Macron who stood in for the former prime minister. Rocard's efforts to remodel the centre-left, and overcome old ideological and partisan divides, Macron said, were a 'precursor' to what he dreamed of achieving. His description of Rocard as a 'rare blend' of statesman and 'convinced, extremely free and committed' politician sounded like a model for himself.

Yet Macron did what Rocard never did. The former prime minister was steeped in the history, iconography and traditions of the Socialist Party, a movement originally founded by Jean Jaurès, as the French Section of the Workers' International (SFIO), in 1905. Macron, by contrast, was utterly unsentimental about the party. He had no tribal attachment to it. He became a card-carrying member only briefly, and soon let his membership lapse. Although many of his young team of advisers came from the Strauss-Kahn wing of the Socialist Party, Macron had no political base there, few allies in the parliamentary party, and almost none out in the powerful regional federations. Had he wanted to mount a bid for the Socialist presidential nomination in 2017, he would have found few friends, and many ready to block his way. Macron's ambition, unlike Rocard's, was not to reinvent the left: it was to render the old division between left and right redundant. He turned his back on a Socialist Party that always considered him a maverick, and in doing so pretty much destroyed it.

Between Ricoeur and Rocard, philosophical reflection and pragmatic reaction, Macron has no political qualms about admitting to complexity and contradiction. Some people 'like their ideas in boxes, neatly organized', Macron told a packed rally in eastern Paris, during one of his last campaign speeches in 2017. 'Well I want to tell you this evening that I will continue to use "at the same time" in my sentences, but also in my thinking. Because "at the same time" simply means that one takes into account imperatives that appear opposite but the reconciliation of which is essential to the good functioning of society.'[34] The crowd began to chant 'at the same time! at the same time!' 'Apparently it's a verbal tic,' Macron declared. 'A verbal tic that means that I'm unclear, I don't know how to decide, and that I'm blurred.' But, he finished, 'yes, I chose liberty and equality; yes, I chose growth and solidarity'. He was not ducking choices, he insisted, but seeking a way to reset the balance between market capitalism and social protection, a new social contract for the twenty-first century.

If the tentative contours of Macronism are beginning to emerge, they are partly based on this: a narrative built upon solidarity as well as opportunity, and on the shared values that set Europe apart. Just as Teddy Roosevelt's turn-of-the-century effort to push a new social contract in America became known as Progressivism, Macron defines his politics as progressive[35]: an attempt to inject Sen and Rawls into French thinking about the relationship between the state and individuals, in a way that unleashes people's capacities rather than hampering them. If the Grande Marche of 2016 revealed a widespread French feeling that lives were 'impeded', Macron's vision of the state is about lifting those barriers. He may be tarred by opponents as the 'president of the rich', and he makes no apologies for cutting corporate tax and transforming the wealth tax. Yet it is interesting to note that, of the five leading candidates during the 2017 presidential campaign, Macron was the one who used the word 'equality' the most.[36] One of the first measures he put in place upon taking office was to halve the size of primary-school classes for five- and six-year-olds in poor neighbourhoods. This, rather than increasing benefits, is his version of anti-poverty policy. If Macronism means anything, it may partly be this: striking a new balance between liberty and protection, in which an enabling state becomes a tool for individual advancement. This is the basis of the overarching narrative that Macron seeks in order to give people the confidence and security to embrace a changing world without turning to nationalism.

Yet it is not solely this. There is another dimension to Macronism, and his attempt to fashion a response to populist politics. Statecraft, in his view, depends not just on policy checklists but on symbols and meaning. He is not the first French leader to grasp the power of iconography. Mitterrand, who did his own solitary walk to the Panthéon after his election in 1981, and held hands movingly with Helmut Kohl at Verdun, was an artful student. Modern French theory has its specialists in semiotics and the decrypting of signs, such as Roland Barthes. French history, monarchical and republican, is peopled by leaders who set great store by the meaning and power of symbols. On hearing of the death of the Turkish ambassador, the French diplomat Talleyrand is said to have asked: 'I wonder what he meant by that?' Paul Ricoeur, who specialized in hermeneutic phenomenology, or the interpretative study of meaning, said: 'The symbol sets us thinking.' And Macron is a faithful disciple. Nothing the president does, no gift he gives, no location he chooses from which to give speeches, is anodyne.

The French were given an early taste of Macron's approach the moment that the president-elect stepped into the courtyard of the Louvre on election night. In 2007, Nicolas Sarkozy had spent the evening of his victory holed up in Fouquet's, a glitzy restaurant on the Avenue des Champs-Elysées, before appearing late in the evening at the Place de la Concorde. Five years later, François Hollande celebrated his election onstage in the provincial town of Tulle with a few awkward and improvised dance steps to 'La Vie en Rose', accompanied by an accordion, with his partner of the moment, Valérie Trierweiler, before flying to Paris for a celebration rally at the Place de la Bastille. Macron, by contrast, offered the French a moment that flirted with grandiloquence. In the former royal palace of the Louvre at night, he crossed the Cour Napoléon on foot, accompanied by the EU's national anthem, and addressed his flag-waving supporters against the backdrop of the modernist plate-glass pyramid. The scene both rooted his presidency in the country's imperial past and its cultural history, and projected it into a (European) future. From that day, Macron slowed his pace, lifted his chin, and began to crease his brow. After the tornado that was the Sarkozy presidency, and the bland mediocrity that was Hollande's, the French found themselves with a leader who aspired to de Gaulle-like heights of incarnation – and Mitterrand-style intellectualism.

The first point about Macron's iconography is that it is unapologetically cerebral and learned. To the foreign ear, his speeches are flights of intellectual fancy. When Macron is in full flow, he can lose his audience with philosophical thought and abstraction. For his first big speech on Europe in September 2017, he went to Athens, spoke of Europe's lost soul, opened his speech in modern Greek, and quoted from Hegel. In interviews, Macron talks earnestly about 'ethereal transcendence' and 'spiritual elevation'. He says, with no apparent irony, that he owes 'many of his emotional philosophical moments' to Kant. When he decided not to take part in the traditional French Bastille Day television interview, in 2017, his aides explained that this was because his thoughts were 'too complex'.

Macron has written three unpublished novels, which he described as 'incomplete' and has shown to very few people besides his wife. He does not seek to conceal his erudition. The president described listening to Bach as 'like looking at a painting by Georges de la Tour: despite all its beauty, there is an extreme austerity. It forces a person to drop any sense of vanity', and he talked about Mozart as being 'to music something like Rimbaud was to literature'.[37] To get a sense of Macron in full flow, here is the candidate, who won third prize as a teenage piano student at the Amiens *conservatoire*, discussing his tastes in music: 'I give Bach a special prize. He has been very important to me. His work for keyboard (organ, harpsichord) and cello is of a precision that does not prevent spiritual elevation, but so to speak favours it. I hear less a mathematical coldness than a musical speech carrying all possible emotions. Bach is a smuggler between several worlds, indefinable and brilliant.'[38]

Macron is a president who wears his culture without complex, and wants the French to know it. Here he is, for instance, on literature: 'Houellebecq is surely the novelist who best describes contemporary phobias and fears. He also succeeds, perhaps like no other, in portraying the post-modern character of our society. He addresses the possibilities of genetics at times, or Islamism, and infuses all of it with a certain amount of absurdity. I get a very strong sense of that in *Submission*.'[39] Macron quotes from contemporary francophone writers such as Leïla Slimani and Kamel Daoud as much as from Victor Hugo or Molière, and says he tries to read fiction or poetry every day. 'I thoroughly believe that reading and literature can help a society to better understand itself.'[40] Macron, said one fellow pupil from his high school, is fundamentally 'an author, more than an author: he's someone who was shaped by language'. His presidency, wrote a French commentator, marked the first time in a long while that 'France has carried to power an authentic intellectual'.[41]

The second aspect of his iconography reflects Macron's aspirations to embody French power. To the outsider, just as his unabashed displays of intellectualism draw derision, this too can come across as excessively grandiose. One British commentator described Macron's walk through the Louvre as 'rather embarrassing'. Even for some of the French, Macron's monarchical excess is laughable. Laurent Joffrin, writing in *Libération*, called the new president 'Emmanuel Bonaparte', and the newspaper described him variously as 'sliding into the proud habits of a republican monarch' and displaying an 'absolutist' characterization of power that was 'forced in its theatricality'. From his analysis of the need for a Jupiterian presidency, it took little to infer that he considered himself to be the king of the gods. From his suggestion that the French regretted the absence of a king, it was only a short leap to conclude that he took himself for a modern-day monarch. On the day he announced he was running for president, Macron dropped in on the Basilica of Saint Denis, the burial place of French kings.[42] Shortly after his election, there he was staging action-man stunts, being winched off a nuclear submarine into a helicopter one day, or dressing up as Tom Cruise in *Top Gun* when visiting a French military air base on another. Jupiter, sun king, action man: Macron's iconography comes hazardously close to bathos. He has his own personal make-up artist to powder his face, who billed the presidency €26,000 for her first three months of work. Even his friends worry about hubris.

It is nonetheless worth considering the possibility that, underneath the powdered presidential cheeks, Macron's obsession with culture, symbols and grandeur is more than just a form of intellectual arrogance, or self-aggrandisement. France expects a degree of both erudition and incarnation from its modern leaders. This is a country that treats its intellectuals like national treasures, devoting hours of talk shows and pages of newspapers to them. Philosophy is part of the national curriculum. Any senior French businessman is as at ease discussing Voltaire as he is analysing spreadsheets. 'The French have high expectations of their presidents. It's an old tradition that pre-dates the republic,' Sylvain Fort, Macron's speechwriter, told me: 'They expect it in symbols and in speech. The mastery of the language is in itself a demonstration of authority.'[43] Macron's ability to embody this cultured sense of national self is a very French way of restoring respect for the presidency and confidence in the country. 'We like our presidents to speak French well, even if we don't understand every reference,' a French business coach once told me. 'It's not political arrogance, but a matter of representing France well.' You didn't need to have read Hegel, in other words, to understand that when Macron spoke in Athens, the cradle of Western democracy, he was reminding the French of their own part in the story of European civilization. 'France is an intellectual country,' one of his advisers told me. 'This isn't Texas.'

France's sense of self is partly built on its ideas and the printed word. It is also about the incarnation of power. Macron argues that the presidency has to be exercised by somebody who, 'without considering himself the source of all things, has to lead society by force of conviction, and action, and give a clear meaning to his approach'. Fundamentally, argued Macron, 'the office of the president is not a normal office'.[44] France is not Germany, where political authority is derived from the application of law. French society, through the historical influence of the Catholic Church, was structured vertically, and retains that expectation of central authority. The French demand more than legalistic leadership, Macron argues: they seek a figure to stand above daily affairs, embody the nation and give political action a sense of direction and meaning. If not, identity politics steps in to take its place. Citizens today, Macron wrote in *Révolution*, expect their leaders 'to give a sense to things'.

Long before his election, Macron was already thinking about the nature of presidential authority, and the need to articulate a vision that transcended policy technicalities. For 17 years, between 2000 and 2017, he was a contributor to *Esprit*, a social-democratic review and incubator of thinking about the moderate, anti-Marxist French left. In a meditation on political action he published in 2011, Macron criticized 'those who assert a facile post-modern critique of "great narratives" … Political discourse cannot just be a technical discourse that lists measures. It is a vision of society and of its transformation.'[45] Ricoeur had taught him to think about storytelling as a means of unlocking people's capabilities.[46] Macron put it this way: 'The function of the president in France is one of meaningful symbolic value … Everything you do, everything you say – but also what you don't say – suddenly has meaning.'[47] From Ricoeur, Macron forged a belief in the need both to hold a microscope to political action, and then to stand back to look at the sweep of history, in order to give the narrative context. 'The great difficulty of politics today lies in the paradox between the permanent need for deliberation, which takes place over the long run, and the urgency of decision-making,' he said. 'The only way to resolve this is to articulate a great horizontal transparency, necessary for deliberation, and to resort to a more vertical relationship necessary for decision-making. Otherwise, you end up with either totalitarianism or political inaction.'[48]

It was in this context that he returned to his point in the autumn of 2016 about the French yearning for a monarch. 'Evidently,' Macron said, 'I don't think we should bring back the king.' But, he went on, 'we absolutely do need to invent a new form of democratic authority based on a discourse about meaning, on a universe of symbols, on a permanent determination to project into the future, all anchored in the history of the country'.[49]

As if to make the point, there he was again in Versailles only weeks after his election, telling a joint sitting of both houses of parliament about French grandeur and its place in the 'history of humanity'. Further into his presidency, Macron developed these thoughts into a plea to liberal democracies to embrace the need for 'political heroism'.[50] 'I don't mean that I want to play the hero,' he insisted. 'But we need to be amenable once again to creating grand narratives.' Without storytelling and symbols, contemporary political leaders, he argued, were leaving a space open to competing darker, dangerous narratives: extremism, fanaticism, even jihadism.

'Our society needs collective narratives, dreams, heroism,' he said in an interview with Le Point, as an alternative to 'fanaticism or a death wish'.[51] Many of those who turned in France to jihadism, it seemed, did so as part of a quest to transform small, angry lives into powerful ones. 'Why do young people from the banlieues leave for Syria?' he asked in the same interview. 'Because the propaganda videos they watched on the internet in their eyes transformed terrorists into heroes.' The error, he judges, is that Western society, in a post-modernist urge to deconstruct, mock and deride everything, has given up on storytelling. 'Why can't there be such a thing as democratic heroism?' Macron asked. 'Perhaps that is exactly our task: rediscovering something like that together for the 21st century.'[52] The challenge for liberal democracies, in his view, is to find a way of speaking, as populist politics do, to the yearning for emotional security and the quest to give meaning to ordinary lives, but in a way that draws on positive emotions, and inclusive identities.

What can he possibly mean by all this? Does France's action-man philosopher president see himself as the star of his own national drama? Does he seek to turn the French themselves into heroes? It all sounds singularly ill-suited to the cynical political age. Yet this may be exactly Macron's point. Political elites, who failed to see Trump or Le Pen coming, have become the victims of their own liberal, urban cynicism, no longer able to see that people need meaning and inspiring leadership to make their lives matter. Before his own presidential election campaign, Macron watched replays of Trump's speeches. He grasps the way in which Trump forged a link with people, using their language and harnessing the anti-establishment rage. What Macron seeks is a counterpoint to the divisive nativism and negativity inflamed by populist leaders: a way to appeal to people's better natures, to overcome what he often refers to as the 'sad passions' of jealousy, distrust and mean-spiritedness.[53] In order to give people the confidence to seize opportunities at a time of anxiety, political leadership needs to provide them with the security and sense offered by symbols and stories: in his case, that of a strong France, heading in a clear direction, and a mobile society which enables all to take part. This is what his talk about a 'Europe that protects' is all about. This is why he constantly reminds the French of their cultural heritage and intellectual tradition, and seeks to restore national pride through embodying French power.

It is perhaps in this sense that his theatrical presidency can also be understood. 'If you want to understand Macron, you need to know that he is a superb actor,' said one friend. On election night, Macron walked down seven broad stone steps before crossing the courtyard of the Louvre to make his victory speech. As he took each step, his eyes fixed ahead and a look of studied gravity on his face, he never looked down at his feet once. This is no easy feat. Most people would trip. It is what catwalk models are trained to do. Had he practised? Had he tried it out before? At the very least, this was a president-elect who had rehearsed in his mind the stage management of his own transformation into a president. 'I think he had assimilated the role for quite a long time beforehand,' said Christian Dargnat, his campaign fundraiser. Shortly after his election, Antoine Marguet, a fellow pupil from Amiens, told me: 'I think it's very clear in his mind. The face he will present as president, to the world, will in my view be a bit different to what he is ... He is somebody who has a clear consciousness of what he will be: anti-normality. François Hollande thought that you could run France like you run your family. Macron is conscious that you are obliged to present an image that is not necessarily the reality of what you are, a character which matches the function of the presidency.'[54]

'It's simplistic to say that it's just communication,' Adrien Taquet insisted. 'He's a guy who has a sense of the history of France, who is saddened to see over the past 30 years a country blocked, depressed, out of work. Yes he has ambition, but it's for his country. Because he believes things can change. He wants to mark history.'[55] Most world leaders do not fret much about their place in history until towards the end of their tenure. Unusually for a young first-time president, Macron seemed to be pondering his as soon as he took office. He chose to place a copy of de Gaulle's memoirs, together with a ticking clock, in the background of his official photographic portrait. Behind Macron's sunny disposition and engaging nature there is both a single-mindedness and a solemnity about him. He seems to carry the responsibility with an outward levity, and inner gravity. 'Being president,' he said shortly after his election, 'is the end of innocence.'[56] It imposes an 'absolute solitude', he remarked on another occasion, and requires a certain detachment. 'You have to be prepared to be disparaged, insulted and mocked; this is in the French nature.' Macron does not overstate the ability of any individual leader to mark history. 'Personally, I don't think that it's possible to do great things alone or through individual actions. On the contrary, I think it is only possible to know what to do in a specific moment once you have understood the zeitgeist,' he said, in full Hegelian swing.[57] But he does really believe that he can make a difference.

Such lofty ambition informs the two features of Macronian iconography: the cultural and intellectual speechifying, and the magnificent talk of common destiny and conjuring civilization from chaos. The philosophy, the literature, the helicopters, the royal palaces: it all invites a mixture of awe and derision. The risk for Macron in his quest to embody something greater than himself, of course, is that he takes it all far too seriously; that, rather than offering ordinary people a sense of direction, hope and national pride from the great heights of the presidency, he appears to look down on them from above. Macron certainly seems to have a habit of causing offence. In Athens, the day after his speech on Europe, he declared that he would 'not give in to the lazy, the cynical, or the extremes'. He once referred to railway stations as places 'where one comes across people who succeed, and people who are nothing'. Who was he calling lazy? Who were the mysterious people who were '*rien*'? The French hold their cerebral presidents in high regard. But they dislike arrogance, and even less disdain. A few months into the presidency, as Macron's poll ratings slid sharply, Jérôme Fourquet, head of polling at Ifop, concluded: 'Whether you call it arrogance or condescension, there is a feeling among certain social categories, where Macron's words are received like a slap in the face, that the president doesn't care.'[58]

Of the various risks to Macron's presidency, one of the greatest is that Macron, in seeking to reach high, cannot find a way to dispel the perception that he is arrogant, out of touch or lacking in empathy. Or, worse, that he reinforces it, that his vanity gets the better of him. Christian Dargnat, his fundraiser, said this: 'I remember one phrase he used. "When you embark on a presidential campaign, when you are a candidate to become president of the Republic, you have to have a dose of narcissism at the start, and I acknowledge that." I have heard him say that in public.' If charismatic leaders base their claim to authority on a compelling vision, a persuasive voice, and a capacity to embody change, they are also by definition more vulnerable to disillusion if their behaviour disappoints. When asked what was the main risk for the Macron presidency, somebody who knows him well replied simply: 'Jupiter'. The Elysée Palace, organized around a front courtyard and backing on to a broad garden, is a curiously solitary and silent place for a building situated in the heart of a capital, just steps from the traffic and tourists of the Avenue des Champs-Elysées. Inside, it is a place of almost absolute silence. Georges Pompidou called it a 'prison'. Macron has very few close advisers and friends who speak to him frankly. If anybody can keep him grounded, said Bruno Bonnell, the deputy, it will be the irreverent, humorous Brigitte Macron. 'She brings wisdom. She lives at a different pace,' Bonnell said. 'And she's rooted in the real world.'

Macron's quest to forge a new social contract, devise a grand narrative to rival the appeal of populism and its darker variants, and bring about a transformation of France, is characteristically immodest. 'Some presidents are better at acquiring power than at exercising it, and some feel that they will have failed only if they aren't re-elected,' Marc Ferracci, his best man, told me.[59] 'I think Macron would feel that he has failed if his reforms aren't implemented.' The president said as much. 'The biggest risk for the next five years,' he told me, 'is not to get things done.'[60] If the embodiment of an anti-Trump presidency fails to deliver results, French populism will be back. In the end, the symbols and statements will count for little if Macron cannot achieve something concrete: puting the economy back on track and the young back into jobs.

7

RE-START NATION

'Macron is trying to encourage disruption as fast as society can accept it.'

Frédéric Mazzella, BlaBlaCar, 2015

The word 'factory' does not do justice to Bugatti's state-of-the-art production site outside the town of Molsheim, in eastern France. There is no grease or grime around the assembly line. The floor is a shimmering white gloss. Light slants in through the picture windows from the forest-clad Vosges mountains, lending the airy space the feel of a museum of modern art. Gleaming eight-litre engines are displayed like so many design exhibits. Workers wear white gloves, as if handling treasures. In fact, they are building the world's fastest supercar.

A Milanese engineer, Ettore Bugatti, founded a car factory in this corner of France in 1909. Germany's Volkswagen, which later bought the brand, chose Bugatti's historic French site to develop the Veyron, a car designed to combine elegance and speed. The French factory turned out every one of these luxury record-breaking cars after their launch in 2005. In 2017 Bugatti unveiled a successor, the Chiron, which pushed the limits of physics and sleek design further still. The car reaches 100 kilometres (62 miles) an hour in two and a half seconds and has a starting price of €2.4 million. Christophe Piochon, head of the French plant, compares the exquisite craftsmanship that goes into the construction of a Bugatti car to haute couture. 'Functional parts,' he told me when I visited, 'should also be works of art.'

Although France has a reputation for making life difficult for business, and struggles to hold on to low-end industries and jobs, it is in some ways well placed to carve out a competitive niche in the knowledge economy – if it can get its policy mix right. Bugatti may be a commercial indulgence for its parent company: a badge of engineering and design prowess rather than the basis for a profit line. But its manufacture in France hints at some of the country's fundamental strengths, notably its traditions in luxury and creative industries, as well as in engineering. France has more winners of the Fields Medal for excellence in maths than any other country except the United States, and has a number of world-class *grandes écoles* for business (HEC, Essec) and engineering (Ecole Polytechnique, Mines ParisTech, Ecole Centrale) that recruit the best high-school graduates after fearsomely competitive exams. French high-end luxury – Hermès, Chanel, Dior, Saint Laurent, Louis Vuitton, Cartier – is unrivalled in the world, and envied these days even by the Italians. The design aesthetic is part of the national mindset. French culture delights in elegance, sensuality, quality and form: the exquisite hand-stitching on the haute-couture dress; the geometrically arranged *tartes aux framboises* lined up in the *pâtisserie* window. The aesthetics of daily life, the *art de vivre*, remains a source of both grand gestures and small stolen pleasures. It is no coincidence that the two biggest and most successful luxury-goods groups in the world, LVMH and Kering, are French.

The world's fifth-largest economy and sixth-largest exporter, France has more big multinational companies in the global Fortune 500 than Germany. The French have long been strong in top-end goods and services: luxury products, food processing, pharmaceuticals, fashion. The giants of the CAC 40, which covers the top-listed French companies, provide the world with tyres (Michelin), shampoo (L'Oréal), yoghurt (Danone), insurance (AXA) and handbags (Louis Vuitton, LVMH). These firms have long been globalized. Moreover, something has begun to stir in corporate France, as the car industry illustrates more broadly. In the past, French car designers had a reputation for a certain cool. When Citroën launched the futuristic DS 'Goddess' in 1955, Roland Barthes, the French structuralist, described it as nothing less than 'spiritual'. After years of turning out dull vehicles and focusing on cost-cutting by shifting production to cheaper countries, French carmakers are beginning to return to form. PSA bought General Motors' European operations. Renault recently launched the Alpine sports car, a retro nod to its 1960s classic, which it is building in the French port of Dieppe. The Renault-Nissan alliance took an early bet on electric vehicles. In the first half of 2017 it became the biggest carmaker in the world. 'A few years ago the motor industry was said to be the steel of the 21st century, but today there's an incredible effervescence in the sector,' Jacques Aschenbroich, head of Valeo, which makes high-tech automotive parts such as sensors for driverless cars, told me.[1] In 2017 half of Valeo's orders were for products that had not existed three years previously.

Yet for all this creativity, corporate France has not fulfilled its potential, and in some respects has been losing ground. Most of the big French companies have been around for a very long time. Saint Gobain, a glass-maker, was founded in 1665 and given a monopoly over the manufacture of mirrors. By 2015 the average age of the top 150 American firms by market capitalization was 91 years, compared to 132 years for the top 70 French firms, according to France Stratégie, a government think tank. Even after excluding Google, Apple, Facebook and Amazon from the American sample, the average age of the top French firms is still 32 per cent older. Not enough French firms have invested in building a digital offering and in technology more broadly. The 2016 World Economic Forum competitiveness index ranked France 21st out of 138 countries for its overall performance, but only 33rd according to a ranking based on the adoption of technology by companies.

Too few new businesses grow to achieve proper scale. France has tied its mid-sized firms in a tangle of rules that deter smaller ones from expanding. The country has less than half as many mid-sized companies as Germany, and half as many firms that export. Most small firms do not recruit enough staff to expand as strongly as they might. By 2012 the average payroll of a French firm listed 14 employees, compared with 41 in Germany. France had 8,480 industrial companies with over 50 employees, compared with 20,340 for Germany. An arresting study by Luis Garicano, Claire LeLarge and John Van Reenen of the London School of Economics, showed that the number of firms employing 49 people was considerably higher than the number of companies employing 50.[2] This was not a coincidence. The Attali Commission report calculated that, once a business in France grew to 50 employees or more, 34 extra regulations and laws came into force. At the start of 2017, a firm had to put in place a *comité d'entreprise* (works council), and hold meetings with it at least every two months, as well as pay for a *délégué syndical* (union representative) to spend ten hours a month on trade union matters. Businesses also had to set up a Health, Hygiene, Safety and Working Conditions committee, with quarterly meetings on company time. A quick glance at the country's Code du Travail, a thick red doorstep of a book containing the French labour code, gave a sense of this regulatory thicket. Running to 3,448 pages by 2017, or 52 per cent more than in 2000, it was longer than the Holy Bible. Each industry and profession has its own branch agreement, the one for hairdressing running to 304 pages, and for bakers to 742 pages. Such rules are patrolled by an army of workplace inspectors, a profession established in 1892. The upshot of all this was that small French firms found it costly to grow, and so didn't.

I began to understand these difficulties when I first met Pierre de Jean, a slight figure with a gentle manner who runs a small umbrella factory in the village of Donzy, in central France. Although only 200 kilometres south of Paris, it is very much in *la France profonde*, and a place that time forgot. Wedged between the wine-growing regions of Sancerre and Pouilly-Fumé and the bleaker uplands of the Morvan plateau, Donzy lies amid the verdant farmland of Nièvre. The village boasts a local goats-cheese maker and walnut-oil producer, and the high street has a *boulangerie*, *pâtisserie* and butcher, as well as hairdressers and a pharmacy. Many shops are shut, as provincial tradition dictates, on a Monday. Guy de Jean, Pierre's father, was a New Wave designer and gave the brand his name in 1962. Today, the artisanal firm still manufactures umbrellas by hand in a modest industrial estate perched on a hill on the edge of the village. Pierre de Jean, who runs the factory with his wife, Catherine, took me on a tour of the shop floor, where 18 employees were stitching lace, ribbons, frills and bows, rolling out and cutting pastel fabrics, and threading spokes into their creations. In 2007, the year I first visited, his firm turned out 150,000 umbrellas a year, 63 per cent of them in Donzy and the rest in China. I asked him how he managed to keep manufacturing in France? 'Through taste,' he replied, 'and folly.'[3]

'Ten years ago we asked ourselves whether we should keep any production in France,' de Jean explained, inspecting the laces on a racy jet-black latex umbrella designed for sale under the Jean-Paul Gaultier brand. 'It was obvious that all the low- and mid-market production was going to move abroad. But we decided to stay, and concentrate on quality and savoir-faire.' In the entrance hall, boxed umbrellas were marked for delivery to Harrods and Fortnum & Mason, stamped with the label 'Lovingly created in artisanal France'. De Jean had no trouble finding skilled labour, nor talented designers, nor suppliers of quality fabric and materials. His great difficulty was getting around the rules that, he felt, hemmed him in at each turn. Back in 2007, he was still feeling the after-effects of the introduction of the 35-hour working week, which meant that he had to close the factory on Friday afternoons. The strict procedures, and uncertain legal outcomes, associated with redundancy laws meant that he was 'afraid to hire', he said, because 'we don't want to have to be in a position to make anybody redundant'.

Five years later, in 2012, I went back to Donzy. The factory was still working at full capacity, and the order books were full. But de Jean was visibly more frustrated. 'We played the game. We kept the site in France, and the same number of employees, out of conviction and desire,' he said. 'But we have no intention of hiring more employees here. Every job created is practically a job for life.'[4] Because of the level of social charges, bureaucratic complexities and personnel difficulties, the firm was outsourcing new demand to Asia. By then, the firm ran production out of two sites in Xiamen, in south-east China. Most dismaying of all for this softly spoken businessman, whose small office jutted on to the shop floor, he had to forego orders in France because of the rigidity of the country's working-time rules. Some of his employees would agree to occasional overtime. But, he said, he had lost clients 'because I couldn't increase production at the site'. Instead of hiring, he let the orders go.

Such experiences were repeated in different corners across the country. France launched plenty of small firms, especially after it simplified the registration of new companies under Nicolas Sarkozy, when the country introduced the 'auto-entrepreneur' regime for new microbusinesses. But it singularly failed to develop a French version of the German 'Mittelstand', those mid-sized, export-oriented, mostly family-run industrial firms. The competitiveness of French industry, and with it economic growth, seemed to be on a path of inexorable decline. Between 2005 and 2010 France's share of world exports shrank by almost 20 per cent, a decline exceeded within the eurozone only by Greece. France's current account deteriorated. From a surplus at the start of the 2000s, it ran the biggest deficit (in cash terms) of any eurozone country by 2012. Four years later, manufacturing's share of employment in France had declined to 12 per cent, higher than in Britain but below Germany's 17 per cent. The French were more productive per hour spent in the office, but spent fewer hours there. While Germany used wage restraint and labour-market reforms to claw back the competitiveness that the country lost after reunification, France brought in the shorter working week. Although French employers secured some flexibility in return, the new rules caused headaches, particularly in the service sector. Many office workers received up to three weeks of extra holiday, in addition to the normal five weeks of paid vacation, leaving companies to juggle constant absences. By 2017 the country had slid from 16th in the World Economic Forum's competitiveness index in 2008 to 22nd place.

As corporate France lost ground, and its attractiveness as a location for foreign investment declined, French politicians often seemed simply to make matters even worse. France earned a reputation as a country that not only had a cultural suspicion of wealth creation, and an ambivalent relationship to work, but also political misgivings about enterprise. Two episodes captured this. One was a row that broke out in 2013, a year after François Hollande had been elected on the back of a promise to impose a top income-tax rate of 75 per cent. Arnaud Montebourg, who was then his industry minister, ended up in a transatlantic war of words with an American tyre boss who had accused French industrial workers of being lazy, overpaid and unproductive. Tall, telegenic and bombastic, Montebourg was no wallflower. He had already got into a public row the previous year with the Indian steel giant, Arcelor-Mittal, over the closure of furnaces in eastern France. The tyre spat began with a letter the minister received from Maurice Taylor, the American boss of a tyre company that was considering buying a French factory, which was leaked to the press. In his missive, Taylor, who was known as 'The Grizz' for his tough negotiating style, held nothing back. 'The French workforce gets paid high wages but works only three hours,' he claimed: 'They have one hour for their breaks and lunch, talk for three and work for three.' On asking the unions about this, he wrote in his letter, he was told: 'That's the French way!' As for the French government's request for talks about his firm taking over the site, he told Montebourg: 'How stupid do you think we are?'[5]

The French Twittersphere went hyperactive, and the airwaves buzzed with indignation. At the French tyre plant, the local head of the Confédération Générale du Travail (CGT), a big trade union with historic ties to the French Communist Party, said that the tyre boss belonged in the 'psychiatric ward'. Montebourg fired back. In an open letter to Mr Taylor, he accused him in return of being 'extremist' and 'insulting'. 'May I remind you,' he went on, that 'the company you run is one-twentieth the size of Michelin, our world-class French technological leader, and one-thirty-fifth as profitable.' If Taylor's firm tried instead to import low-cost tyres to France, Montebourg warned, he would make sure his officials monitored its every move.

Montebourg may have had a point. But, despite a measure of hyperbole and gratuitous insult in Taylor's letter, so did the tyre boss. It was an absurd exaggeration to state that French industrial workers spent only three hours a day doing anything productive. Yet it was the case that the 35-hour working week, combined with an entrenched role for unions within companies and intrusive labour rules, made life particularly difficult for French managers. When Taylor claimed that the French government seldom confronted unions with the painful truth that it was better for them to make concessions than to watch potential investors flee and factories shut, he was not far off the mark.

A second saga exposed the political damage being done, not to old industry this time, but to new. It arose over pigeons. Or, to be precise, a movement led by French entrepreneurs who styled themselves *les pigeons*, or 'suckers', and used the back-slang hashtag #geonpi. This was an online revolt against the government's plan to double capital-gains tax to some 60 per cent. Led by Jean-David Chamboredon, a venture capitalist, the rebellion went viral. 'I've never seen people so depressed. They've had enough, they are leaving,' warned Marc Simoncini, an internet entrepreneur and founder of the online dating site Meetic. The government seemed unaware that entrepreneurs rarely paid themselves a salary, investing earnings into the capital of their business, and thus that this tax would be deeply damaging to French start-ups. Had the fiscal revolt been led by corporate giants, it might have been dismissed as special pleading. But the 'Pigeon' movement captured the imagination thanks to its spontaneity, grass-roots nature and youthfulness. The biggest single age group backing the movement on Facebook was 25- to 34-year-olds. Four days later, the government, embarrassed, said it would think again.

Thanks to such poor and inconsistent policymaking, France damaged both its image, and its real economy. Over a period of 15 years from 2000, the French economy went from being one of the OECD's stronger economies to one of its underachievers. Within the eurozone, France was no better than a middling performer. The euro had secured France low inflation and currency stability. But, by giving up control of monetary policy, the country could no longer devalue its currency to retain competitiveness, as it was able to with the old French franc. Failure to fix the competitiveness problem with domestic reform condemned France to mediocrity. In the two decades after the single currency's launch in 1991, the French economy avoided the spectacular collapse witnessed in Greece, Ireland or Portugal, or even Italy and Spain. But it failed to keep up with the eurozone's robust performers, including Germany and the Netherlands. France's economy bumped along in the middle, doing less well in upturns, and less badly during downturns, including the financial crisis that began in 2008. Broadly, three brakes on French growth have kept its economy from realizing its potential: a rigid labour market, an overly large public sector, and overprotected professional and state-linked industries.

On the first point, France is a classic case of what labour economists call a two-tier jobs market, in which insiders enjoy the comfort of strong protection but to the detriment of outsiders, whether the young, unskilled or unemployed. For those aged between 25 and 54, France's employment rate (79.8 per cent) is above the OECD average, and indeed marginally better than that in the United States (78.7 per cent). The real problem concerns older, and above all younger, workers. Little over half of workers between the age of 55 and 64 are employed, well below the OECD average of 60 per cent and 70 per cent in Germany or 77 per cent in Sweden. At 62 years, the official retirement age is well below the European average. On weekdays throughout the warmer months, tour buses across the country disgorge groups of sprightly French 60-somethings in trainers into cobbled squares and historic cathedrals. For the under-25s, at the start of their working lives, permanent jobs are scarce. French youth unemployment reached 25 per cent in 2016, more than three times that in Germany. Whereas only 5 per cent of the over 50s were on short-term contracts in 2016, the share was nearly 30 per cent for those under 25, who often find themselves stuck with years of back-to-back temping and short-term work. In other countries, temping is a route to a permanent job. In France, only a fifth of temps are in permanent jobs three years later.

Short-term contracts are a scourge that touches those with and without skills alike. In 2015, I came across Ange-Mireille Gnao, an energetic 28-year-old French woman of Ivorian origin, who had a master's degree in communication strategy. When I met her, she had been looking for a permanent job for three years, but found nothing. Permanent jobs, she said, were impossible to find in France. To keep herself busy, she had set up her own communications consultancy, but yearned for the 'stability' that a permanent job would bring. 'Psychologically, it can create a real lack of confidence,' Ange-Mireille told me. 'If you don't have a permanent contract in France, it's impossible to rent a flat, or get a loan.'[6] The culture of temping also made it difficult for young people to move out of the family home, she explained, putting strains on their relationships and hampering their independence. Her 29-year-old friend, Florence Moreau, who lived in the Paris *banlieue* of Créteil, was also looking for work, and said that she 'would take anything, as long as it is permanent'. She had gone through no fewer than eight consecutive short-term contracts. 'Now,' she said, 'people think that I have an instability problem.'

Because the labour code offers little flexibility, firms use temporary contracts to get around it. These accounted for over four-fifths of new contracts in 2017. Many of these short-term positions last for less than a month, and firms use them as a means to circumvent the rules that deter them from creating proper jobs. So France's overprotected labour market keeps the young in precarious work – and the unemployed out of a job at all. The financial risk of taking on new permanent staff is particularly high for small firms, which can be crippled by the payouts assessed in

French labour courts for unfair dismissals if they get the redundancy procedure wrong. Termination cases can be brought up to two years after an employee is fired, and awards vary massively. Sylvain Camos, who runs an events business with 25 employees, explained that an employee he had fired was awarded €200,000 for unfair dismissal, a sum halved on appeal, but nonetheless huge for a small business. Jérôme Veneau, who ran a tiny one-man barber shop in Paris, told my colleague that he had never taken on another employee after his first one claimed to have been injured at work, and was awarded €17,000 in damages by a labour tribunal. In short, the excessive protection of insiders, along with the rules that weigh down on companies when they reach a certain size, deter job creation and contribute to structurally high levels of unemployment in France. It is a problem that will only be accentuated in the digital, data-driven economy. As intelligent machines and algorithms replace people, and job obsolescence accelerates, firms will be even more reluctant to take the risk of permanent hires.

The second constraint on growth has been France's over-heavy public sector. For years the French argued, with some reason, that the excellence of their public services justified the scale of their public spending. Back in 2000, as a share of GDP, French public spending was below that in Sweden, whose stripped-pine model of social welfare was more comprehensive still. Yet over the better part of the following two decades, Sweden grasped that its model was unsustainable, and decided to rethink its state in a way that did not jeopardize solidarity. While France continued to hire civil servants and build grandiose headquarters for its regional governments, Sweden kept its public nurseries and generous paid paternity leave but trimmed spending elsewhere. By 2017 the two countries had swapped positions. France's public spending, at 56 per cent of GDP, was seven points above that in Sweden.

Up to a point, the French accept high taxation, and the platoons of bureaucrats needed to administer it, as part of the bargain that brought them good hospitals, roads, ambulances and schools in return. France was built by a strong centralizing hand and it is part of national mythology that the state steers the economy, and shepherds society, through a form of hyper-centralization that survived the transition from monarchy to republic.[7] Jean-Baptiste Colbert, Louis XIV's finance minister, put the Gobelins tapestry firm under royal control in 1662, founded the Saint Gobain mirror factory in 1665, and approved the building of the Canal du Midi in 1666. The Napoleonic code, established in 1804, imposed a systematic set of civil laws and rules to unify the nation. Over the course of the twentieth century, the country's *acquis*, or social rights, were incrementally enshrined by law and the protections afforded by the state became a mark of progress towards a better society. Léon Blum introduced the two-week paid holiday for all workers in 1936. François Mitterrand extended this to five weeks in the early 1980s, and brought in retirement at age 60, and the 39-hour working week, which Martine Aubry reduced to 35 hours.

After 1945, France drew on this *dirigiste* tradition to transform a war-battered country, publishing five-year plans for the economy that were run from Paris, and setting up a social-security system directly inspired by the *résistants* of the National Resistance Council. Entitled 'Les jours heureux' ('Happy Days'), this was designed to ensure 'to all citizens the means of existence in case they are unable to procure it through work'. These progressive improvements buttressed France's sense of the state as a guarantor of progress, carrying the country forward, however fitfully, like an 'endless cortège proceeding towards the light', in the words of Jules Ferry, the nineteenth-century educationalist. Faith in the state did not, of course, preclude revolt against it. The French harboured ambiguous feelings towards central authority, lurching from veneration to uprising, torn between the 'cult of the State and the inclination to rebellion'.[8] Alain Peyrefitte, a former minister under de Gaulle, put it well when he wrote that the French are 'passively submissive to their administration, and in (disappointed) love with authority; rebellious towards their State, at the same time unfit to live without this irksome tutor'.[9] All the same, a strong, well-financed central state remained intricately linked in the French mind with the idea of progress and the guarantee of a decent life. What was the point of France, after all, if it was not to demonstrate to the Anglo-Saxon world how to run a society in a more civilized way: less individualistic, more protective, more *solidaire*?

By the early years of the twenty-first century, however, the cracks in the model began to emerge. Michel Pébereau, a banker and former civil servant, put it bluntly in a 2005 report on French public finances: 'Each time a new problem has arisen in the past 25 years, our country has responded with more spending.'[10] France did indeed supply its citizens with a first-class health system, fast trains and comprehensive public services. In 2016 no country in the world spent a greater share of its GDP on social, health and pension programmes. At 31.5 per cent of GDP, French social spending was far higher than in either Norway (25.1 per cent) or Sweden (27.1 per cent), the Nordic countries that Macron seems to want to emulate. While Sweden and the Netherlands reduced their share of social spending between 1990 and 2016, in France it just kept on rising. Thanks to generous benefits, a low retirement age and high longevity rates, French spending on pensions imposes a particular burden.

Yet successive governments created the illusion that this was sustainable by running up hefty debts and taxing their citizens with abandon. By the end of 2016, the overall French tax take as a share of GDP was higher than any other EU country. An employer who pays a worker twice the minimum wage, or €2,400 a month, has to contribute nearly half as much again to the state in social-security contributions; the employee, for his part, has to hand over 22 per cent of his pay in social-security contributions, on top of income tax. A French pay slip typically runs to over 40 itemized lines, with deductions for pension, unemployment, social-security, work-accident, work-medical, transport funds and so on.

Were the state taxing the French in order to service debts incurred for long-term investment, it might make sense. Yet most borrowing pays for current operations, not research and development, higher education or infrastructure. Overseeing all of this is an administration that keeps on growing. Over two decades to 2012 the state hired nearly a million extra civil servants, bringing France's total to five million. In the Ministry of Agriculture alone, which serves an ever-shrinking number of farmers, the number of staff grew by 8 per cent. France boasted a post office for every 3,530 inhabitants, twice as many as Germany, yet fewer of its letters arrived the next day. It numbered 90 civil servants for every 1,000 inhabitants, compared with 50 in Germany. Over one in five French workers was employed by the public sector. A *mille-feuille* of public administration, which reached from the mayor in the town hall, to the *département*, via the region, to the top layer of national government, sustained a public sector with a voracious appetite for taxes, paperwork, forms and rules. The French state taxed their people more, and spent more, than any other country – yet still did not generate better economic growth in return.

At the same time, the state overprotected and intervened in industry, the third check on French growth. In 1856, Alexis de Tocqueville wrote about the country's 'regulating, restrictive administration, which seeks to anticipate everything, take charge of everything, always knowing better than those it administers what is in their interests'. To this day, the state sets the dates that shops can hold sales; prohibits supermarkets from selling paracetamol; limits the number of Paris taxis (hence the anger of those taxi-drivers who did hold precious licences at the arrival of Uber); and prevents chemists from owning more than one pharmacy. It retains a deep portfolio of public shareholdings in private companies, which it does not always manage well. According to a 2017 report by the Cour des Comptes, the official public auditor, the French state had investments in nearly 1,800 firms, holdings that together were worth almost €100 billion. Nearly 800,000 people in France worked for firms in which the state held a majority shareholding, more (in absolute terms) than in America or Germany. Yet the Cour des Comptes was scathing about the public management of these state assets, pointing to 'chronic weaknesses', including failures of oversight and a lack of vision over strategic purpose. Between 2011 and 2016, when the overall value of the CAC 40 rose, the state's portfolio lost value. The state, it concluded, 'has difficulty being a good shareholder', and 'needs to break with an inappropriate vision of its role as a shareholder and with its desire to intervene under the pressure of the moment for fear of appearing impotent'.

The underwhelming performance of some of France's publicly owned firms is an awkward reality for the country's *dirigistes*. Even some of the former crown jewels of French industrial policy, such as its nuclear-energy firm Areva (now known as Orano), 83 per cent owned by the state, have become strategically weak and financially precarious. Nuclear energy provides three-quarters of the country's electricity, a level that Macron's government had promised to reduce to half by 2025 until it realized that such an ambition was unrealistic. Yet the French model of large pressurized water reactors, expensive to build and decommission and prone to delays and cost over-runs, is increasingly being challenged by the more nimble mini-reactors offered by American and Asian firms, and by the big switch to gas and renewables, notably solar power. Vast sums of taxpayers' money are still being pumped into Areva (Orano) to keep it going. The SNCF, which operates all those fabulous TGVs, also devours big state subsidies while piling up debt. Despite the collapse in letter-writing, La Poste, the French public postal service, is still the second-biggest public employer in the country, with 250,000 employees. All this is overseen by a caste of highly trained elite managers, part of a system well suited to the *dirigiste* planning of the post-war years, which protects its own in the upper echelons of the administration and the boardrooms of publicly controlled firms.

In the years leading up to the 2017 election, the thinking in France was beginning to evolve. Competition, long considered somewhat suspect, brought cheap mobile telephony, to the delight of a new generation. In 2009 the state awarded a licence for a fourth mobile telephone operator to Free, a phone company launched by Xavier Niel, who went on to become godfather to the Paris tech scene (and a friend of Emmanuel Macron). Niel built the business against the odds, and the resistance of incumbent operators. With no university education, no family money, and a background that included marketing sex shops and chat lines, Niel was originally treated as a disreputable outsider, and existing operators lobbied hard against him. 'If I commit suicide, or if I die in a car accident in the next three months or so,' he told my colleague a year before he won the licence, 'you will know the threats were serious, because I am not feeling at all suicidal, and I drive very slowly.' France came late to competition for service and utility providers compared with most other European countries, and had to be prodded into action by the European Commission. But French consumers have begun to understand the benefits. Over the six years following the launch of Free, the price of telecommunications in France fell faster than in Germany, Italy or Spain.[11]

At the same time, the Greek debt crisis awakened the French to the risks of high levels of public debt. When France lost its triple-A credit rating, and worries about debt-servicing costs rose, this became a subject of fevered political debate. The French began to realize that they could not defy forever the rules that applied to their neighbours. Indeed, Macron judged that public opinion was a step ahead of the politicians, and that the weaknesses of the costly French model ought to be discussed during the election campaign. When it is no longer oriented to serve the right purpose, he wrote in his book *Révolution*, the state machinery in France 'becomes an obstruction and a weight to the whole nation. Hundreds of structures exist that should disappear. Agents carry out useless tasks. Rules invade everything, because it is more convenient to write a law or a decree than to set a direction. Bureaucrats find in all this a raison d'être and politicians an opportunity to justify their privileges ... The country lives for the administration and not the administration for the country.'[12] The candidate was clear. The question was: what would the president do about it?

* * *

On a winter's day before Christmas in 2003, a young French computer-science graduate from Stanford University was working flat out for a software consultancy in Paris and hadn't much time to think about travel plans. He didn't own a car, and had been hoping to take the train to join his family in the Vendée, in western France, for the holidays. By the time he got round to booking, though, the trains were full. He persuaded his sister to take a detour via Paris to pick him up for the ride and, as they headed down the motorway for the 500-kilometre journey, Frédéric Mazzella noticed how many other cars on the route were empty apart from the driver. That moment, he recalled later, was when the idea came to him of launching a long-distance ride-sharing service that could link passengers to empty seats. Three years later, BlaBlaCar was launched. By 2017 it was the biggest ride-sharing service in the world, with 60 million users.

The idea behind BlaBlaCar is simple: the driver 'sells' empty seats to cover petrol and road tolls, but not at a profit; the passenger gets a cheap trip, even last minute. The business model is that of Airbnb: BlaBlaCar takes a cut on transactions; trust is built through peer review. Mazzella told me that he sees his firm as a disruptor of the mobility business rather than a competitor to trains, coaches or taxis. What he does is open up the inventory of empty car seats. In 2016 a funding round valued BlaBlaCar at $1.5 billion, making it one of the rare French 'unicorns', those privately held tech start-ups with a valuation equivalent to $1 billion or more. Within Europe, there are still far more unicorns in Britain. And Europe's are dwarfed by the number in America. BlaBlaCar itself has more recently had to rethink its branding and operations, after running into expansion difficulties. But what the start-up managed in France, where the genial and fashionably bearded Mazzella became the public face of the newly emerging French tech scene, was to transform the image of corporate success. 'What has really changed is that students from the best schools in France, who five to ten years ago would have joined L'Oréal or BNP Paribas, are now looking at start-up jobs,' Mazzella told me, 'Things have really changed.'[13] Mazzella, like many French tech types of his generation, is also close to Emmanuel Macron. The pair appeared together in 2015 at an investor event in London, designed to promote the country's emerging start-up scene. Together, they were the new faces of a more open, innovative France.

There has been no better example in recent years of how smarter incentives, and fewer burdens, can release French economic growth than the country's tech entrepreneurs. High taxes on stock options and bureaucratic rules used to make France a difficult place for them to operate, as the Pigeon protest made clear. For years, London and Berlin had a far better buzz, and French tech types could be found setting up in converted warehouses in Shoreditch and Hoxton. But the boost Macron gave the sector when he was economy minister has helped bring about a cultural shift. By 2015 a quarter of graduates of HEC, the top business school, had started their own company, up from one in ten a decade previously. Many spoke good English, and had an uncomplicated approach to doing so. From 2014 onwards, venture-capital investment in France increased sharply. By 2016 it had reached €2.7 billion, more than was invested in Germany. That year saw 590 rounds of capital-raising in France, more than any country in Europe. Venture capitalists in London, who had until then shied away from Paris, became bullish about France for the first time. Sheryl Sandberg, COO of Facebook, said the country now had 'some of the most innovative technology companies in the world'.[14] Tony Fadell, the inventor of the Apple iPod, moved to Paris to work with entrepreneurs in the French capital. In 2009, he said, French corporate life was all about big, old companies, and 'felt like the Dark Ages'. Now, he declares with all the passion of the convert: 'I'm telling everyone, "Do you know what's going on here?" One day, it's going to take just one big company that comes out of here or any of these incubators around France.'[15] Xavier Niel told me: 'There has been a transformation of mentalities in France.'[16] He has become an evangelist, urging young people to take risks, think big and break conventions and describes a 'new alchemy' in France.

What Macron understood during his time as economy minister, and from the contact he had with the likes of Niel and Mazzella, was the scale of economic upset being brought about by the digital revolution. He argued that the country both needed to open up to innovators and embrace these changes, but also to put in place a proper regulatory framework. Macron spent a lot of time hanging out with tech types at the time. When I interviewed him in the autumn of 2015, I asked him what he had read recently on the subject. Most French ministers would have quoted a piece of French research, or more commonly a French government report. Macron cited *The Second Machine Age*, by Erik Brynjolfsson and Andrew McAfee. He had a good grasp of the pace and nature of technological change, as well as its implications for jobs and society as machines hollowed out the salaried working middle. French policymakers have long tended to favour producers over consumers, and to protect incumbents from newcomers to the market. This, he judged, made it difficult for tech innovators, and needed to change.

At the same time, as ever, Macron argued that rules needed to be 'fair'. It would be short-sighted to consider everything about start-ups as 'supercool' and to shy away from regulation as a result. This was a line he was to take to the presidency, pushing strongly for a hard line towards Google, Amazon and Facebook over tax. But regulators would nonetheless need to start putting consumers first. 'They vote every day, by taking Uber,' Macron said back then. The French might reason more like producers, but workers were transformed after office hours into shoppers and users of services that had to start to respond to them. To side only with those threatened by technology was to favour conservatism and defend insider privilege. 'Rules need to evolve with society,' Mazzella told me in 2015. 'Macron is trying to encourage disruption as fast as society can accept it.'

In office, Macron has been guided by an approach that puts the need to encourage business, risk-taking, entrepreneurship and job creation at the centre of policy. In doing so, he has begun to deal with the first two big checks on French economic growth: labour-market rigidity, and the outsized, ill-adapted state. On the first count, just four months after he was elected, his flagship labour reform was discussed, fine-tuned, adopted and put on the statute books. The new law was designed to give companies more flexibility over staffing, in order to encourage them to create more permanent jobs. Among the various measures, the law brought in a cap on court-awarded redundancy payouts for unfair dismissal, in order to reduce financial risk; simplified worker representation in companies; gave small firms the right to bypass union agreements; and introduced a more straightforward procedure for hiring people for specific projects. Although the unions secured a role for branch agreements in some areas, the underlying principle was that employers were to be trusted to reach deals with employees. Small firms were freed of many constraints. The basic concept of a single labour code for all, progressively enshrined since the time of Napoleon, had been challenged. France could not stand still while technology dislocated the job market, Macron argued. 'For 30 years we've suffered from the sickness of mass unemployment,' the president said. 'That's the French problem.'[17]

There were two arresting features to this piece of legislation. The first was the shift it represented in French thinking about employment policy. In 2000, when the Socialist government of Lionel Jospin introduced the 35-hour working week, the underlying idea was to share existing work in order to create more jobs. Martine Aubry, the Socialists' labour minister at the time, described the shorter week as a 'project of solidarity towards the unemployed'. This was in keeping with a long-standing French preference for public spending as a tool to combat unemployment. Directly subsidised jobs were favoured over a loosening of the rules that deterred firms from creating such posts themselves. France operated a menagerie of such schemes for subsidising jobs. The names came and went, as governments of the left and right rotated in and out of power: *contrats jeunes*, *contrats d'avenir*, *contrats aidés*, *contrats de génération*. Bold was the French politician who defended the idea that firms might be more willing to hire more staff if redundancy rules were less punitive. 'Who could imagine that making redundancies simpler will favour jobs?' wrote a group of politicians and intellectuals in *Le Monde*. Macron's labour law, though, involved no new project to subsidise jobs, a policy that the labour minister, Muriel Pénicaud, described as 'the least efficient of all employment policies'. The idea, rather, was to take some of the uncertainty and risk out of taking on staff. The new law was designed 'to liberate the energy of companies to invest and create jobs', said Pénicaud. Contained in five 'ordinances', it was passed using an accelerated parliamentary procedure to speed up implementation.

The second element was the method that Macron used to get his reform through. Most observers were expecting an outpouring of anger and protests on the streets in the autumn of 2017, as tradition dictated. There was even discussion of whether a 'Thatcher moment' might be helpful for the new president, a way for him to show his determination not to cave in. On the far left, Jean-Luc Mélenchon tried to drum up support for his campaign of protest known as *les casserolades*: a noisy banging of saucepans in the streets. Protesters, he promised, would show the president that his economic reforms 'ruin our life and keep us from dreaming, so we will stop you from sleeping'. A few protests and strikes took place that autumn, but none took hold, and the numbers dwindled by the week. Some 223,000 took part in protests across France on 12 September 2017 according to Interior Ministry figures; by 21 September the figure had fallen to 132,000. A month later, on 19 October, only 38,000 turned out. Philippe Martinez, secretary-general of the hard-line CGT, who sports a Mexican moustache, promised that he would 'keep going to the very end'. But the movement failed to capture the broader imagination. Macron had obtained a clear mandate for the reform and for the use of the fast parliamentary procedure to pass it. 'I do what I say. In effect, that's quite new,' Macron said afterwards, sardonically.[18]

This tactic not only gave him legitimacy; it also disarmed his opponents. Pénicaud, a personnel specialist respected in the industry for handling difficult negotiations while head of human resources at the dairy giant Danone, held around 100 meetings with union leaders during the summer, which resulted in some concessions. She found a constructive partner in the Confédération Française Démocratique du Travail (CFDT), a moderate union, which in 2017 overtook the CGT as the biggest union in the private sector for the first time since it was founded in 1895. Midway through the talks, I went to see Laurent Berger, the softly spoken head of the CFDT, at the union's headquarters in eastern Paris. Recalling that the country had stepped 'very close to darkness' that year, a reference to the presence of Le Pen in the presidential run-off, he seemed to sense a historic responsibility. 'The French elected the president because they wanted something new,' he said. 'I'm convinced they want that novelty elsewhere too, including from unions.' Jean-Claude Mailly, leader of another big union, Force Ouvrière, also chose not to block a deal. In the end, Macron did not negotiate his labour reform so much as neutralize its opponents. Faced with a democratically elected president who was doing what he had said he would, the unions struggled to mobilize.

It would be premature to suggest that Macron has turned the page on theatrical conflict resolution in France. But a smarter way of managing, and explaining, reform seems to be emerging. Macron applied it to his second set of early decisions, designed to rethink the role of the state. This began with a bold shift in fiscal policy. As adviser to Hollande during the presidential election of 2012, Macron had tried to nudge economic policy in a more business-friendly direction. For all the philosophy, or perhaps precisely because of his Ricoeur-like belief in crossing experience with theory, Macron's attitude as president was often pragmatic, rather than ideological. He had argued clearly during the campaign that those who took risks, invested in the productive economy rather than property, and earned profits, should be encouraged, not punished. 'My predecessor massively increased the wealth tax,' the president said, a few months after his election. 'Did that bring in a lot of money? No. Why? Because people who succeeded left.'

All the same, by 2017, the politics of taxation in France remained highly charged. The only previous time a government had tried to abolish the wealth tax, in 1986, it proved so unpopular that the politician who dared to do it, Jacques Chirac, was roundly beaten at the presidential election two years later, and the tax was promptly brought back in. Nicolas Sarkozy once promised to get rid of the *impôt de solidarité sur la fortune* (solidarity tax on fortunes), to give it its full name; but he never did. By 2017 this tax was levied each year – and on top of a separate income-tax bill – on a household's combined assets worth over €750,000, including property, securities, cash and furniture. The tax rate ranged from a base of 0.55 per cent to 1.8 per cent for assets over €15 million. Back in 2004, a Senate report showed that the tax prompted a steady flow of exiles to lower-tax Belgium and Switzerland, deploring a 'loss of dynamism for the French economy' and warning that, in the long run, 'the situation is not sustainable … if we want to preserve the attractiveness of the country and hence French jobs'. Yet there was little, if any, public sympathy for those who had to pay it. When it emerged shortly after Hollande's election that Bernard Arnault, the founder and chief executive of the iconic luxury group LVMH and one of the country's richest men, had applied for Belgian nationality, the left-leaning newspaper *Libération* rejoiced. It ran a front page with a picture of Arnault under the headline '*Casse-toi, riche con!*', which translates roughly as 'Sod off, you rich bastard'. Fed up with French taxation, Gérard Depardieu, star of *Cyrano de Bergerac* among many other films, fled the country, swapped his French passport for a Russian one, and took up residence in neighbouring Belgium.

In office, Macron was unrepentant. He had spelt out during the campaign that he would transform this tax, and duly did so. His first budget, for 2018, abolished the wealth tax, and converted it into a property tax. 'I don't believe in a French jealousy that says there are rich people, let's tax them and everything will be better,' he explained on prime-time television. Macron hoped that this might encourage wealthy French people to invest in home-grown start-ups, as they do in London or America. At the same time, he introduced a flat tax of 30 per cent on financial income, on which higher-band earners had been paying tax at a rate of 60 per cent. The government also began to reduce the corporate tax rate, which Macron said would drop from 33 per cent to 25 per cent over five years. In order to tax work less, and inactivity more, the payroll burden was eased by transferring some social charges to a more broad-based tax (the *contribution sociale généralisée*), which includes – to the dismay of the retired – pensions. To make this tax-cutting programme, perceived as a gift to the rich, more palatable, Macron also began to phase out the *taxe d'habitation* (council tax), a regressive tax that disproportionately touched the worse-off. Luck, as ever, came Macron's way too. Economic growth helped the government both to cut taxes and to bring down the budget deficit to below 3 per cent – for the first time in ten years.

If Macron has managed to shift the balance of French taxation, he has so far been less convincing on public spending. Judged by words and ambition, he seems plain enough. 'There are no magic finances which allow the reduction of taxes without touching spending,' Macron told a gathering of mayors. By 2022 the president plans to have curbed the share of GDP consumed by public spending to a more Swedish-style 52 per cent, and stabilized the public finances. Yet exactly how he intends to do it remains unclear. Macron's plans to trim the civil-service headcount have been slow to firm up. He has rejected the option of raising the retirement age as a way of saving on the public pension bill. And he puts great faith, as governments always do, in the idea of efficiency savings.

Nor is it yet clear that Macron is willing to take on the third constraint, and shake out the industrial-administrative complex. Although he forged his political reputation on the back of the deregulation of protected professions, most notably the coach industry, he has yet to show that he is willing to go much further. Indeed, as economy minister, Macron used publicly held stakes to engineer industrial results, taking an extra 5 per cent in Renault in 2015 in order to give the state and other long-term shareholders double voting rights, and prompting a spat with Renault's boss, Carlos Ghosn. At the time, the minister insisted that this would be a short-term holding. By the start of 2018 the stake was still on the books.

Macron may well decide to pick other battles rather than to take on the industrial lobby and what is known in France as the 'techno-structure' of the elite civil service: the strata of high-flyers that supplies bosses to many of the big industrial firms, but has an uneven record of managing them. France's nuclear industry is highly cosseted. Areva (Orano) in particular has been plagued by technical and financial difficulties. Some big industrial and defence firms that depend on state contracts still also own media assets, giving them exaggerated lobbying power. The same firm, for example, that makes Mirage fighter planes for the French army (Dassault) also owns *Le Figaro* newspaper. Plenty of other sectors – such as the pharmacy industry, with its monopoly on many non-prescription drugs – still hide behind professional protection. Macron has promised to sell off some 10 per cent of state holdings, and may be ready to let go of industrial assets, especially if they remain in European hands. As president, he nodded through the merger of the French firm Alstom with the railway business of the German company Siemens, on the grounds that it could forge a European champion to rival the likes of the Chinese state-owned CRRC rail firm. But the president's willingness to unlock value by upending other industries and professions could turn out to be limited, and will test his professed belief in the power of disruption.

Perhaps the most arresting ambition behind Macron's talk of transformation is his effort to rethink the role of the French state, in order to 'emancipate' people's capacity to make the most of their lives. His central insight is that France needs to adapt its system of rules and safeguards, designed in the post-war years to protect jobs, in order to meet the needs of the new economy and focus on the protection of individuals instead. 'The term *Etat-providence* has a maternal connotation, one of hyper-protection, one that disempowers, that I'm not fond of,' Macron told me in July 2017.[19] 'I would rather talk of a state that offers security, that makes things possible, that gives autonomy. That's what I want to do.' His guiding principle is to try to break down the protection system that defines jobs by rank and status, improve flexibility and mobility in and out of jobs and careers, put choice in the hands of users, and transform an insurance-based welfare system into one based on universal, portable rights. This is why he wants, for instance, to unify the country's baroque system of 35 different pension regimes.

If the post-war welfare state was born to deal with accidents of life, Macron wants his twenty-first-century version to be a flexible safety net that treats movement in and out of jobs and spells of unemployment as a normal feature of working life, and the need for new skills as a lifelong affair. Protecting people, not jobs, is the central concern. This draws heavily on ideas that have long been put in place in other European countries, notably the Danish 'flexicurity' model, with its emphasis on training and retraining to get the unemployed back into work and keep their skills updated. The French labour minister Pénicaud visited Denmark, Switzerland and Germany to look at how others do it. France spends a hefty €32 billion a year on state-mandated training programmes. Yet 62 per cent of this goes on those who already have jobs, and only 14 per cent on the unemployed. France's complicated rules create only half as many apprenticeships as in Germany, often at higher cost and with poorer results. If anything, as the economy picked up in 2017 and 2018, French employers began to report an increase in unfilled vacancies, pointing to a widening skills gap. Putting in place a credible scheme for improving apprenticeships and vocational training, especially for the low-skilled and the young, will be a good test of Macron's capacity to update the French model.

It is too early to judge whether Macron is on to something really new, or whether it is just new for France. Transforming one of Europe's heaviest, most bureaucratic states into a nimble, user-friendly public service for the digital era will require a transformation of mindset. If the state is to be an enabler, a facilitator, a liberator and a simplifier, it needs to change the way it treats its citizens. One early attempt to nudge the public service this way was a law that Macron introduced known as the '*droit à l'erreur*', or the right to make a mistake in dealings with the French bureaucracy, in order to temper the feeling of punishment that tends to prevail. 'Who hasn't suffered when filling in enrolment forms for the umpteenth time at the start of the school year?' sighed the prime minister Edouard Philippe on Twitter, as he launched a consultation on making the bureaucracy less soul-destroying. People will be able to book training courses via a smartphone app, using a personal credit account topped up by the government. It is an exciting project, to be watched closely. To do this properly, though, will require deep shifts in public-service habits, a willingness by government to take on resistance from the public sector and unions, as well as sustained policy follow-through.

If France under Macron can start to get even half of this right, the prize could be significant. With its top-class mathematicians, the country has particular potential in sectors set for rapid growth over the next decade, notably machine learning, artificial intelligence (AI) and big data. In 2015, Facebook set up its only European research lab into AI in Paris. After I toured their offices, complete with an outside deck overlooking the zinc rooftops of Paris and the Eiffel Tower, Antoine Bordes, who runs the lab, told me that Paris was chosen because of the excellence of the university research in this field already taking place in France. Britain and Germany, he judged, did not have the same depth of doctoral research nor diversity of existing AI expertise. The lab in Paris is one of only three AI research centres that Facebook runs in the world, and Bordes is planning to triple staffing levels there over the next three years. Elsewhere, young French graduates are increasingly shunning corporate life and trying their luck with their own start-ups. One day I had a meeting scheduled with Hugo Mercier, the French engineer who launched Dreem, a headband that uses promising neuro-technology to improve deep sleep; he turned out to be 25 years old. Such entrepreneurs, a new generation of tie-less French youth, can be found huddled over their laptops in the open spaces and cubic break-out rooms of a disused railway building in the east of Paris, where Xavier Niel opened Station F, the world's biggest incubator for start-ups. Macron introduced special grants to international researchers, with a focus on climate change and green tech, as part of his 'Make our Planet Great Again' initiative. 'Within five years,' claimed Niel with his customary flourish when I spoke to him shortly after Macron's election, 'France will be the top country in Europe for start-ups.'

Until recently, France had underperformed for so long that it seemed to have lost the will to make such heady claims, or when it did they sounded like the hype of state-run marketing agencies. By 2018 they appeared less absurd. 'There is every reason in the medium run for economic growth in France to match or exceed the average in the eurozone,' François Villeroy de Galhau, the governor of the central bank, told me.[20] If growth in the French economy were to reach this average, combined with labour market reforms, he said, the effect on unemployment could be 'spectacular'. Macron has yet to face real domestic conflict, so his will to push through tough measures, particularly over public-sector reform, remains untested. Michel Crozier, a French sociologist, once argued that his country was a 'blocked society': too many top-down bureaucrats bred popular distrust and created a system that was unable to reform except through crisis. Macron nodded to this idea when he launched En Marche, vowing to 'unblock' France. Others blamed the problem on themselves. Asked in a 2006 poll why reform in France was so difficult, respondents identified the biggest single reason as the 'state of mind of the French'. Macron has said that France 'is a country that reforms less than it transforms itself, in sudden spasms'. His ambitions are immodest, and the risks of disappointment plain. Macron is working with administrations, and against lobbies, that have entrenched habits and interests to defend, at a time when the shifting balance of global economic power and pace of digital dislocation will not be forgiving. Perhaps most intractable of all, he is trying to bring all this about in a country that, as the election revealed, remains deeply fractured.

8

Fractured France

'The further you live from an SNCF train station, the more likely you are to vote National Front.'

Hervé Le Bras, French demographer

'It's simple until you make it complicated', reads a poster pinned to the wall of the hangout room. Purple and green cushions lying on the sofa are printed with other injunctions, such as 'Less meeting, more doing'. There are deckchairs, coffee machines, a figure of Yoda from 'Star Wars' and other must-have accessories of the start-up office. The main concession to local culture, says Jérôme Vuillemot, a young tech entrepreneur in Lyon, is a table-football game, a staple of the traditional French café. On the twentieth floor of the city's second-tallest tower, these are the offices of Vidcoin, a start-up he co-founded in 2013, which uses zero-latency technology to allow advertising videos on smartphones to launch instantly. By 2017 the Lyon firm had 75 million users a month worldwide, its revenues had doubled each year, and its biggest market was America.

The former capital of Roman Gaul, in the Rhône valley of south-eastern France, Lyon is a thriving, cosmopolitan regional city that feels broadly at ease with change. Between 2008 and 2015, a period when unemployment rose across the country, the net number of jobs there increased by 5 per cent. The city enjoys fast trains and slow food, and introduced a bike-sharing scheme long before Paris or London. Perched at the sharp point of the confluence of the Rhône and the Saône rivers is a futuristic new plate-glass museum, the Musée des Confluences, designed to represent a 'crystal cloud of knowledge'. Along the nearby quay, an experimental driverless bus conveys passengers to and fro. A converted sugar refinery has opened as an arts centre, and an old boiler factory is being refitted as an incubator for start-ups. At the presidential election, as many as 84 per cent of the city's population voted for Macron.

The city's affinity with the new president is not coincidental. In many ways, it was a laboratory for his politics. Gérard Collomb, Lyon's Socialist mayor from 2001 until he became interior minister in 2017 at the age of 69, was one of Macron's earliest supporters. He ran the city by building a majority across the political divide – a tradition begun by his predecessor, Raymond Barre, who was French prime minister from 1976 to 1981 – showing that this was possible well before En Marche was launched. 'We've done this for a long time and it feels quite normal here,' David Kimelfeld, who replaced Collomb as head of Lyon Métropole, told me.[1] A Socialist senator while also running the city, Collomb brought Macron useful political support, lending the young outsider his political network and a measure of credibility when others in the party considered him a no-hoper. It was in Lyon in September 2016, thanks to Collomb, that Macron made a powerfully pro-European speech as guest speaker at a conference organized by the Gracques, a French centre-left grouping. Five months later, it was also in Lyon, at the Palais des Sports on 4 February 2017, that the candidate held his most electric campaign rally in a hall so packed that hundreds of supporters were turned away at the door.

Collomb, like Macron, did not shy away from backing business in his city either. Lyon retains a heavy industrial base, but has built new strengths in robotics, life sciences and clean tech. New office space is being opened in the city every year. With 17 Michelin-star restaurants, well-ranked business and engineering schools, a freshly scrubbed Opera House, and quick links to the Alps and the Mediterranean coast, as well as to Paris, Lyon is a place that is comfortable with globalization and modernity. Certain neighbourhoods still have a neglected air. But the transformation of a once-sleepy backwater is arresting. 'Lyon used to feel like a provincial town,' Bruno Bonnell, the En Marche deputy who is also the founder of a local robotics firm, told me in a burst of enthusiastic hyperbole. 'Now it could become France's Shanghai.'[2]

Such breezy confidence can be found in a string of other provincial French cities these days: Grenoble, Montpellier, Toulouse, Lille, Rennes, Nantes and Bordeaux. Thriving cosmopolitan cities, with their smart pedestrian centres, tech hubs and gourmet food have renovated the regions. Criss-crossed by shiny trams and well supplied with smoothie bars and co-working spaces, they are the new metropolitan face of a country whose geography was once famously summed up as *Paris et le désert français* (*Paris and the French Desert*), the title of a book by Jean-François Gravier, a geographer, published in 1947. Between 2006 and 2011 the number of jobs in the 13 largest French regional cities – Lyon, Marseille, Toulouse, Lille, Bordeaux, Nantes, Nice, Strasbourg, Rennes, Grenoble, Rouen, Montpellier and Toulon – increased on average by 5 per cent, at a time when in France as a whole jobs were lost. These are cities that have managed to carve out a specialized niche in the global service economy – for medical technology in Grenoble, or green tech in Lyon – and can lure and keep creative types looking for a cluster of similarly minded people. These metropoles are home to 85 per cent of France's computer engineers and 75 per cent of its IT professionals. 'It's the French California here,' a young start-up entrepreneur told me in Bordeaux, when I went to look at the expanding tech sector in the city. 'After work, you can be surfing on the ocean in less than half an hour.' Thanks to the TGV, and regional airports, such places are well connected to Paris and cities abroad. In 2017 a new TGV line opened linking Paris and Bordeaux, 580 kilometres apart, with a journey time of just two hours.

France's dynamic regional cities have become hubs for liberal values and politics too. Before the 2017 presidential election voters in such metropolitan centres elected moderate mayors with an open outlook, whether from the left (Lyon, Nantes, Rennes), the greens (Grenoble) or the centre-right (Bordeaux). This French pattern matched that noted in America by John Judis and Ruy Teixeira, who showed in 2004 how the socially liberal politics of growing post-industrial big-city America were being shaped by the university-educated voters attracted to their service-based economies: 'the new professionals who live according to the ethics of post-industrial society'.[3] The parallel with France is inexact. But just as America's fast-growing service-based urban centres voted for Barack Obama and Hillary Clinton, so France's thriving regional cities, with their uncomplicated links to globalization and technological change, are Macron territory. In the second-round presidential vote Macron scored a massive 90 per cent in Paris, 88 per cent in Rennes and 86 per cent in Bordeaux. Such places are deeply at ease with his business-friendly globalism. Another side of France is not.

Travel 10 kilometres east of Lyon, to the *banlieue* of Décines-Charpieu, home to the brand-new Groupama stadium for the Olympique Lyonnais football club, and Macron's second-round presidential majority begins to taper off. Continue for another 10 kilometres, beyond the city's airport to the town of Colombier-Saugnieu, and it disappears. Here, Marine Le Pen secured a hefty 57 per cent of the vote. Carry on up over the Crémieu plateau, which looks out towards the snow-capped Alps, and down to the village of Briord, with its single main road, café-bar-tabac and car mechanic, and you reach deep Le Pen country. The FN leader came top in first-round voting in the surrounding department of l'Ain. In the 2017 run-off, 61 per cent of Briord's voters backed her for president.

If Macron appealed to confident, optimistic France, Le Pen's territory is the France of anxiety and neglect. This fracture running through the country, between prosperous and confident metropolitan centres and the fragile towns and deserted rural areas, will be one of the greatest challenges to the Macron presidency in the coming years. It divides the France that is at ease with his talk about openness, globalization and change, and feels equipped to face coming dislocations, from the part of the country that is baffled, fearful and alone. If Macron can't find a way of reversing the sense of abandon in these territories, he will leave them open and responsive to the message of the political extremes: the National Front on the far right, and Jean-Luc Mélenchon's Unsubmissive France on the far left.

Few parties have understood better the potential for harnessing disillusion for political ends in France's peripheral regions than the FN, one of Europe's oldest populist parties. For years, it campaigned broadly in two strongholds, both touched by high levels of unemployment and immigration. One was the Mediterranean fringe, where the party has a petit-bourgeois sociological base and an ultra-conservative, Catholic outlook. The second was the industrial rust belt of the north and east, including the steel areas of Lorraine and mining basin of the Pas-de-Calais, where the FN began to scoop up the working class disappointed by the French Communist Party. Under Marine Le Pen, who took over the party in 2011 after a dynastic feud with her father, the FN's vote continued to correlate broadly with high unemployment and a lack of qualifications. Only 9 per cent of those with a three-year degree or more voted for her in the first round of the 2017 presidential election, next to 30 per cent of those without the *baccalauréat*, or high-school diploma. The most startling change on Marine Le Pen's watch, though, was the FN's push into small rural communities, where pavements, logistics parks and retail sprawl give way to farmland.

Marine Le Pen managed to bring an improbable mix of homespun nativism, Euroscepticism and star appeal to France's forgotten territories. Her father was never interested in a methodical strategy of electoral conquest. Jean-Marie Le Pen, a former paratrooper, set up his first political movement back in 1957 in defence of French Algeria, and co-founded the xenophobic FN in 1972, obsessed with nationalism, the loss of overseas territory and conflict with the Arab state. For years, the daughter who most resembles him lived in her father's shadow. When I first interviewed Marine Le Pen, in 2003, she was running the FN legal service from a dark office at the end of a corridor, and was a gravelly voiced chain-smoking divorcee, with an untidy shock of long blonde hair, trying to find her place in a party of macho, family-values traditionalists. By 2015, when I found her at the European Parliament in Strasbourg, platinum blonde and neatly coiffed, her tall, broad frame somehow outsized for the tiny sixth-floor office, she had turned a patriarchal fringe movement into an established feature of French party politics. In doing so, she found a way to speak to France's left-behind.

Finely grained maps produced by Hervé Le Bras, a demographer, based on voting in the country's 36,000 communes during the 2015 regional elections, show that the FN vote had by then spread into the sprawl on the periphery of towns as well as semi-rural and rural areas across France. Towns and city centres, as a rule, resisted the FN. But they were ringed by FN-voting areas that fell beyond the outskirts – often with very low immigrant populations. In the Paris region at these elections, the FN vote rose according to the distance from the city centre. The party scored just 14 per cent in the capital itself. In a ring of *communes* between 40 and 50 kilometres from the centre of Paris, it won an average of 32 per cent of the vote. In places 80 kilometres or more away, the FN reached on average 41 per cent. It was not just proximity to the city centre that matched the strength of the party's vote. Distance from a train station also seemed to matter. In *communes* with a railway station, the FN vote averaged just 23 per cent. In those situated more than 10 kilometres from a railway station, it reached 35 per cent. 'The further you live from an SNCF train station,' Le Bras concluded, 'the more likely you are to vote FN.'[4]

Isolation, in other words, seems to boost FN support. With its high-quality public services, France is a country whose citizens have matching expectations for the fabric of their lives. When that tissue thins – when the doctor leaves town, or the local butcher closes – neglect is keenly felt. An analysis by Le Bras and Jérôme Fourquet, of the Ifop polling agency, showed that the FN vote was closely associated with the absence of local services, such as a pharmacy, bakery, post office or café. A common factor behind the FN vote in such places, said Fourquet, is 'a sense of abandonment, of being left behind by an elite that doesn't care'. When Jean-Marie Le Pen was first elected to the National Assembly, in 1956, it was on a list led by Pierre Poujade, who evoked this tradition when he spoke up for 'the little people': 'The downtrodden, the trashed, the ripped off, the humiliated.' This 'France of the forgotten' was zealously courted by Le Pen's daughter, who played a classic populist hand, appealing to ordinary people's sense that the elite was neglecting them, and promising to evict the establishment 'in the name of the people' (her 2017 campaign slogan). It was no coincidence that Marine Le Pen held more rallies during the 2017 presidential election in villages – Monswiller in Alsace, La Bazoche-Gouet in La Sarthe – than she did in big cities.

These are the areas that Christophe Guilluy, a geographer, calls 'peripheral France'. Many of the factories that have closed over the past decade are found in these in-between zones, not in France's cities: the Lejaby lingerie factory in Bellegarde-sur-Valserine, in the foothills of the Alps; the Moulinex factory in Alençon, in southern Normandy. This is not the dreamy France of cobblestones and cathedrals. It is a sort of drive-past country, a battered second tier of towns, marked by betting shops and half-empty cafés, which the casual visitor to France seldom sees. The photographer Raymond Depardon called it 'in-between France': the bar-tabac-presse draped in lottery ads on the corner of a run-down street; the car-less new roundabout amid empty fields; the empty plastic chairs lined up for the infirm inside the *boucherie-charcuterie*. Once, the motorist would travel along the *routes nationales* that passed through such small towns, Michelin guide in hand, stopping perhaps for a *plat du jour* on the way to somewhere else. Today, these are regions that the TGV, fibre-optics and 4G mobile connection passes by, where people sense that globalization and automation have dealt them a blow. It is a world in which Uber, bike-share schemes, organic cafés and co-working spaces are nowhere to be found, where mobile reception is poor, and the young, and better educated, have left. As jobs and confidence have drained away, so has faith in the mainstream parties. This is where the FN has now taken hold.

Few places better capture this sense of abandon, and the political forces that can thrive on it, than Hénin-Beaumont, a red-brick town in the mining basin of northern France. The turn-off to it from the A1 motorway, south of the city of Lille, is marked by a vast slag heap covered with whiskery grass, which looms as a defiant historical reminder of the region's muscular past. Hénin-Beaumont once supplied jobs and dignity to local residents. Coal was first discovered in the Pas-de-Calais basin in 1842, and the town's railway station, built by the Compagnie des Chemins de Fer du Nord, opened nearly two decades later. By 1913, before the outbreak of war, the mining basin employed 130,000 miners and supplied 67 per cent of France's national coal output. Industry prospered too, with brewing, sugar-processing, tanning, glass-making and metal-working factories all setting up for business nearby. On the central facade of the turreted grey-stone town hall, a statement of municipal grandeur built in 1926, are carvings of bare-chested miners in tin helmets.

Today, the mining has long gone. Between 1962 and 1990 the number of people directly employed by the mines in Hénin-Beaumont collapsed from 55,000 to just 1,000. With its neat rows of terraced brick houses and discounted clothing stores, the town has lost jobs, factories and hope. In recent years over 200 jobs disappeared at a luggage-manufacturing plant. Another 200 went at a paper-printing factory. Each closure was a local trauma, fiercely contested by employees. At the Samsonite luggage factory, a strike by workers lasted 44 days. Today, the biggest nearby employer is the regional office of the miners' social security system, followed by Auchan, a large French hypermarket selling global brands, many of them manufactured abroad. By 2013 the unemployment rate had reached 18 per cent, well above the national average. The long-term jobless rate is higher still. Most social and economic difficulties crowd into this small town of 26,000 inhabitants. A quarter of its population lives below the poverty line; 24 per cent depend wholly on welfare payments for their income. Local residents have fewer skills, and lower median incomes, than the region as a whole. They also die younger.

At the municipal elections of 2014, Hénin-Beaumont elected its first FN mayor.

How this happened is a lesson in how working-class disillusion in left-behind parts of fractured democracies can be yoked to populist politics. It also points to the difficulty Macron faces if he hopes to coax such places back into the liberal fold. Hénin-Beaumont's town hall was run by the Communist Party after the end of the Second World War, and then by successive Socialists and governments of the left. The names of its streets bear witness to this political history: *rue de l'Humanité, boulevard Gabriel-Péri, place Jean Jaurès, rue Jules Guesde*. The town's Socialist mayor from 1969 to 1989, Jacques Piette, was a pillar of the French left, who fought against Franco and fascism in Spain and worked underground for the Resistance during the Nazi occupation of France. During the second round of the presidential election in 2017, 62 per cent of Hénin-Beaumont's voters backed Marine Le Pen for president.

On my first visit to Hénin-Beaumont, in 2012, when the town hall was still run by the left, I came across the blonde-haired, blue-eyed Laurent Brice in the FN's unmarked office on a side street in the town. He was only nine years old when the French elected François Mitterrand as the country's first Socialist president, in 1981, and can remember his family throwing a party that night, the dancing and celebrations spilling into the street. His grandfather was a miner in the local pits. His father worked as a metalworker, and his mother as a cleaner. The FN, which was seeking at the time to anchor itself in the old industrial heartlands, offered him identity politics of a different sort: a form of patriotic talk that combined right-wing nationalism with a left-wing denunciation of big corporations, globalization, and their disregard for the workers. Brice joined up and never looked back, becoming the local FN department representative and then, in 2015, a member of the elected regional assembly.

'They say that we are a fascist party, but we're too young to know anything about that,' he insisted. 'We're just patriots.'[5] Flanked by piles of new membership forms, he had been handing out leaflets at the Renault factory in nearby Douai, after workers finished their shift. The French car company had just announced that it was transferring some of its production to a new factory in North Africa, and he was whipping up outrage. 'The state holds 15 per cent of Renault, but does nothing. It's absurd,' he said. 'Our workers are sometimes obliged to take time off because there isn't enough work, and yet they are opening a new factory in Morocco.' Neither the Communist Party nor the Socialist Party, he claimed, was ever seen outside the factories. The Socialists catered to local notables and public-sector employees, but were 'non-existent' for the working classes. Today, he said, 'our voters are in the factories'.

'French workers betrayed by the system' was an FN flyer handed out one day by Marine Le Pen outside a car factory near Hénin-Beaumont, and the message rang true.[6] Voters, fed up with corruption and job losses, grew suspicious of the politicians who had long been in office. Gérard Dalongeville, Socialist mayor from 2001 to 2009, had been arrested in 2009 on charges of forgery, misuse of public funds and extortion, and later sentenced to prison for corruption. The Socialist Party, Marine Le Pen told the town in a speech in 2011, 'has once again turned its back on the workers'.[7] Spearheaded by Steeve Briois, a local son whose father worked in a food-processing factory and whose grandfather was a miner, the FN methodically planned its conquest of the town hall. His model was the Communist Party, which had used cultural tools such as outings and dances to build loyalty and then political support.[8] The FN set out to do the same. 'Every day the phone rings at the FN office because people have trouble paying their bills, or with their heating,' said Laurent Brice. 'This is where people call.'[9] Marine Le Pen was parachuted in from party headquarters to motivate the FN on the ground. 'Indignation needs to be organized,' she told them on one training day.[10] When Marine Le Pen took over the FN leadership in 2011, she appointed Briois its national secretary-general. Three years later, in Hénin-Beaumont, he was elected mayor.

In the dark, austere, wood-panelled mayor's office, where I found him shortly before Christmas in 2015, Briois stuck to much of the traditional FN script. Disarmingly reserved in conversation, he railed against the migrant camp at the port of Calais, 100 kilometres from Hénin-Beaumont. He denounced the influx of immigrants, and the way Europe had opened its borders to Syrian refugees. But his signature policies in Hénin-Beaumont were rather less obnoxious: Sunday dances for the elderly in neighbourhood municipal halls, a 'beach' in the town centre for children during the summer holidays, and a Christmas market complete with a skating rink. 'As a mayor, one has limited powers,' Briois told me. 'But we have managed to bring back a sense of confidence to our inhabitants ... Here in the mining basin there are people who never go to restaurants, who put their children in the school canteen because they know that at least they will eat there. It happens frequently. There's a precariousness here that you cannot imagine.'[11] The FN was turning social disadvantage in the rust belt into a source of far-right political mobilization.

It was market day when I visited Hénin-Beaumont in 2015, and stall-holders were wrapping up fat slices of rabbit terrine, others unpacking discounted hairspray and nail varnish from cardboard boxes. The local branch of *La Voix du Nord*, the regional newspaper, was in open warfare against the mayor. There were concerns about the ending of municipal subsidies to human-rights groups. Yet in the Café de la Paix, opposite the church, which was busy at lunchtime serving its *formule du midi*, it was hard to find anybody with a harsh word about their mayor. Down the street at the Turkish kebab restaurant, I asked Mahir Kurtul, the manager, what had changed in the town under Briois. His reply: there were now municipal flowerpots on the lamp posts, and new speed bumps on the roads.

To try to understand why there was so much approbation for the FN mayor, I looked up his retired predecessor, Eugène Binaisse. He had taken over at the town hall after the corruption scandal, and I first met him in the mayor's office when he was trying to clear out the mess. Three years later, he was still living on a terraced street in the town, and I went to visit him in his home; he dressed in a suit for our meeting. 'Their mission is to do nothing that can be criticized too much,' Binaisse explained, because they want it to be a laboratory town. 'Marine Le Pen is careful about what she says; but it's all about innuendo.'[12] The symbolism wasn't always subtle. In the town-hall entrance that year, Briois had installed a giant *crèche* (nativity scene), with colourful life-sized figures of Mary and the three kings – a breach of the country's strict secular laws that keep all religion out of public life, and which was later ruled illegal in court.

What the FN has established in Hénin-Beaumont is a potentially resilient form of municipal populism that blends identity politics and left-wing welfarism, and speaks to the left-behind. Pauline Guibert was a history student when I came across her in Hénin-Beaumont, and each of these strands drew her to the FN, where she was helping stuff envelopes as a volunteer. It was a party, she said, 'that supports the people' at a time of 'more and more unemployment and crime, and more and more poverty', which politicians had done nothing about. At the same time, France was 'favouring foreigners over French people' and giving them bigger pensions than local farmers. Marine Le Pen helped to transform economic disappointment into rage against the political system, immigration and Europe. They have betrayed you, she told them; we offer you hope. Fear of immigration remained the chief driver of the overall FN vote in 2017. But the country's geographical fracture offers a way for populist politicians to divide society, between the winners and losers of globalization, which will remain potent in the years to come.

Marine Le Pen's calamitous performance during the televised duel with Emmanuel Macron before the 2017 presidential election, and the splits and recriminations that this unleashed within the FN, mask a raw political fact. No fewer than 10.6 million French voters, or 34 per cent, backed her at that election – over 5 million more than her father had drawn when he too reached the second round, in 2002. In the first round of voting she was the favourite among blue-collar voters. Marine Le Pen may not end up as the one who leads the FN into the presidential elections in 2022. The baton could well have been passed on by then, perhaps to her strident young niece, Marion Maréchal-Le Pen, who wears her blonde hair in a ponytail and her ultra-conservative politics on her sleeve. But the FN's strategy of using identity politics and municipal welfarism to meld the conservative, Catholic bourgeoisie and the working class remains a powerful force for abandoned France.

The FN, of course, is not the only party working the territory of the left-behind. The firebrand Jean-Luc Mélenchon, whose Unsubmissive France won 17 parliamentary seats in 2017, toils on much the same ground. A razor-tongued former Trotskyist, with a taste for revolutionary-style Mao jackets and a weakness for Latin American autocrats, he advocated a top income-tax rate of 100 per cent during the 2017 campaign, described America as a 'dangerous power', and called for a 'Bolivarian' alliance alongside Venezuela and Cuba. This seemed to be just what young people wanted to hear, and the 65-year-old Mélenchon turned into a sort of French Bernie Sanders. He also dug deep into the Socialist vote, securing working-class support in industrial cities and areas that were losing jobs. The seven million votes that Mélenchon drew in the first round of the 2017 presidential election were only 600,000 short of Marine Le Pen's score. Between the pair of them alone, they scooped up a massive 41 per cent of the first-round vote. Add in other minor candidates, and nearly half of all votes went to the extremes. These disillusioned voters, whether in Hénin-Beaumont, the village of Briord in the valley east of Lyon, or hundreds of other small towns and villages across France, have not gone away. And the radical left and far right alike will be ready to tap into their exasperation again.

What can Macron, whose liberal internationalism does not speak to such places, hope to do to reconquer these parts? The most important response, of course, is his labour reform, which he hopes will create more jobs. That he takes the broader problem seriously is reflected in his appointment of Julien Denormandie, one of the co-founders of En Marche, as 'junior minister of territorial cohesion', tasked with such policy matters. Their underlying strategy is *désenclavement*, or breaking the sense of isolation. One of Denormandie's first moves was to work with the telecoms regulator to force mobile-phone firms to extend their coverage into all corners of France, including those forests, mountains and farmland that are known as 'white zones' for having no reception at all. Mobile operators will also be asked to make 4G networks the norm. Both these obligations, backed by sanctions, were to be a condition of the renewal of mobile operating licences. The government also secured an agreement between private telecoms operators and local government, part-financed in rural areas by central government and EU regional funds, to bring fibre-optic broadband into all homes by 2022.

A second raft of policies is designed to reinforce the visibility and presence of public services. Macron plans to double the number of health centres in rural areas, in order to stem the loss of family doctors, as well as to develop more online and remote medical-advice services. In his first year, he promised not to close any more primary-school classes in remote parts of the country. All towns and villages in such areas have been promised a single national office to deal with when it comes to projects to improve roads, waterways or other infrastructure. And the government intends to make it easier for towns to revive their centres and keep their neighbourhood shops going. In a country built on administrative complexity, setting up such structures, let alone getting them to operate efficiently, will be a challenge. More doctors and better mobile connections would seem a flimsy response to populism. But, on the ground, there may be no better public-policy answer to isolation and political disillusion.

* * *

Far from the metropolitan centres and the rural heartlands, a second fracture also runs through France. Lyon, the municipal prototype for Macron's national politics, is no stranger to this one either. Beyond the city's ring road lies Vaulx-en-Velin, an angular *banlieue* originally built to house workers recruited from North Africa, Spain and Portugal for the textile industry and public works. Vaulx-en-Velin made a mark on the collective French mind after riots broke out there in 1990. Since then, huge sums have been pumped into renovating the area. In 2016 brutalist tower blocks were demolished with explosives. Open spaces have been landscaped, saplings planted and park benches put in. Huge, brightly coloured plant pots were installed in front of one concrete parade of shops, where men gather at shaded tables outside a kebab restaurant. Yet unemployment in Vaulx-en-Velin, at 20 per cent, is nonetheless still twice the national average. Nearly two in five adults have no school-leaving certificate. In the first round of the presidential election Jean-Luc Mélenchon topped voting there. The abstention rate, high in many *banlieues* across France in 2017, was nearly twice the national average.

Such intractable problems have been powerfully captured over the years by French films, from Mathieu Kassovitz's angry *La Haine* (1995) to Céline Sciamma's tender *Bande de Filles* (2014). Physically removed from the elegant tree-lined boulevards of central cities, French *banlieues* house a population that is poor, jobless, angry and, mostly, of North or West African origin. In these 'sensitive urban zones', as officialdom coyly calls them, youth unemployment reaches a staggering 40 per cent, four times the national jobless average. These are places marked by long rides on suburban trains to reach central Paris, soulless tower blocks, shuttered shop fronts and faceless fast-food joints open late into the night. When I spent a day in Sevran, which lies north-east of the Paris *périphérique* and ranks as one of France's poorest places, an official in the job centre told me that she had recently organized a visit to the Louvre museum for unemployed youngsters. Of the 40 young people who made the 32-kilometre trip, 15 of them had never left Sevran before, and 35 members of the group had never been inside a museum.

It is a world as socially isolated in its own way as the mining basin of northern France. Over mint tea and Moroccan pastries at the Othmane mosque, just next to Vaulx-en-Velin, I met Azzedine Gaci, the softly spoken rector and imam. He was much exercised by the breakdown of family authority. 'There are lots of single-parent families, and sometimes mothers who work nights,' he told me, 'so parental control is difficult.'[13] Recently he had been out with a group of concerned adults after teenagers had torched three vehicles and thrown lighters into bins to set them alight. 'What are children as young as eight years old doing out at night at 1 a.m.?' Gaci asked. 'Unemployment is high. There is drug dealing. There is an absence of positive authority figures.' A local social worker described 'an identity crisis in these neighbourhoods ... Politicians have abandoned the *banlieues*.'

France has stored up these problems for many years. After three weeks of rioting, which led to the introduction of a state of emergency in 2005, *la banlieue* became associated in the French mind with torched cars, angry youths and high-rise housing projects. So much so that a local clothing line, branded 'Produit de Banlieue', launched hooded tops and baggy T-shirts with the slogan 'Extremely dangerous material'. Originally a medieval word, meaning a place a league (*lieue*) away from a city, but subject to the authority (*ban*) of the city's feudal overlords, the geographically peripheral modern *banlieues* were built to house workers brought to work in French factories in the 1960s and 1970s. *La Haine*, the stylized black-and-white drama about youth, guns and police brutality, written and directed by Kassovitz when he was just 26 years old, opened French eyes to the rage that these places had generated. The *banlieues* were on the capital's doorstep. But they felt like a world apart.

Clichy-sous-Bois, where the 2005 riots first broke out, is only 15 kilometres north-east of the art galleries and chic boutiques of central Paris. But when I went there shortly after the violence began, it took me nearly an hour and a half by public transport. The suburban RER train went only as far as Le Raincy; then it was a slow, winding uphill bus ride to Clichy-sous-Bois. The high-speed TGV travelled from Paris to Lille, 220 kilometres away, in less time than this. In Clichy, the disconnection from the capital was keenly felt. 'I'm not Parisian, I'm from 9-3,' said one young man, referring to the number of the department of

Seine-Saint-Denis that covers the northern Paris *banlieue*. At the time, Clichy had no police station, nor public job centre. The unemployed had to catch a bus to a neighbouring suburb if they wanted to check job vacancies. Many of those who made the effort said that their applications got nowhere; they suspected that a foreign-sounding name, or the local postcode, put employers off. A report in 2004 by the Institut Montaigne exposed job discrimination on the basis of address or name on 'an undreamed of' scale. France has no monopoly on a ghettoized, isolated underclass, but its high unemployment rate makes life in its *banlieues* particularly difficult. 'The only integration that means anything is a job,' Samir Mihi, a youth worker at Clichy's town hall whose parents came to France from Algeria, told me.

Over the years, governments have appointed cities ministers, devised 'Marshall plans', and invested billions in regeneration schemes. Yet from 2008 to 2011 the gap between unemployment rates in French 'sensitive urban zones' and surrounding areas simply widened. Schools suffered from a high turnover of often inexperienced teachers. Job centres were hopelessly understaffed. Drug dealers competed with careers advisers to recruit teenagers. 'Here, drug trafficking has always helped circulate money,' Stéphane Gatignon, the Green Party mayor of Sevran, told me. 'It's how people scrape by.' Over 70 different nationalities, and many faiths, crowd into Sevran. At the dimly lit Sevran-Beaudottes station, where posters advertise Vita Malt African bottled drinks, fast RER trains tear through, carrying travellers from the airport direct to Paris. 'We have to wait for the slow trains that stop at the stations in-between,' said a woman from Sevran who commuted out to the airport for work each day. 'There's too much theft here, and they want to keep the tourists safe.'

Emmanuel Macron laid out his approach to some of these difficulties in the autumn after his election. He argued that the answer was not to devise yet another 'policy for cities', but to use broader policymaking – improved education, labour-market reform – to treat the problems concentrated in such places.

A more deregulated labour market may in time help more firms create stable entry-level jobs, particularly for the young. Smaller primary classes in such areas should improve schools in the long run. His planned overhaul of the inefficient training system, and more apprenticeships, could help get people into work. Macron has also promised to ensure that public services, like the post office or public library, are available in all such neighbourhoods, and to put policemen back on the beat in an effort to defuse the high levels of tension that exist between law-and-order forces and local communities.

As well as working his way through this list of promises, Macron is also hoping to send a different sort of message to the *banlieues*: less to do with public subsidies and more about harnessing local initiative. Part of the thinking is to identify and back nascent entrepreneurs and start-ups in the *banlieues*. He has a model in his own government, in the shape of Mounir Mahjoubi. The son of working-class immigrant parents from Morocco, and a software geek, Mahjoubi helped to engineer En Marche's defence from hacking during the election, and went on to become Macron's minister for digital affairs. 'Digital can be a tool to overcome discrimination,' Mahjoubi told me, explaining the trouble he had getting a job because of his 'Arab-sounding name' and how this prompted him to launch his own start-up. Thanks to a maths prize he won at the age of 13 run by a children's magazine, he bought a computer and taught himself to code. After earning degrees in law and business, Mahjoubi went on to co-found La Ruche qui dit Oui, a sharing-economy start-up that links farm producers and online consumers. That technology could be a way to get round discrimination was a principle that Macron had seen for himself as economy minister. He often used to comment then that it was easier for young people in the *banlieues* to 'get a client than a job'. Uber drivers in Paris, for example, disproportionately come from such neighbourhoods. A study by Augustin Landier, an economist at the Toulouse School of Economics, and colleagues discovered that a third of Uber drivers were under the age of 30, and a quarter were previously unemployed. He concluded that 'driving on the Uber platform can be used as a way to escape unemployment'.[14]

The toxic mix of policy failures found in France's *banlieues*, along with the discrimination that is felt, is a challenge in itself. But it also worries those who see disaffected young people in such places as vulnerable to radicalization. 'The *banlieues* represent a collective failure,' said Amine El-Khatmi, a young deputy mayor in Avignon who grew up on a housing estate in that Provençal, former papal city, 'because we are losing a generation.'[15] His father was a truck driver who arrived from Morocco in the 1970s, bringing his mother, a cleaning lady, over to join him after their marriage in 1985. Today, El-Khatmi told me, in the *banlieue* of Avignon where he grew up, there is an upswell of rejection of France among some of the French-born children of North and West African immigrants. 'These are people who don't feel French,' he said, 'and are told that the country doesn't love them.' This worries observers such as Gilles Kepel, a prominent scholar of Islam and the *banlieues*, who detects the hand of ultra-conservative Salafists behind this message, recruiting on French soil. According to a comprehensive study of French jihadists who returned home after going abroad to fight in Syria and Iraq, conducted by David Thomson, a broadcaster and writer, many of his subjects, harbouring feelings of deep social humiliation, were drawn first to the Salafist doctrine of 'rupture' with French society.[16] Thomson's contacts with his interviewees subsequently led to death threats, police protection, and the need for him to go into hiding outside France.

A few weeks after the Charlie-Hebdo terrorist attacks in 2015, I spent the day in Trappes, a pocket of poverty that lies south-west of Paris and, improbably, not far from the marble and gilt of Versailles. A working-class enclave that grew up around a railway yard, Trappes has the vibrant mix of languages and faiths common to many such neighbourhoods. Once heavily Portuguese, today's population mostly has family roots in Morocco and Algeria. The share of children born to at least one foreign-born parent in Trappes grew from 9 per cent in 1968 to 61 per cent in

2005. Nearly two-thirds of housing is publicly owned. The poverty rate of 24 per cent is almost twice the average for the Paris region. On the housing estates of Les Merisiers, near a newly built mosque fringed by mini-palms, the poverty rate has reached 42 per cent. Soon after the Charlie-Hebdo attacks, two young men left Trappes for jihad, presumed to be heading for Syria. One had been employed by the town hall supervising after-school activities.

Their departure prompted much soul-searching. For, in Trappes, the picture was not one of straightforward public neglect. The *banlieue* had benefited from vast amounts of public money, pumped in by governments following the 2005 riots. After 2006 some €350 million ($400 million) had been spent renovating tower blocks and digging new roads. A developer was putting up private housing, as part of an effort to lure better-off families. In Les Merisiers, cycle paths had been laid out, and the municipal gym revamped. New equipment had been installed in the playgrounds of the primary schools, whose buildings were adorned with the French motto '*Liberté, Egalité, Fraternité*'. On the main square, where I found halal *foie gras* for sale at the Maghnaoui butcher, stood a brand-new post office. Such changes had improved daily life. Staff at the modern red-brick town hall, which juts on to the busy dual carriageway that tears through the middle of the *banlieue*, talked encouragingly of a return of 'dignity', and noted that the freshly painted walls of the estates were free of graffiti.

Yet Trappes remained troubled. Two summers previously, riots broke out there after a man violently resisted a police check on his wife, who was wearing a niqab. 'Poverty does not explain everything,' Guy Malandain, the veteran Socialist mayor, told me. 'It's as much a question of ideological excess and manipulation.' Nothing about the town-hall employee who disappeared had suggested that he was preparing for jihad. He had no previous criminal record. But young local people seemed to be receptive to a hard-line Islamist message, and a tiny minority of those to the jihadist promise of 'revenge, power and status', as Thomson puts it. In the road outside the Trappes town hall, near the 'So

Good' fast-food restaurant, whose delights included a 'Big-biggy burger', I found parents waiting to pick up their children from school. One father, whose own parents arrived in France from Morocco, told me that he was worried about local youngsters who 'are becoming radicalized through rejection'. He had enrolled his children in the local Catholic primary. In towns like Trappes and *banlieues* across the country, the French felt their vulnerability particularly acutely. President Hollande and his prime minister Manuel Valls had to face unimaginable horrors on their watch, and did so largely with dignity.

On matters of security, Macron has taken an uncompromisingly tough line. He called the struggle 'against Islamist terrorism' his first security priority. Within months, he passed a hard-line counter-terrorism law, designed to bring an end to the state of emergency, but which incorporated a number of its provisions. As a candidate, he had argued that the emergency laws had brought only 'modest' results. So liberals were taken aback to see him entrench sweeping powers for the police to restrict individuals' movements with electronic tags, and search people and vehicles within security perimeters if they perceive a terror-related threat, as well as to shut down temporarily places of worship deemed to be inciting violence or acts of terrorism. Less controversially, Macron has also set up a National Centre for Counter-Terrorism, a coordinating body based in the Elysée Palace and run by a respected former chief of counter-espionage, Pierre de Bousquet de Florian. Poor operational coordination between rival services was identified by parliament as one of the failures in 2015. The French intelligence services' terrorism watch list contains no fewer than 18,000 individuals. France, like other European countries, is up against big numbers, small and shifting cells, and low-tech operations such as knife attacks and the use of vehicles to kill pedestrians. They are all but impossible to prevent.

Macron approaches the broader questions with a more open outlook. He had urged the French, back in 2015, to take a long, hard look to see what part they may have had in creating the 'fertile soil' on which terrorist networks seem able to recruit. The answer, he seems to think, is partly about ensuring that French Muslims feel better integrated in France, and enjoy the same opportunities to get on as any other citizens. It may also require a less rigid application of the French secular creed of *laïcité*, which separates religion and public life, in a way that is not felt by the country's Muslims to be stigmatizing. Entrenched by law in 1905, this principle was the product of a long anti-clerical struggle with the Catholic Church and the forces of obscurantism. It formed the basis for the French ban on the wearing of the burqa in public, and the headscarf (and other 'conspicuous' religious symbols) in state classrooms. At times, the country's ultra-secularists push *laic* principles to illiberal excess. After the Nice terrorist attack of 14 July 2016, some mayors in beach resorts tried to ban the 'burkini', before being overruled in the courts. Such measures, and the scandal they provoke, play into the hands of those who seek to portray France as anti-Muslim.

Before he took office, Macron argued that France needed a better balance between freedom of religious expression and the enforcement of secular rules. The function of *laïcité*, he said, was not to curb religiosity, but to protect freedom of religion, within the framework of French secular law. 'If the state should be neutral, which is at the heart of secularism, we have a duty to let everybody practise their religion with dignity,' Macron declared in a campaign speech in Montpellier. He described the debate over the burkini as simply 'crazy'. Entering into conflict with French Muslims stirred up exactly the sense of victimhood that jihadists sought. Policy was better directed at making sure that Muslims were properly integrated in France, with access to training and jobs. France, he said in a speech in the northern town of Tourcoing after he became president, had to accept a 'part of the responsibility' in the radicalization of some of its young. The 'Republic has given up' in certain neighbourhoods, he said, leaving citizens vulnerable to becoming prey to those who offer a competing narrative and twist Islam for political ends. The fact that the vast majority of the millions of people living in the country's *banlieues* have nothing to do with radicalization, the president declared, should not be a pretext for ignoring the problem.

These are daunting and complex problems. No single European country has found a satisfactory approach to ensuring that its Muslim minorities get the same chance of making a decent life for themselves as any other citizens. The legacy of the Franco-Algerian war, which has left behind deep distrust, grievance and hurt, makes for a particularly complicated relationship between France and its citizens of Algerian origin. Each crisis over migration renders the subject more sensitive still. France's double fracture – that between its thriving regional cities and its neglected peripheries, where populism has taken hold, and the one between its metropoles and their *banlieues*, targeted by radical Islam – serves as a sobering reminder. For all the optimism Macron's victory rekindled among metropolitan liberals, the threat of populism on the far left and the far right, as well as the dark fascination with political Islam, remain potent. Each will continue, in its own way, to lure some of those who have been angered, disillusioned or repelled by liberal Western society. And each raises intractable policy challenges. As David Thomson says of radicalization: 'The reality is that nobody knows how to solve the problem.'[17]

9

THE TYRANNY OF NORMAL

'We have a tendency in France to think you need a single solution for everyone.'

Nicolas Sadirac, Ecole 42

The most startling feature of Sandy Sablon's classroom at the Oran-Constantine primary school, on the outskirts of Calais, is the collection of old tennis balls that she has wedged onto the legs of all the little chairs. At the start of the school year, the teacher spent a weekend gashing and fitting the lime-green balls in order to cut down noise. This became a problem when she introduced new teaching methods that broke with established French pedagogy. Out went desks in rows. Instead, she grouped children of a similar level of achievement around shared tables, which meant pupils got up and moved about much more. 'When we just did dictation,' she tells me with a laugh when I visit, 'there wasn't any noise to worry about.'

All the strains of post-industrial France crowd into Fort Nieulay, the Calais neighbourhood surrounding the Oran-Constantine school. Red-brick terraced houses, built for the families of dockers and industrial workers in the 1950s, jut up against rain-streaked tower blocks. On the estate, the Friterie-Snack Bar is open for chips, but other shop fronts are boarded up. The children's swings are broken. This is not ethnic disadvantage, but France's '*misère blanche*', or white destitution, an educationalist says: the hidden side of French poverty. Sophie Paque, the primary school's energetic head teacher, tells me that a staggering 89 per cent of her 330 pupils live below the poverty line. Obesity is a growing concern. There are cases of scabies, a disease spread by mites that fester in old bedding. 'We give them a structure they don't have at home,' she says.[1] Outside a garage on the local housing estate, three adults in ill-fitting tracksuits sit on plastic chairs, watching, or maybe waiting. Youth unemployment in Calais is over 45 per cent, twice the national average. In Fort Nieulay it touches 67 per cent.

In the autumn of 2017, however, Oran-Constantine, like 2,500 classes in other priority schools nationwide, became the beneficiary of Macron's promise to halve class sizes to 12 pupils for five- and six-year-olds. The new policy caused a certain amount of chaos elsewhere, as head teachers tried to find space for the extra classes. But Oran-Constantine was ready, and keen. It had already been part of a pilot experiment launched in 2011, based on smaller class sizes, a rigorous new scheme to teach reading, and more personalized learning. This experiment was put in place under Jean-Michel Blanquer, who went on to become Macron's education minister. Using voice-recognition software on tablet computers, the project allowed faster learners, wearing little headsets, to practise pronouncing sounds in the corner of the classroom, thus freeing up their teacher to help weaker classmates. Smaller class sizes enabled teachers to spend more time with individual pupils. The pilot also broke with the country's tradition that put the *maîtresse*, or teacher, at the blackboard and the children in rows. 'French teachers tend to advance like steamrollers: straight ahead at the same speed,' Christophe Gomes, from Agir pour l'Ecole, the partly privately financed association that ran the government-backed pilot scheme, tells me. At Oran-Constantine, he says, 'pupils set the pace'. Some teachers feared at first that technology was threatening their jobs. In fact, it freed them up to do their jobs better. One year into the experiment, the number of pupils with reading difficulties at the 11 schools in Calais that took part had halved. Gomes is visibly proud of what they have all achieved: 'It's a little revolution.'[2]

The Calais experiment feeds directly into the plans that Blanquer and Macron have drawn up to improve education in France. By international standards, these may seem uncontroversial and no more innovative than those introduced long ago in countries such as Finland or Singapore. Yet in France they challenge central educational tenets, which will have to be confronted if the country is to lift school standards. For many years, French education has been subject to what might be called 'the tyranny of normal'. Ever since compulsory, free, secular primary education was introduced in the 1880s, uniform schooling countrywide has been part of the French way of doing things. The nineteenth-century *instituteur*, or schoolteacher, was regarded as a sort of missionary figure, a guarantor of republican equality and norms. Teachers were trained in *écoles normales*. The Ecole Normale Supérieure, today one of the most prestigious and selective French higher-education institutions, was established in 1795 to train the young republic's educators. To this day, the mighty Ministry of Education in Paris sets standardized curriculums and timetables for state schools across the country. All 11-year-olds, for example, spend exactly four and a half hours on maths a week. Experimentation is frequently regarded as suspect. 'Classes are not laboratories', noted a report by the conservative education inspectorate a few years ago, 'and pupils are not guinea pigs.'

Yet 'in reality our standardizing system is unequal,' the professorial Blanquer told me, when we sat down on teak chairs in the shaded garden of the ministry shortly after he took over the job.[3] In cities around the world, from New York to Hong Kong, French *lycées* are regarded as places of excellence, and a gold standard for uniform global education. The centralized, top-down approach means that the French elite can move their children around the world knowing that all schools will be teaching seventeenth-century French tragedy and comedy to pupils in their fifth year of secondary school. Yet, at home, France is failing its young. By the age of 15, some 40 per cent of French pupils from poorer backgrounds are 'in difficulty', a figure six percentage points above the OECD average.

French schools, with their demanding academic content and testing, do well by the brightest children, who end up winning places in the fiercely selective *grandes écoles*, but they often fail those at the bottom. Performance in international maths tests fell significantly between 2003 and 2012, and has stagnated at around the average, despite public spending on education matching that elsewhere. In a 2016 international study of reading, known as PIRLS, French pupils lagged in 34th position, behind schoolchildren in Spain, Portugal and Italy. Their level had dropped by 14 points since 2001. France is an 'outlier', said Eric Charbonnier, an OECD education specialist, because in contrast to most countries, inequality in education has actually increased over the past decade. Those who fail to learn to read in the first year of primary school often never make up the learning gap later. Fully 20 per cent of children leave primary school without being able to read or write properly. Too often, pupils who drop out of secondary school without any qualifications are the ones who struggled in primary school. When the French Armed Forces tested all high-school leavers in 2016, as it does every year when teenagers turn up at their local military base for the country's compulsory 'defence and citizenship' day, it found that one in ten still had difficulty reading.

A technocrat, with a quiet passion for education and a curiously extensive knowledge of Latin America, Blanquer had previously worked for years within the education establishment, as head of the Créteil *académie*, or local education authority, running various pilot experiments. Formerly also director of ESSEC, one of the country's top business schools, he helped Emmanuel Macron draw up his education manifesto during the campaign. They decided to put reform of primary education at the centre of their policy to combat school failure and improve life chances. Along with smaller primary classes, Blanquer plans to encourage a more rigorous way to teach reading, with more regular nationwide tests. As education policy goes, none of this is revolutionary. But for France even halving class sizes felt like a radical shift. The minister plans to extend the programme to the second year of primary for the school year starting in September 2018.

Smaller class sizes is just the start. Unusually for a French policymaker, Blanquer has studied what works abroad, and how such lessons might be applied in France. He has sought out his counterpart in Singapore, and has praised methods used in Finland. 'Egalitarianism,' he told me, taking on a creed shared by much of the teaching profession, 'is the real enemy of public service.' Blanquer is keen, rather, on autonomy and experimentation, which put the educational establishment on edge. He told primary schools, which had been ordered by the government to introduce classes on Wednesdays, traditionally a day off, that they could return to a four-day week if they preferred. Or not: it was up to them. Secondary schools were allowed to bring back bilingual classes, along with ancient Greek and Latin, which had been cut back as too elitist. Blanquer was nicknamed 'Ctrl Z' for deleting what had come before. The idea that schools might be free to decide such matters was disconcerting for a profession that had long been run along almost military lines. An army of 880,000 teachers is centrally deployed to French schools across the country. Head teachers have no say in staffing. In the course of their careers, teachers acquire points that enable them to request reassignment. Newly qualified ones without such points are sent to the toughest schools, and turnover in such places is depressingly high.

During his campaign Macron promised to give schools more autonomy over teaching methods, timetabling and recruitment, and to stop newly qualified teachers from being sent to the toughest schools. At the Oran-Constantine primary school in Calais, Sophie Paque, the dynamic head teacher, calls the system a 'straitjacket'. She has 48 members of staff in her school, and yet none report to her. Paque can neither recruit them directly, nor evaluate them, and certainly not get rid of them. Instead, teachers apply for jobs via a vast centralized and computerized deployment system, known as I-Prof. 'Sometimes teachers leave and they don't tell me,' Paque tells me. She had no institutional authority to impose the pilot teaching experiment at Oran-Constantine, and had to use her impressive powers of persuasion to convince sceptical teachers. Her pupils now leave primary school with a reading level that is within the national average, an astonishing result for a school in this sort of socio-economic catchment area. Not all French head teachers, however, are like Paque, and the existing rigid system gives even the ones who are limited scope for transforming a school. 'Head teachers do not have the solid means to lead a team, although they are the only ones in a position to do so,' noted a report by the Cour des Comptes, the public auditor, in 2017.

If France is to introduce greater freedom for schools to experiment, and adapt an ossified system for the innovation age, this will require quite a change in mindset. It will doubtless also at some point provoke a battle with the country's teaching profession. Blanquer's plan to redesign the *baccalauréat*, the final school-leaving exam, for those graduating from secondary school in 2021 makes for explosive reading in a French context. Currently made up of around 12 final exams, the *bac* will become more modular, centred on a smaller core of four subjects (of which philosophy, naturally, remains compulsory), with more specialism, and a big dose (40 per cent) of continuous assessment. The preliminary recommendations of the report into designing the new *bac* make for uncomfortable reading for those used to the traditional ministry-driven command structure. 'A system piloted from the centre never diversifies, it turns into an everlasting hierarchy,' it states.[4] The document goes on to declare: 'It makes sense to let *lycées* move at their own rhythm and according to their own ideas ... It seems to us neither legitimate nor appropriate to make precise suggestions about either the number of hours for each subject or the organization of semesters or the exact choice of subjects offered.' By French standards, this was ground-breaking.

Not surprisingly perhaps, Blanquer was accused of being reactionary and ideological. The head of curricula at the Education Ministry resigned in protest, even before the reforms were unveiled. Teaching unions, fearing a creeping increase in the hours they would be expected to spend in the classroom and worried that continuous assessment would aggravate inequalities between schools, decided to go on strike. Old habits, backed by strong lobbies, will be hard to shift. Only 20 per cent of French teachers currently adjust their methods to individual pupil ability, according to the OECD, compared with over 65 per cent of those in Norway; and far fewer work in teams. Such weaknesses will need to be fixed if Blanquer is really to make French timetables less rigid, classes less dull, teachers more involved, head teachers more autonomous, classrooms more connected, and the curriculum more adapted to the coming digital disruption.

The government may also try to make school a less crushing experience. Before he became a minister, Blanquer published a book about reforming French education, deploring the lack of confidence that his country's schools generate.[5] Between the extreme rigour of some Asian teaching systems, and the pupil-centred approach of American and Northern European schools, France, he suggested, could offer a middle way: 'between tradition and modernity, fulfilment and rigour, effort and liberty'. At the start of the first school year on his watch, Blanquer called his project that of building 'a school of confidence'. French tradition is for teachers to grade harshly, and praise with extreme moderation. For a *dictée*, a piece of dictation read out by the teacher to test pupils' written French, points are taken off for each mistake, so a child can end up with zero. This approach prompts excessive anxiety. No less than 75 per cent of French pupils worry that they will get bad grades in maths tests, according to an OECD study, close to the level reported by stressed-out South Korean schoolchildren (78 per cent). A government-commissioned report on a small pilot experiment in some French secondary schools, where ruthless grading had been shelved in favour of a more encouraging system, noted with some surprise that weaker pupils were absent from school less often, more confident in the classroom, and 'less stressed when faced with failure'.

The government seems to have taken on some of these weaknesses. 'Pleasure in learning is a condition for pupils' success,' Blanquer stated shortly after taking office, as if unveiling a fresh discovery. 'To create a favourable environment, schools must offer a benevolent framework and inspire pupils' confidence.'[6] The reforms will be a heroic task, and require deft handling of sceptical teaching unions, as well as some wary parents. However, if Blanquer gets it right, France might be able to find a new, more productive balance, one that keeps the best of Cartesian rigour and cultural breadth – where else can a physicist quote Rousseau and Voltaire? – while injecting a much-needed dose of creative thinking, autonomy and even fun.

At the other end of the education ladder, a hint of how creative autonomously run French education can be when left to itself can be found inside a boxy building on the inner edge of an unfashionable stretch of northern Paris. This is 42, a 'coding school' in which students learn advanced computer programming. It is named after the number that is the 'answer to the ultimate question of life, the universe and everything', according to Douglas Adams's science-fiction classic, *The Hitchhiker's Guide to the Galaxy*. The entrance hall at 42 is all distressed concrete and exposed piping. There is a skateboard rack, and a painting of a man urinating against a graffiti-sprayed wall.

The school is everything that traditional French higher education is not. It is entirely privately financed by Xavier Niel, the tech entrepreneur, but free to pupils. The school holds no classes, has no teachers, fixed terms or timetables, and does not issue formal diplomas. All learning is done through tasks on screen, at students' own pace. 'Graduates' are often snapped up by employers before they finish. There are no lectures, and the building is open round the clock. The school is hyper-selective and has a dropout rate of 5 per cent. When it opened in 2013, *Le Monde* newspaper described it politely as 'strange'. 'What's difficult to understand is that we're not about the transmission of knowledge,' Nicolas Sadirac, the hirsute director in a baggy T-shirt tells me. 'We are co-inventing computer science. The robot age isn't about repeating tasks, but innovation. We need individuals who create, not ones who replicate.'[7] He likes to call computing a 'creative industry', and 42 an art school.

On a spring weekday morning when I drop in on 42, I find Guillaume Aly, dressed in shorts and trainers, swiping his security badge at the entrance. He takes off his headphones to answer questions. Aly had been in the army for eight years before he applied, and went to school in Seine-Saint-Denis, a nearby *banlieue* just over the Paris ring road, where joblessness is well above the national average. He heard about 42 after seeing a documentary about the school on television. 'I'm 30 years old, and you don't have much hope of training at my age,' he tells me. But 42 shows a deliberate disregard for social background or exam results. It tests applicants anonymously online, then selects from a shortlist after a harsh month-long immersion in what is known as the *piscine*, or the 'swimming pool'. Each year 50,000–60,000 people apply and just 900 are admitted. At the back of one of the school's big rooms of computers, I come across three students puzzling over an online challenge. Léonard Aymard, originally from Annecy, explains that he was a tour guide when he applied. Sitting next to him, Loic Shety, who hails from Dijon, tells me that he won a place at 42 even though he lacked the school-leaving *baccalauréat* certificate. 'It's not for everyone,' says Mathilde Allard, who is from Montpellier and one of a minority of female students. She slept in the school for four weeks, as many of the students do, when she was going through selection in the *piscine*. 'But we work together so we don't get lost.'

To understand quite how innovative 42 is in a French context, I cross the river Seine to the capital's fashionable left bank to visit the University of Paris-Descartes. A world away from 42, it is run from an eighteenth-century building in the 6th arrondissement, whose amphitheatre was begun under Louis XV. In the president's reception room, a grand piano stands in the corner and eighteenth-century tapestries adorn the walls. Home to one of the most prestigious medical schools in France, places at the university are highly sought after by the capital's brightest, and it is a world-class centre of research in medical and life sciences. As at all French universities, tuition there is free, bar a small enrolment fee, so students do not graduate burdened with debt like their counterparts in America or Britain. Yet a glimpse at Descartes also shows how French higher education can tie the hands of innovators, including the university's president, Frédéric Dardel, a molecular biologist.

Like universities the world over, Descartes receives far more applications each year than it has places available. Yet unlike university heads in other countries, Dardel is not permitted to select undergraduate students at entry. Ever since Napoleon set up the *baccalauréat*, which is awarded by the Education Ministry, this exam has served not so much as a school-leaving diploma but as an entrance ticket to university. Students can apply for any course they like, regardless of their ability. A university place is considered a right. And a centralized system allocates Dardel's students to his institution. This routinely overfills certain courses and causes overflowing lecture halls. When a university cannot take any more, those at schools nearby are supposed to be given priority. Such is the demand that places have increasingly been allocated through random selection by computer, known as *tirage au sort*. By 2017 this was happening to 169 degree subjects across France. 'It's an absurd distribution system which leads to failure,' Dardel tells me.[8] He calculated that the average dropout rate at Descartes over the previous six years had been 45 per cent. Students took on average four and a half years to complete what should be a three-year degree, mainly due to retakes. The total extra cost during that period of non-selection was, on Dardel's estimates, €100 million.

An admirer of 42, Dardel nonetheless argues that there is still a place for theoretical maths in computer science. In year three the computing degree at Descartes puts a heavy emphasis on mathematical theory, as perhaps a university named after one of the fathers of analytic geometry should. Yet, because the university lacks the right to select those who attend, too many students fail, breeding disillusion and waste. In 2014, 81 of the 268 students allocated to the maths and computing course at Descartes did not have the *bac* 'S', the maths-heavy version of the school-leaving exam. After the first year as undergraduates, only two of those 81 passed their exams.

France's university system encapsulates many of the drawbacks of its over-centralized, bureaucratic model. The country has 71 universities, catering to 1.6 million students, nearly twice the number in 1980. All universities are public, and all the lecturers are civil servants. Universities are barred from selecting undergraduates at entry. Enrolment fees amount to less than €200 a year, and tuition is paid for by the state. Medicine and law aside, the brightest pupils opt instead for the upper tier of institutions known as *grandes écoles*, which cater to a tiny fraction of the student population. They are highly selective, and supply the French elite in government as well as in the board-room. Entrance exams to such places as Polytechnique and Mines ParisTech (engineering) or HEC and ESSEC (business) are so stiff that they require two years of preparatory study. Such schools are regularly rated and ranked. But they serve only about 8 per cent of the student population. Selection and excellence are acceptable for the elite, it seems, but not for everybody else. Elie Cohen, a French economist, put it well when he once told me: 'The French accept the brutality of selection on condition that we maintain the illusion of formal equality.'

For years, this two-tier higher-education system has led to top jobs for the few, and confined most students to courses that ill prepare them for the world of work. I began to under-stand this only after visiting the elegant, pink-bricked city of Toulouse in south-west France to look at two universities that lie just a few kilometres apart. Both are big: Toulouse 1 Capitole, a quick walk from the Place du Capitole in the city centre, has 21,000 students; Toulouse-Jean Jaurès, known as Le Mirail when I went there and a short metro ride away on the city's outskirts, has over 30,000. Both were spun off as sep-arate universities after France's 1968 student riots, which led to the break-up of many of the country's giant universities. Both cover, broadly, the social sciences: Toulouse 1 offers economics, political science, law and management; Jean Jaurès spans litera-ture, philosophy, history, human sciences, arts and maths. But there the similarities end.

Toulouse-Jean Jaurès, a low-rise 1960s campus of squat grey concrete blocks when I visited, looked like a demonstration model of France's difficulties with its university system. It has pockets of research excellence, such as in archaeology, and has adapted to international standards by introducing the Europe-wide structure of bachelor's and master's degrees. But it concentrates on mass teaching in subjects – philosophy, psychology, sociology – whose graduates find it hard to get jobs. Over 5,000 students there study psychology alone. Lecture halls at Jean Jaurès were overcrowded. In one vast 800-seat amphitheatre, steeply banked rows of students sat impassively while a lecturer mumbled on a distant platform. Each year, 46 per cent of new students dropped out. The university did not seem to consider this to be its problem. 'This is a left-wing university which has a social project,' its director at the time told me. 'It is not an institution designed for professional training.'

Yet jobs seemed to be a worry for its students. A generation ago most university graduates could have gone on to secure work. But the rapid expansion of numbers passing the *bac* – from 26 per cent of the relevant age group in 1980 to 79 per cent today – has flooded France's non-selective universities. School-leavers who might in the past have done an apprenticeship sign up instead for courses in social sciences that ill prepare them for the job market. Across France, as Jean-Michel Blanquer likes to recall, an astonishing 70 per cent of those who start an undergraduate degree still do not finish it in three years. 'Unemployment weighs on our minds,' said the student-union leader at Jean Jaurès at the time. 'We're the first generation that lives worse than our parents.' Student unions blockaded the campus at Toulouse-Jean Jaurès during university sit-ins in 2006, and again in 2018. Graffiti sprayed on the walls declared: 'We will strike against capitalism' and 'We do not want to return to life as normal'. It was hard to find anybody satisfied with the way things were. Teachers were fed up because they were poorly paid and felt treated as second-class citizens. Students did not feel they got enough support.

The 4,000 new undergraduates who arrived there each year got no tutorial help or careers advice. There was no bar on campus. The library was light, airy and brand new. But it closed at 6 p.m. on weekdays, and was shut at weekends.

On the other side of the Garonne river, at Toulouse 1, bicycles were leaning against red-brick courtyards and students sat cross-legged in the shade of plane trees. This university had not found a solution to all the difficulties that Jean Jaurès faced. Yet, across all disciplines, 82 per cent of undergraduates got their degree in three years. During the student revolt, the Toulouse 1 campus was shut for just a brief period. In the Toulouse School of Economics (TSE), a faculty within the university, it has a world-class department of economics. One of the TSE pioneers, Jean Tirole, won the 2014 Nobel Prize in this field. Indeed, the history of the TSE, which arose from an institute originally set up in 1990 by Jean-Jacques Laffont, shows both how France has tied its hands with the existing system, and how to circumvent it. Instead of accepting its lot, the school's founders decided to work around the rules. They sought private sponsorship for research, setting up research centres as associations, officially outside the university management structure and therefore not subject to civil-service rules. I first met Tirole when he and his colleagues were flying up to Paris for fundraising meetings, to solicit research contracts directly with private firms. French universities are handicapped in international rankings, because most research goes on not within their walls but in the many excellent national public-research bodies. So the TSE encouraged its lecturers and researchers to work and publish together, and under its name, in order to lift its position. In a final twist, the school used a transfer procedure to lure top researchers, as it was unable under French civil-service rules to recruit them directly. In short, the struggle to stay competitive internationally, and to subvert the system, required relentless creative efforts.

Under Nicolas Sarkozy's presidency, universities were in 2007 given a degree of autonomy from such central state control, which made life simpler for places like the TSE. Universities were free to recruit more of their own lecturers, and to set up private foundations – with tax breaks for donors – to complement public finance. Some merged, including the three universities of Strasbourg and three of the four in Bordeaux, to give themselves critical mass. Other merger projects struggled to overcome internal divisions and rivalries. Yet selection at undergraduate entry remained taboo. And autonomy turned out in reality to be partial. As the Cour des Comptes pointed out in 2015, eight years after the law on university autonomy was passed, an average of 82 per cent of university budgets were still paid directly by state subsidy, the bulk of this being staff salaries. 'The financial flexibility of universities in reality appears to be limited', it concluded.[9] Meetings of the board of governors were too often dominated by national politics and union concerns rather than the strategic place of higher education. This made outside governors 'flee' the job. Almost all university buildings and premises remained the property of the central state.

Ten years ago, I asked a top education official at the ministry in Paris whether France would ever allow universities to pick undergraduates at entry? 'Oh là là!' he replied. 'It's not in the French mentality.' Macron's government has now decided to break the selection taboo. Within months of taking office, it put in place a new online post-*bac* application system, known as *parcoursup*, for all pupils enrolling at universities from the autumn of 2018. Out went the algorithm and the randomized allocation of places. In came the right for universities to study applications themselves and make pupils offers, as well as to impose something coyly referred to as 'requirements'. The ministry put it this way: universities, it declared, 'will henceforth have the possibility of making enrolment conditional on a special educational programme in cases where they judge that the applicant does not have what is required'.

Nobody was under any illusions. Although the ministry could not quite bring itself to say so, this was code for universities to be able to start a form of selection. At the very least it will make it possible for a university's maths department to require an applicant for a maths degree to have a minimum level of maths. Once this principle is established, more meaningful selection may be possible later on. Above all, the reform of the *bac* and university entrance go hand in hand, and have been designed together. The new *bac*, based on a three-year cycle to begin in 2018, will involve grading some subjects earlier in the school year, to give universities a fuller idea of the applicant's abilities. At that point, France may be able finally to get over its selection hang-up.

The real question for French education is how far President Macron is prepared to go. Not all institutions can be as creative and experimental as 42. And not all students could survive there. But Xavier Niel has understood what many French education ministers in the past have not: that the world of work is being upturned, and education has to be too. 'We have a tendency in France to think you need a single solution for everyone,' Nicolas Sadirac, the director of 42, told me. His school points to how it is possible in French education to overcome the tyranny of normal in order to make more of what the system does well, and minimize what it does not. Macron's approach is not to devise an entirely new model. He seeks to innovate largely within the existing institutional system. Yet this still leaves much space for novelty. There is plenty of thinking about how to break free from standardization, and make teaching more individualized, without losing the excellence and cultural breadth that French education provides. The underlying challenge is to persuade public opinion, students, parents and teachers that variety, autonomy and experimentation are not a threat to equality but a means of restoring it to an education system that has lost sight of it. If Macron can do this, he will have gone a long way towards improving the lot of people in places like the housing estates of Calais whom the system currently fails.

10

A Certain Idea of Europe, and Beyond

'Europe needs to wake up!'

Emmanuel Macron to the author, 21 July 2017

'In every beginning dwells a certain magic.' Germany's Angela Merkel quoted these lines from 'Stufen', a poem by Hermann Hesse, when she welcomed Emmanuel Macron to Berlin on the evening of his first full day in office. The doyenne of European leaders, she was by then on her fourth French president, having worked first with Jacques Chirac in 2005. The link with her second, Nicolas Sarkozy, was volatile; with François Hollande, lopsided. The election of Macron, who praised Germany for 'rescuing our collective dignity' during the refugee crisis and whose supporters waved EU flags at rallies, came as a relief, a source of promise but also a reckoning.

In his first three months, Macron met Merkel nine times, more than twice as often as the leaders of the United States and Italy, and three times more than those of Russia and Great Britain. This was a return to the traditional European reflex of French presidents under the Fifth Republic. After the Second World War, France had dealt with its insecurities towards its mighty neighbour by building the European Union, a project through which it sought to bind in Germany and amplify French power. By pooling their steel and coal production, declared Robert Schuman, the French foreign minister, from the *salon d'horloge* of the Foreign Ministry in 1950, France and Germany would render war 'not merely unthinkable, but materially impossible'. The French regarded shared sovereignty as a means of reinforcing, not undermining, their nation state, and the Franco-German axis was the foundation of the project. It was General de Gaulle and Konrad Adenauer, his German counterpart, who codified this link when they met in 1963 under the crystal chandeliers of the presidential palace to sign the Elysée Treaty. 'My heart overflows and my soul is grateful,' averred the General, adding that the treaty 'opens the door to a new future for Germany, for France, for Europe and therefore for the world'.

Emmanuel Macron would probably not put it very differently. He twice took his election campaign in 2017 to Germany. The lanky, bearded former mayor of Le Havre who is now prime minister, Edouard Philippe, was educated at the French lycée in Bonn. The smooth-talking finance minister, Bruno Le Maire, is also a fluent German speaker. The president's veteran diplomatic adviser, Philippe Etienne, arrived at the Elysée from Berlin, where he was ambassador. Sylvie Goulard, who was (briefly) Macron's defence minister and is now deputy governor of the Bank of France, is well-connected in Germany. Macron has a long-standing fascination with German literature and culture, and considers the two countries 'united' by their common 'taste for freedom and the universal, in art as in philosophy'.[1] As a boy, he told Michaela Wiegel, one of the first books his grandmother gave him to read was the resistance novel *Le silence de la mer* by Vercors, about a cultured German officer quartered in a provincial French home under the Occupation, which was published secretly in 1942. 'Civilization and culture,' he said, 'are stronger than the idiocies of certain leaders and the people who follow them.'

Macron and Merkel may make for an unlikely couple. He, hailing from the left, is grandiose, literary, florid and tactile. She, from the conservative right, is understated, scientific, cautious and reserved. But they have established a strong bond. They speak in English to each other, in their meetings or during their very frequent telephone calls. Before Macron gave a big speech on Europe at the Sorbonne in September 2017, he sent Merkel a draft to read through first. 'She wants to trust France,' claims one of his aides. 'She's very straight and technical. So you have to be precise, know your stuff, and follow up. He respects that. Whenever there's a disagreement, he always talks to her first.' Whatever the question in Europe, the first answer for Macron seems to be Germany.

The new French president took office determined to restore balance to what had become an uneven Franco-German relationship, tilted towards mighty Germany. His objective was to reach a 'new deal' with his neighbour, as part of a wider plan to transform the European Union from an object of indifference, frustration and disappointment into a project that can offer growth, jobs and meaning to its citizens. Macron summed up the core bargain he sought when he was still economy minister, with the phrase '€50bn of spending cuts for us; €50bn of investment for them.' A fuller version goes something like this: France restores its lost credibility in German eyes by sticking to its promises to reform France; in return, Germany supports closer integration of the 19-member eurozone, with more fiscal convergence and joint investment, and in time some form of common budget, even finance minister and parliament, for the currency area. Despite a robust economic recovery in 2017–18, both countries recognize that the eurozone remains vulnerable to future financial shocks, and that growth is not what it could be. Where Paris and Berlin diverge is over what to do about it.

Macron's first step was to keep to his word at home. 'He will surprise them, because the Germans don't believe it will happen,' one of his aides told me shortly after he was elected. 'They have been disappointed by France too many times before.' Nobody in Berlin expected Macron to pass his labour reform without provoking chaos on the streets. They had heard too many French governments in the past promise reform only to back down. Nor was there much confidence that France would keep to its promise to bring down the government's budget deficit to below 3 per cent in 2017. France's chronic inability to do so over the years had become a source of German exasperation. The European Commission first slapped France on the wrist over this, under what is known as 'excessive deficit procedure' (EDP), in 2009.

Successive French governments kept lobbying to be allowed to go on breaching the rules. When in 2015 the commission agreed to give France an extra two years to get its public finances in order, this was the third time it had indulged the French. By mid-2017 the commission had taken all offending countries out of the EDP, including Greece, bar two: Spain and France. Why would Berlin trust Macron to be any different?

Just days after the French election, the cover of *Der Spiegel*, a German weekly, summed up the views of many east of the Rhine. It featured Macron under the heading '*Teurer Freund*' – which can mean either dear, or expensive, friend. In Berlin, French talk of greater integration is generally understood as a 'transfer union': a sort of giant sucking movement through which Europe's profligate south would extract cash from the thriftier north. When France talks about more risk-sharing, Germany hears bigger bills to pay. When Germany insists on more control and rules, France hears a refusal to accept solidarity.

Macron called Germany's bluff. He passed his labour reform four months after his election, followed it with tax cuts for businesses and investors, and delivered the first budget deficit below 3 per cent in over a decade. As a frequent visitor, Macron knew Germany well enough to know that it would take delicate nudging to get Berlin to shift. After sending a draft of his Sorbonne speech to Merkel, he 'deliberately left open the technical implementation on some points', he said, by which he meant his ideas on reforming eurozone institutions. Talk of eurobonds or debt mutualization, toxic in most German quarters, has been muted. Macron's underlying strategy is nonetheless clear: the more reason that France can give Germany to trust it, the more it can hope to get from Berlin.

The French president's ambitions for 'transforming' a dysfunctional eurozone, and the unloved European Union more broadly, are not modest. 'Ambition is never modest,' he told *Der Spiegel*. 'If modesty means having middling success, then I can only say: I'm not interested.' He seems to have cast himself as the man of the hour, less a king than a sort of modern-day de Gaulle, who will rescue Europe from its demons, and conjure hope from crisis. Around him, nationalists and populists are on the rise, sitting in government in Poland, Hungary and Austria, and in parliament in Germany, where they hold more seats than at any time since the Second World War. Forces of fragmentation, from Britain to Catalonia, are undermining the EU's common purpose. Internal economic strains within the single-currency area are testing its unity. Instability on Europe's southern shores and eastern borders threatens its security. Migrants from Africa's Mediterranean rim menace its resilience. Macron surveys all this and concludes what exactly? Not that Europe is too divided, rigid, ageing or set in its ways to be able to hold its own. But that 'France is back', and with it Europe.

'Europe needs to wake up!' Macron told me in July 2017, the pitch of his voice rising. With the United States under Donald Trump volatile and morally adrift, Britain in retreat due to the all-absorbing complexities of Brexit, and illiberal powers on the continent's doorstep, the French president senses an unusual – and probably brief – opportunity for the European Union: a chance to fashion a stronger centre, and reassert itself and its values as a guarantor of the democratic liberal order, but also as a place that needs to secure decent lives for its people. And, because there is a hidden romantic inside the French president, to help them to dream a little. 'What world are we living in?' he said to me. 'Our responsibility is immense. We need to stop holding crisis summits around hyper-technical subjects. We need to define another horizon together. We can be the leaders of tomorrow's world.'[2]

In this respect, Macron can sound quite impatient with his mighty neighbour. 'Germany is faced with a real choice: whether it wants a European model with a German hegemony which isn't durable, because it rests in part on courageous reforms that Germany did a dozen years ago, and in part on the imbalances in the eurozone,' he told me. 'Or whether Germany wants to partici-pate with France in a new European leadership which rebalances Europe, with more solidarity and also a project of stronger convergence.'[3] If the current situation of imbalances continues, he said, 'Europe will fracture'. It was up to Germany, he argued, to decide 'whether it is ready to join France in a remaking of Europe around a great moment of convergence'. As economy minister, he had battled against the German line (and his own president) to try to impose less harsh terms on a struggling Greece in order to keep it in the eurozone. Macron has no illusions about the price of failure. The choice, he judges, is about whether liberal democratic politics can prevail, and whether Europe can hold together.

In the autumn after his election, Macron laid out this vision in two landmark speeches. Before the backdrop of the Parthenon in Athens, and to an evening chorus of cicadas, he articulated the more lyrical and very Macronesque rendition. This was not the punchier version he later took to Davos, but a musing on Pericles, Hegel and History with a capital letter. Recalling words uttered by André Malraux, a writer and French former minister of culture, at the same spot in Athens in 1959, Macron spoke of these places of memory that 'demand that we listen to them ... because it was here that the risk of democracy was taken'. Europe was built on the triumph of hope over failure, and unity over war. Yet new risks are emerging, old certainties fading. For too long, Europe's leaders have failed to listen to their own voters, who rejected treaties and constitutions, and were simply made to vote again. 'Did we listen?' Macron asked in that speech. 'No, we did not. Those who led Europe at the time decided not to respect their choice. They pretended nothing had happened, and sought compromises aside from the people, so as to continue a method that for decades had worked so well: building Europe a little to the side, and explaining it afterwards.'

Instead, Macron argued, Europe's leaders need to repair the broken democratic link with their citizens, and find a new way to make the EU meaningful for them. Not by presenting them with structures and treaties designed only by experts and lawyers. Such technocrats have a job to do, but talk of summits and rules is what puts people off. Citizens also need to feel that they have their say, and that the EU works for them. Macron has his own grand designs, but he also wants to replicate his grass-roots 'Grande Marche' tactics across Europe. What actually matters to people? He has some ideas: the protection of data, online privacy, fair taxation of tech giants, safe food, clean air, easy and safe ways to travel, communicate, study and share with fellow Europeans. If those sound prosaic rather than visionary, Macron has an answer to that too. 'Look at the time that we are sharing. It is the moment of which Hegel spoke, the moment when the owl of Minerva takes flight,' he declared in Athens. 'The owl of Minerva provides wisdom but it continues to look back,' he declared, 'because it is always so easy and so comforting to look at what we have, what we know.' Instead of surveying the past, like the owl, he urged Europeans: dare to dream.

This was vintage Macron: grandiose, historically sweeping, overly intellectual, stylistically extravagant, baffling, but also admirable. It was the sort of speech that most other European leaders, Merkel among them, would never choose to make. What emerged from it was Macron's unapologetic desire to line up with Europe's thinkers and visionaries, not its technocrats. There are few questions that vex him more than being asked whether Europe needs a new treaty. Europe, he will reply irritably, is not primarily about institutions and rules: these are just tools, which should be at the service of grand ideas. Nor does he have much time for those who try to temper his ambition. Of course there will be discussions, debates and disagreements. His proposals are the start of a conversation. To get lost in the thicket of jargonese, or political bickering, or crisis management, is for Europe to lose its citizens all over again. Instead, the philosopher-president wants to get Europe to face the big existential questions first – what do its citizens want from it? what is its purpose? – and from there to work out how to achieve it.

For Macron's second big presidential speech on Europe, he chose another seat of civilization: the great amphitheatre at the Sorbonne, a college originally founded in the thirteenth century, in the historic Latin Quarter of Paris. In an address brimming with ideas, both old and new, the French president described the EU as 'too weak, too slow, too ineffective', and spelt out a breathless list of policy ideas to transform it. The French love *grands projets*, and this speech was full of them: a shared European military budget, a European intelligence academy, a joint intervention force based on a 'common strategic doctrine', a European asylum office, a new agency for 'radical innovation', six-month exchanges for young people, an environmentally friendly carbon tax at the EU's external border, a 'trade prosecutor', a eurozone budget and finance minister, fiscal harmonization, and more. If this speech was more technical, its impulse was nonetheless political. Macron reminded his audience that the 'sad passions' inflamed by 'obscurantism' were being awakened across the continent. Europe's leaders, by blaming Europe when things went wrong and failing to give it credit for success, had to accept responsibility for having created the conditions for such forces to prosper.

The overarching message at the Sorbonne was threefold: that Europe needs to revive its democratic legitimacy; shore up its unity after a period of damaging division; and assert a new form of European sovereignty that will enable it to defend its values in the face of American clout and an assertive China. Europe's leaders are not there to pander to popular anxieties. But they do need to take such fears into account, Macron argues, if voters are to start believing in Europe again. So global tech giants, whose technology brings benefits to consumers but also dislocates jobs, careers and work practices, should be made to pay their 'fair' share of taxes. And Europe should be able to protect itself from the dumping of Chinese steel, or to vet Chinese investment in strategic industries and infrastructure. 'He believes that if you want to keep Europe open to trade and migration, you need to protect people,' says an aide. Hence Macron's mantra: a 'Europe that protects'. The crisis of advanced capitalism that has unfolded since the financial crisis, he argues, requires a recalibration of the balance between the market and the state, between competition and protection, innovation and preservation. 'I believe very profoundly in the innovation economy. I believe very profoundly in an open world,' Macron told the Sorbonne students. 'But an open world is only worth it if the competition that takes place there is fair.' If Europe cannot protect its citizens, as well as offer them opportunities, fanaticism and extremism will continue to hold a dark fascination.

What might a Europe reshaped by Macron look like by 2024, the year that Paris hosts the Olympic games and by which he hopes to have helped bring it about? His starting principle breaks with French tradition in one important respect, by leaning in a federal direction. De Gaulle rejected the supra-nationalism envisaged by some of Europe's founding bureaucrats, including France's own Jean Monnet, in favour of a 'Europe of nations'. Although the General denied ever using the phrase *'Europe des patries'* that is often attributed to him, he did oppose supra-nationalism. Countries, he declared, could not simply be blended 'like chestnuts in a purée'. This preference for an inter-governmental approach, whereby decision-making is done chiefly by nation states, has guided French policy on Europe over the years. The years of Europe's federalist push under Jacques Delors, another Frenchman and head of the European Commission, which began with the Single European Act of 1986, were in many ways the exception. The wily François Mitterrand did back the creation of a single currency, which was written into the Maastricht Treaty of 1992, but not for ideological reasons: it was a means to counterbalance the growing might of a reunified Germany. Mitterrand had an almost obsessional fear of German unification, telling Britain's Margaret Thatcher at a summit of European leaders that it felt like Munich in 1938. France was not ready to accept both a bigger Germany and the dominance of its currency; the creation of the euro to deal with the latter was Mitterrand's condition for endorsing the former. French policy on Europe has traditionally been marked by a lingering Gaullist resistance to federal ideas, and a suspicion of the European Commission.

Macron approaches Europe with the French Finance Ministry's more federal-leaning views. He is not only willing to talk about ceding sovereignty to a better integrated eurozone: he sees it as a condition for the strengthening of Europe's core, if not its survival. Brexit, in some ways, provides both an opportunity and an impulse for continental Europe to do this, since integration involves lots of projects that the British instinctively dislike. Among the unintended consequences of Britain's decision to leave the EU has been not only an enhancement of Europe's popularity among other member states, and an improbable solidarity among the 27 other members, but also a willingness to think practically about what is known as 'reinforced cooperation'. Under Macron's multi-tier plan, the 19-member currency area would be deepened by harmonized rules and common projects, as well as – in time – new institutional structures. Other EU members would be arranged in a more flexible constellation, choosing to join certain integration schemes as and when they liked. No member would be forced to take part, but none would be allowed to hold back the more enthusiastic either. Binding this all together would be a strengthened common approach to certain matters central to EU unity, including border security, migration and asylum.

To secure political backing for his scheme, Macron is trying to reach beyond Germany. He sees his immediate neighbours often, and has toured Central and Eastern European countries that his predecessors largely ignored. He also hopes to bring En Marche-style disruption at elections to the European Parliament in 2019. The unloved parliament is generally perceived as a woefully remote gravy train, disconnected from voters and filled with second-rate, unknown legislators elected on a low turnout. Members of the European Parliament are elected nationally, yet they are supposed to represent a Europe-wide *demos* that does not really exist. They also now have real powers, among them voting rights over the selection of the commission's head, a job occupied by Jean-Claude Juncker until 2019. If Macron wants to influence the make-up of the next commission, which acts as a sort of super-powered EU civil service, he needs to pull off what looks all but impossible: the creation of an En Marche-style European Parliament grouping, which peels away deputies from other established parties on the left and right, just as he did in France in 2017.

If France over the past 15 years has often been too weak a partner for Germany, the country in the coming years may turn out to be too ambitious. Macron's wish list is dizzying. He knows that he needs to build relationships, and believes in working through multilateral institutions, to get things done. He may have said 'I don't think it's possible to do great things alone', but it's not clear that he really believes this. There are shades of the self-belief of Nicolas Sarkozy about him, or Tony Blair, comparisons that raise their own concerns. Pascal Lamy, the French former head of the World Trade Organization, and a fine observer of political forces in Europe, told me that to understand Macron you need to know that 'his method is motion'. His solutions may not be optimal, his vision ambitious. But he believes that once things begin to move, possibilities open up.

Does Macron stand any chance of setting off the motion he wants in Europe? Germany is not the only country sceptical about his plans for eurozone reform, which would ultimately require new institutions and some form of treaty. Other Northern Europeans too have their doubts about what Mark Rutte, the Dutch liberal prime minister, has called deeper integration and other ideas 'coming from France'. It may be easier in the short run to make progress on less controversial elements designed to protect the currency area from future shocks, such as the transformation of the eurozone bail-out fund into a proper European Monetary Fund, as well as some form of common investment vehicle. Far more difficult will be winning Germany round to a substantial eurozone budget, which Macron would like to be worth 'several points of GDP', let alone a finance minister or parliament for the currency area.

Some ad hoc integration projects might well work. French officials point to defence cooperation as a model. An old idea, it was revived in the summer of 2017 as a joint Franco-German proposal, based on pooling some defence capabilities, such as rapid-reaction forces, as well as joint development work. Both France and Germany fret about Trump's disdain for NATO, as well as the underlying, structural disengagement of the United

States from Europe, and share a desire to strengthen European defence co-operation as a result. 'We Europeans have to take our destiny into our own hands,' Merkel declared when campaigning for re-election in 2017. By November that year 23 member states, including Poland, had agreed to what is known as Permanent Structured Cooperation (PESCO), designed to complement NATO and involving binding budget commitments.

Yet such initiatives will not transform Europe's defence capability, which remains essentially guaranteed by the continent's only two major military powers – Britain and France – under the North Atlantic security umbrella. As it is, the EU has its hands full containing trouble on its borders – from migration to Russian meddling – along with internal worries, from the independence movement in Catalonia to hard-line governments in Hungary and Poland. It may also be that Macron's haste and ambition lead him to push too hard in ways that are divisive. He will rattle free-marketeers with his call for a 'Europe that protects'. To Northern European ears, this smacks of old-style French protectionism and cuts against the principles of the EU's single market. Such member states are sceptical too about the way Macron seems to regard the single market as a tool of convergence, rather than of competition, and his use of trade policy as a vehicle to protect citizens from the impact of globalization. They looked with concern at the way he nationalized a French shipyard in the summer of 2017, albeit temporarily, in order to renegotiate a Franco-Italian deal. Macron is willing to let go of French assets, it seems, but only if this creates European champions of the sort that can compete with Chinese and American rivals. Such a strategy has its own logic, but it will generate misunderstanding and conflict.

As it is, the French president's scheme for a multi-tier EU, centred on an integrated eurozone, carries the risk that countries outside the single-currency area – which include Sweden and Denmark, as well as most of Central and Eastern Europe – will be treated as second-class states. This may turn some into difficult partners, and isolate nationalist governments outside the euro further still. Macron secured backing from Slovaks, Czechs,

Romanians and Bulgarians for his reform of the 'posted workers' directive in 2017. Yet this also left damage in his wake, particularly in Poland. Beata Szydlo, who was then Polish prime minister, accused Macron of being 'arrogant' after he spoke out against her government's infringement of liberties. If Macron is to contribute to European unity, he cannot afford to have too many brooding, resentful governments within the club.

And then there is Brexit. The French stress that this is neither a preoccupation for them, nor an issue that consumes much of their time. But negotiations over Britain's departure will nonetheless continue to absorb EU energies, as the 27 member states work out what sort of arrangement they will offer Britain after it leaves in March 2019. On a trip to Britain in early 2018, Macron appeared at one point to have endorsed a 'bespoke' deal, raising hopes that he might be willing to cede some ground in Brexit talks. In reality, he has consistently kept to the EU-27 script. The French president regrets Brexit, claims not to want to punish Britain, and says France would welcome its cross-Channel neighbour back if the British people ever changed their mind. But he is clear that any deal for a country that chooses to leave the EU, which will by definition be 'special' even if based on a Norway or Canada-type trade agreement, cannot involve the same rights enjoyed by those who belong. Access means accepting the rules. 'Europe is not a supermarket,' he says. On this point, France and Germany understand the value of sticking together and are likely to hold their firm line, more so than other member states, not least because Paris still hopes to lure business from post-Brexit Britain, while Berlin wants to protect the integrity of the single market. Macron may be fond of the UK. He speaks English and has visited London often. But anybody in Britain who hopes that the French president can therefore be prised away from the EU line on Brexit negotiations is likely to be disappointed.

If Macron is likely to stick to the rule-book on Brexit, he is keen not to isolate Britain as a result. He warmed up a Franco-British summit at the UK's Sandhurst military academy in early 2018 by offering to loan Britain the Bayeux Tapestry, telling guests at a reception, in English, how much he valued the close link that French and British people have forged by living, working and setting up home in each other's countries. Macron values, and hopes to deepen, crucial Franco-British defence and intelligence cooperation after Britain's departure from the EU. Hence the unusual meeting at Sandhurst between British Prime Minister Theresa May and President Macron, attended by the heads of all five of both countries' intelligence services. The French president will not be willing to let the British government use future bilateral defence cooperation as a bargaining chip in discussions over a post-Brexit deal with the EU. But he does understand the importance of the Franco-British security tie – a genuine success built on the bilateral defence treaties signed at Lancaster House in 2010 – and is keen to ensure it survives Britain's departure. It was in this spirit that, on the day he was elected, the second person he called after Angela Merkel was Theresa May.

If Macron can make a success of his European ambitions, or even some of them, he could reap big dividends. Diplomatic leadership is there for the taking. Merkel needs a stronger France to help share what Berlin considers to be the burden of EU leadership. Post-war Germany has never been comfortable with the idea of being the EU's de facto leader, does not see itself as a world power, and has yet to entrench a new willingness to use force abroad. Britain in the foreseeable future will be too distracted by Brexit to be a fully engaged diplomatic partner. If Brexit goes ahead, France will become the EU's only member with real military muscle: the only permanent member of the UN Security Council, the only country with an independent nuclear deterrent, and the only one that maintains a proper military force that can be sent abroad to fight at short notice. Despite an initial squeeze on military spending, Macron has promised to raise the French defence budget to 2 per cent of GDP by 2025.

How far might Macron be able to project such influence? The French leader arrived in the presidency new to foreign and security policy, and untested as commander-in-chief. During the campaign his foreign policy had to be invented from scratch, a process that one insider described as 'shambolic'. The people in his close circle were young and smart, but had no experience in global strategic affairs. Macron wanted a free hand to set his own agenda, and establish his authority. In office, he talks to a number of veterans within the French foreign-policy establishment. But, besides his official diplomatic adviser, Philippe Etienne, there is no single elder statesman acting as his guide.

Nobody doubts that Macron is deft at using diplomatic symbols. Inviting Vladimir Putin to Versailles, against the backdrop of an exhibition celebrating Peter the Great's 1717 visit to France, spoke of respect for great, or once-great, powers. As is his way, Macron used the occasion both to flatter, and then reprimand, speaking at a press conference with the Russian leader about 'organs of influence and propaganda' before his ashen-faced guest. The muscular handshake he gave Donald Trump on their first meeting, which was 'not unintentional', Macron said later, because 'that's how one gets respect', was straight from the alpha-male diplomatic playbook. His offer to loan the Bayeux Tapestry to Britain, or his gift of a gelding from the elite Republican Guard cavalry corps to President Xi Jinping, who had admired the horsemen who escorted his visit to Paris in 2014, were smart. Each, says his team, was his own idea.

Macron's emerging diplomacy seems to rest above all on dialogue and pragmatism: a belief in keeping the door open to all-comers, however unsavoury, on the premise that isolation breeds even greater danger. 'He doesn't want to lock himself into a doctrine, which is a good thing,' notes François Heisbourg, the security analyst. Macron comes to French diplomacy with few of the complexes harboured by his predecessors, including the use of English. Jacques Chirac, on principle, refused to speak a word of English, even though he could, having spent a summer in Boston as a student, working part-time in a 'Howard Johnson's' fast-food restaurant. Sarkozy, in office, struggled with the language, once memorably telling Hillary Clinton as she arrived at the Elysée Palace in the rain: 'Sorry for the time' (*le temps* meaning both 'weather' and 'time' in French). Macron, like many Frenchmen of his generation, has no hang-ups about speaking English, whether on the phone to Trump or while hosting global CEOs in Versailles, to a point that some French traditionalists find inappropriate or showy. But Macron probably secures a fair amount of goodwill by doing so, in diplomatic talks as well as foreign television interviews. It also lends France a less culturally defensive tone.

If there is not yet anything that can be defined as a Macron doctrine, the contours of his geo-strategic policy are emerging. He is enough of an Atlanticist to be committed to NATO, but enough of a realist – and admirer of both de Gaulle and Mitterrand – to know that Europe needs to strengthen its independent capacity to prepare for a diminishing American security guarantee, which began before Trump. He sees no contradiction between a commitment to both the trans-Atlantic security shield and European defence. In his dealings with Trump and Putin, he has shown that he believes in building relationships rather than moral grandstanding, and on doing so by calibrating his approach. He does the back-slapping bonhomie with Trump; with Merkel, he plays the respectful gentleman, or favourite son. In the Middle East and the Gulf, where France has some long-standing regional interests and ties, Macron's policy is not to choose sides. Sarkozy set great store by his ties with Qatar. Hollande invested in a relationship with the Saudis. Macron seeks to keep lines open both to Saudi Arabia and to Iran, and to each of the Gulf states. He talks regularly on the telephone to the Iranian and Turkish leaders, and has said that he is prepared to visit Tehran. The French president is a realist, who knows that he needs to work with authoritarian regimes against complex global threats such as terrorism or climate change. And he judges that such leaders are more dangerous when ignored and isolated. Macron has made himself an interlocutor in Europe for Trump on this basis. 'He likes to engage with people, with the good guys and the bad guys, with everybody basically,' said a diplomatic aide. 'He's not naïve. He knows it's not enough. But whenever Macron picks up the phone to Trump, he answers.'

If Macron is pragmatic, and opportunistic, he also seems to be working from some underlying principles. The first is a rejection of what he calls 'the neo-conservatism imported into France over the last ten years': the idea that Western powers can impose democracy and the rule of law on authoritarian sovereign states. Macron calls the intervention in Libya in 2011 'a historic error', on a par with that in Iraq in 2003, which the French under Jacques Chirac at the time tried to prevent.[4] Outside interference of this sort, he judges, based on a moralizing attempt to teach lessons to regimes deemed 'evil', ends up creating new threats: internal and regional conflicts, political instability, mass migration, and a breeding ground for jihadism. 'Democracy isn't built from the outside without the people,' he says. 'France didn't take part in the Iraq war, and that was right. And France was wrong to go to war in Libya in this way. What was the result of those interventions? Failed states where terrorist groups prospered.'[5] To this end, he has reversed the French policy pursued by Hollande of calling for the removal of Bashar al-Assad, arguing that this should not be a precondition for diplomatic efforts in Syria. 'It's not me, in Paris, in an office, who is going to choose the successor to Assad! It's the Syrian people. What I want to do is to create the conditions so that the people can choose.'[6] By turning the page on neo-conservatism, Macron is marking a return to foreign policy built around diplomacy, multilateralism and international law, more in the Gaullo-Mitterrandist tradition, which reached its high point in the passionate speech against the Iraq war at the United Nations in 2003 made by Dominique de Villepin.

Does ruling out interference in the internal affairs of sovereign states not risk emasculating his defence and security policy? Macron thinks not. From inside the Elysée Palace, he watched with dismay as the West failed to punish Syria for using chemical weapons in 2013. France at the time had its fighter planes ready to take part in an American-led bombing campaign. But Barack Obama decided to seek congressional approval first, and David Cameron failed to win parliamentary authorization in Britain. So the strikes never took place. As president, Macron laid down his own red line – the proven use by Assad of chemical weapons – and declared that, were Syria to breach international law on this point again, he would not hesitate to order the French armed forces to destroy chemical-weapons stocks. All the while, the French president hopes to be able to gain diplomatic traction in the region, talking to the Turks, Russians, Jordanians and others over Syria's future.

The second focus is an attempt to normalize relationships strained by the weight of history across the Mediterranean, in order to minimize the friction and instability this engenders. To that end, during the 2017 campaign, Macron spoke of French colonization as a 'crime against humanity', and chose to do so on a campaign stop in Algeria, a country with which France has long, painful and complicated ties. Algiers is as close to Marseille as Marseille is to Paris. Algeria is also the country of origin of France's biggest Muslim minority, and is run by an ill and ageing president whose departure could prompt instability. Macron needs to handle that relationship carefully, as well as those with other nations in the region, which he would like to see take on a greater share of the security burden. Concerns about jihadism, and migration pressures, in North and West Africa, where France has permanent military bases, have kept France engaged there as a sort of regional gendarme. Macron would now like structures such as the G5 Sahel force – composed of troops from Mali, Chad, Burkina Faso, Niger and Mauritania – to take on a bigger role so that France, which keeps 4,500 soldiers there under 'Operation Barkhane', can scale back its own contingent. On a tour of West Africa in 2017, Macron told students in Burkina Faso that he wanted to break with the approach of his elders more generally. 'There is no longer a French Africa policy,' he declared. 'I belong to a generation that does not want to tell Africans what to do.'

Africans, of course, could be forgiven for saying that they have heard it all before. 'They all say that. Let's wait and see,' one head of a West African state told me sceptically, as he tucked into a three-course dinner at Macron's One Planet Summit in late 2017.

Sarkozy and Hollande each in their time promised to turn the page on *françafrique*, the cosy web of political networks, business contracts and arms deals that has long linked France and French-speaking Africa. But the habits are hard to shift, and Macron has his work cut out if he is to persuade Africans that he is serious about making a break. The French president may think he is *décomplexé*, bringing in a breath of fresh young air. But such is the sensitivity in parts of French-speaking Africa about a supercilious France that even an off-hand comment can sour relations. While in Burkina Faso, Macron was asked by a student at the University of Ouagadougou what he planned to do about the country's repeated power cuts. 'You speak to me as if I'm a colonial power, but I don't want to deal with electricity in Burkina Faso,' Macron replied. 'That's the job of your president.' As the audience laughed, President Roch Marc Kaboré left the hall, prompting Macron to joke: 'He's left to fix the air-conditioning!' Macron later called the local social-media frenzy this prompted 'ridiculous': a relation of equals, he said, means being able to 'laugh at one another'. African citizens will want to see evidence that France is ready to stop propping up their undemocratic leaders if they are both to indulge his sense of humour and believe his talk about turning the page. Given the level of security concerns in the Sahel region, France is likely to remain involved there for a long time yet.

A third principle of Macronist foreign policy is his effort to carve out a role where he can for France, and by extension Europe, by using soft power and innovative diplomacy. An early example was his climate push, prompted by Trump withdrawing America from the Paris climate deal, which kicked off with his cheeky social-media appeal to 'Make the Planet Great Again' and the offer of fellowships in Paris to international researchers into climate change. The One Planet Summit that Macron held on an island in the Seine in December 2017, designed to keep the issue alive, was part of what he calls 'participative multilateralism'. Rather than putting heads of state around a table to read out prepared statements, he told them they were invited to listen, and to speak only when they had a specific commitment to make. The rest of the time he handed the floor to NGOs, start-ups, businessmen, city mayors, regional leaders or anybody with a pledge. Macron likes this sort of disruptive diplomacy, even if the heads of state present looked rather less amused.

A diplomacy of gestures and nudges seems to have won France friends. A poll by the University of Southern California's Centre on Public Diplomacy ranked France, under President Macron, as the world's leading 'soft power' in 2017, noting that 'a more dynamic and energized France' could take on 'a leading role in the EU and perhaps show greater global leadership overall'. But what can France realistically hope to secure in broader diplomatic pay-back for all this fresh activism? Macron, after all, is not the first modern French president to believe in his special powers of diplomatic persuasion. Sarkozy's energetic arrival in the presidency led to inflated expectations about what he could achieve. His dream of a 'Union of the Mediterranean' that would unite the countries around the sea was visionary, but unrealistic and poorly thought out. Sarkozy also imagined he could win over authoritarian leaders by bringing them out of isolation, inviting Gaddafi to plant his tent in the garden of a presidential mansion in Paris, and treating Syria's Assad to the 2008 Bastille Day parade. Three years after his visit, Sarkozy and Cameron sent their fighter jets to destroy Gaddafi, in an operation that ultimately left Libya a 'shit show', as President Obama later described it.[7] Diplomacy based to excess on personal relationships can end in disappointment and betrayal. 'His great difficulty is accepting that there are limits to what one can do,' says François Heisbourg of Macron. 'It is a worry.'[8]

Arguably, Macron's most skilful early diplomatic exploit was the extraction of Lebanon's prime minister, Saad Hariri, from Saudi Arabia, where Lebanese authorities suggested he was being held under duress. With American diplomacy largely on hold, Macron stepped in, dropping in for talks in Riyadh on his way back from Abu Dhabi, inviting Hariri to Paris, and helping to devise a technical pretext on which the prime minister could rescind his resignation, thus helping the Saudis save face. This may hint at the sort of diplomatic role the French president can usefully play in places where France has historic levers to activate. Global campaign issues, such as climate, are also well suited to his cajoling style of leadership. France's long-standing diplomatic channels may be able to help with some of the major regional geo-strategic threats, as it showed during the drafting of the agreement to curb Iran's nuclear programme. Ultimately, though, on the big issues, France, and Europe, still need the credibility and heft of America.

This is why the improbably warm relationship that Macron has established with Trump may turn out to be so important. The French president enjoys enough political capital at home to be able to act as a friend to Trump, at a time when few Europeans are rushing to hold his hand, let alone to try to reach a better part of the American leader's tortured self. Trump and Merkel are at odds with each other. After an initial love-in, the British prime minister Theresa May has had a rocky relationship with the American president. Trump tweeted to May: 'don't focus on me, focus on the destructive Radical Islamic Terrorism that is taking place within the United Kingdom. We are doing just fine!' Yet he called the French president 'a friend of mine, Emmanuel' and 'a great guy … Smart. Strong. Loves holding my hand.' The French seem willing to let Macron see what he can make of this relationship. He has understood that Trump relates to affection, and is awed by raw displays of power. 'It was one of the greatest parades I've ever seen,' the American leader gushed after attending the Bastille Day parade. 'It was two hours on the button, and it was military might, and I think a tremendous thing for France and for the spirit of France.'

The French president judges that the greatest danger would be to isolate Trump. By keeping him inside the club, exposed to the views of liberal democrats, Macron hopes at worst to contain some of the damage he can do and, at best, to bring him back on board. To this end, he urged Trump to go to Davos, which he did. He has not given up hope of coaxing him back into the Paris climate agreement, and tried hard to stop him from breaking the Iran nuclear deal. He claims to have kept him involved in efforts to make diplomatic progress on Syria. Macron calls Trump often by telephone, addresses him as Donald, and speaks to him in English. The phone calls are short. 'I'm always extremely direct and frank' with him, the French president told the BBC. 'Sometimes I manage to convince him, and sometimes I fail.' Macron sees himself as a sort of 'interpreter in Europe, sifting through the brash pronouncements to find places of common interest', said an aide.

They make an unlikely pair, the nationalist and the globalist, the casino owner and the philosopher, the impulsive tweeter and the literary intellectual. Their world views are fundamentally divergent. Where Trump argues for borders, walls and America first, Macron preaches openness, liberal internationalism and the defence of the planet. Each is building his politics around an appeal to opposing aspects of human nature: Trump, in anger, on insult and division; Macron, in earnestness, on cooperation and *bienveillance* (goodwill). And yet each was also an insurgent against the establishment, defying the odds, and elected to the presidency at his first attempt. The pair have formed an unlikely bond, Trump, flattered and goggle-eyed at the parade of tanks and fighter planes the French president treated him to on Bastille Day in 2017; Macron, the first foreign leader Trump invited for a state visit to Washington D.C. There is something about the strange alchemy between these two leaders, the sunny liberal intellectual and the scowling former reality-TV host, that raises a small hope. Could Macron become the leader who can help to summon Trump's better nature? Trump, Macron told me carefully, is 'atypical'. He is 'somebody who operates through emotion, who decides alone, but who listens. If we speak often, he hears things, and that in itself is important.'[9] Against the odds, Macron seems to have found a way to handle him. The French president is not naive about where this can lead. But he seems to mean it when he says, almost despite himself, that he has established 'a personal, affectionate link; we like each other'.[10]

Of course, Macron is not the first European leader to think that he can rein in an American president. And if he fails to win anything in return, he will not be the first to disappoint either. He cannot alone be the tamer of Trump. But if Macron is smart, he could well become a key political intermediary between Europe and Trump's America. The more that Macron can turn France around, and get his European project moving, the more he may be able to build on what is already an encouraging start. As a weakened Merkel enters her twilight years, there is an unusual opportunity for him to establish a new balance in Europe, and a leading role for France, on issues where Washington sees no interest or is in disagreement with Europe. If he can build credibility through a stronger Europe, Macron could turn out to be a global leader with real influence.

If he cannot make progress in Europe, though, the best Macron may be able to hope for is to keep pushing on international campaign issues, such as global warming, while stepping in to help with points of friction as they emerge, as he did on Lebanon. This would cast the French president as a useful facilitator, go-between and campaigner. Which would not fit Macron's global ambitions. But it may, in the end, be as much as any European leader can realistically hope for. Macron may not be able, de Gaulle-like, to restore fully France's past glory in world affairs. But his starting point is promising. And, with 73 per cent of the French approving of the way he handles French diplomacy, they seem to think so.

CONCLUSION

'Everyone sees what you appear to be, few experience what you really are.'

Niccolò Machiavelli, *The Prince*

PARIS, JANUARY 2018

'I'm a bit like my dog,' Emmanuel Macron declares suddenly, 'a half breed.'[1] It is an overcast wintry Saturday afternoon, the Elysée Palace is silent, and the French president is dressed for work in his sober navy suit and tie. On the first-floor marble landing, a *huissier*, or usher, in a wing-collared white shirt and bow tie, tails the colour of anthracite and a ceremonial chain, is pacing about slowly. Since the last time I sat down to talk to the president, in his first-floor interconnecting corner office, I seem to have been upgraded. Today, we are sitting in the sumptuous *salon doré*, whose ceiling-high mirrors reflect the intricate silk uphol-stery and gilt-decorated wall panels, lending the whole room an overwhelming golden glow. This is where he received Donald Trump for one of those handshakes. It is also the spot where the newly arrived presidential dog once urinated against the fireplace. But today Nemo, a black Labrador-Griffon cross that Macron adopted from an animal shelter, is nowhere to be seen.

I have asked the president what he meant when he once described himself as a '*métèque*', an outsider in ancient Greece with only partial rights. 'I'm not a thoroughbred,' he replies. Then he is off, comparing himself to his mongrel dog, and reciting

263

the lyrics to 'Le Métèque', by the Franco-Greek singer Georges Moustaki, 'a magnificent song by the way': *'Avec ma gueule de métèque,/De Juif errant, de pâtre grec'* ('With my face of a foreigner/Of a wandering Jew, of a Greek shepherd'). The French president may now be one of the most powerful leaders of the free world, but he sees himself as an interloper, a misfit, someone who does not quite belong. 'The problem for the *métèque* is that others don't like him,' Macron says coolly. 'People' did 'everything' to make sure he would not succeed in politics, 'because I was not one of them'. He had the same welcome when he turned up at Rothschild's, and his colleagues said 'he's a strange guy, not really a banker', and then that he was 'a thief' when he pulled in his Nestlé deal. And he felt it again, he says, when he took up his job as adviser in the Elysée Palace, and 'they called me the banker, because I was not of the same species, I hadn't done the right things.' All his life, he declares, 'I have always had that, it has always stuck to me.'

For a split second, I wonder whether he is trying to cultivate sympathy. Am I supposed to feel compassion? For the lifelong professional outcast who is sitting opposite me upon a silk-upholstered Empire sofa in a presidential palace? But it is obvious that what Macron really wants to say is that he is free. He doesn't care what others think. Or at least he doesn't care what other politicians think, or the *bien-pensants* in Paris. In fact, he cares a lot about what the *French* think. Earlier in our conversation he speaks at length about how he tries to get out of the Elysée Palace as much as possible, and away from France's big cities and the 'bubble' of protocol, to get a feel for what people are really concerned about on the ground. He has just come back from the snow-covered Puy-de-Dôme in central France, where he spent the night. Indeed, when I turn up for my appointment earlier this afternoon, I find a commotion in the street outside, with policemen carrying assault rifles and a knot of excited shoppers and tourists on the pavement; Macron has stepped out to greet passers-by. At this point in our conversation, though, what the French president is trying to convey I think is his sense of liberty to take decisions, to antagonize if necessary, and do what he has to do.

The great advantage of not fully belonging, Macron continues, is that it helps him 'to avoid the mistakes of habit'. There is nothing more 'idiotic', he says, 'than people who are all the same and think they belong to the same club; I've always hated that.' When you are different to others, and unbothered by that, you take your own decisions freely. Has he always felt different? 'Yes,' he replies, 'not because I wanted to be different, but because the choices I have made have always led me to be, *voilà*, a bit apart.' He never went to *boums*, or early-adolescent parties, as a child, he says, preferring 'piano and literature' and 'time with my grandmother than with my classmates'. That is how he was then; that is how he is now. He does not owe any political party, or union, or lobby, or financier, for his job. Being different, he says, 'has given me strength, and made me independent'. When I remind him later that he described Trump as 'not a classical politician', he replies: 'Neither am I. Perhaps that's what nourishes our relationship.'

Listening to Macron speak, it occurs to me that what he is saying feels both disingenuous and plausible. He is at once a product of the French system for manufacturing its elite, and an insurgent against it. One of them, and yet not quite. 'I have never sought approbation or truth in the eyes of others,' he claims. Of course it cannot be true for any elected leader that he does not seek the approval of others. Maybe he doesn't mind much whether the French *like* him. 'As president,' he told *Der Spiegel*, 'you cannot have a desire to be loved.'[2] But Macron will doubtless want to be re-elected in 2022, and at the very least he needs the French to think he has done a good job – which requires a form of approbation. He comes close to conceding as much when he confesses to 'an obsession with being understood, in order to be followed'. People can hardly approve of, or back, a leader they can't understand at all.

Besides, Macron, the disciple of Ricoeur, is a keen student of meaning. And if he can't get the meaning right, and make himself understood, then he is going to be in trouble. So when I ask him whether he is ever wrong, his answer surprises me. 'Yes, often,' he replies. Which is not the impression he gives in public, this president who seems to have an answer for everything, does not like to be caught out and appears to doubt nothing, least of all himself. Such as, I ask? There is a long pause. Macron looks at the ceiling. He puts a knuckle into his mouth, and he seems to be biting it. The question seems to require a great presidential effort.

He thinks that he was wrong, he says finally, not to have launched sooner a review of French prisons. And he reproaches himself, he adds, for 'not doing things sufficiently early' – a regret that many leaders make, but usually once they have left office, yet Macron is only eight months into his term and, by most measures, has already done a great deal. Then he adds that he is 'always wrong when I get annoyed, which does happen'. This is interesting for what it may, or may not, say about the self-control so many people attribute to him. Perhaps that composure of his requires more of an effort than it appears to. Finally, Macron comes up with the last thing I was expecting: that he was wrong to have said, as president, that a railway station is a place where those who succeed pass by 'those who are nothing'. It's not what he thinks, he tells me, the line was improvised, and he now realizes that it was taken for condescension. The same goes, he says, for his comments about the 'lazy'. 'I never treated the French as lazy,' he insists, 'and it's not what I think, so I was wrong not to have been explicit. And I never thought that when you do not succeed you are nothing. It was precisely to denounce those who think that, but it was not understood. So it was a mistake.' Perhaps the Jupiterian president is a little more self-critical, more attuned to the perception of haughty arrogance, than he lets on.

At any rate Macron seems to be continually running his presidency through the scanner, evaluating and adjusting as he goes. Not just to assess progress on policy, although 'execution' is a word Macron uses frequently in our conversation, talking of the need to 'keep up this level of intensity' and 'not to grow accustomed to inertia'. He speaks a lot about the need to keep 'pushing', and 'following up', not to be defeated by the 'weight' of the system and those 'who are used to saying it's not possible', in order to make sure that the 'execution is perfect'. It sounds to me a lot more like the job of a hands-on line manager than that of an exalted de Gaulle-like figure who rises above the mundane and the quotidian to a higher sanctified place of guidance. 'Nothing enhances authority more than silence,' wrote de Gaulle. 'Prestige cannot exist without mystery.' For all Macron's flighty rhetoric about the need for a regal incarnation of presidential power, he likes to micro-manage, to supervise everything, to run it all from the Elysée Palace. Before I can point this contradiction out, he anticipates my question. 'The function has changed. Before, one would have been able to lay out the principles, to give a direction, and delegate the execution elsewhere.' If he wants to restore faith in public action, in a hyper-connected transparent era, he thinks it is his job to make sure that actions match words.

The more that I listen to Emmanuel Macron speak, the more it strikes me that he has in this short time grown into the role. There are no evident signs of fatigue. His face is not drawn. He has not visibly filled out on presidential banquets. He still manages to fit in some tennis when he is in Le Touquet, and when he says tennis he means an intense coaching session, not Sunday after-noon doubles. (He was once ranked 15/1, which under French rankings is good amateur competitive level.) Macron may have a high self-regard, but he tempers it in conversation with a relaxed good humour. Perhaps this is theatre too. After all, he describes the need for 'a crazy energy' in the job, and confesses, this man who has a reputation for needing little sleep, to feeling tired some-times in the evening. In the month of January alone Macron has found time for a three-day tour of China, a stop-off in Rome, a Franco-British summit in England and a quick trip to Davos, for a very long speech, before heading off for three days to Tunisia and Senegal.

The man in the presidency is, like his party, *en marche*, on the go. All this moving, and pushing, and 'getting traction'. It's that concept of motion again, which Pascal Lamy, who knows

Macron well, spoke of. And this, of course, is deliberate too. Partly because Macron wants to show his country that he is serious about turning France around, and that politics can make a difference. But also because he hopes to stir the French from torpor and defeatism. In this, Macron seems to have discovered his inner Norman. The French, he declares, 'have a passion for conquest'. They are 'a people of adventurers, of discoverers, of explorers, of engineers, of scientists, writers, philosophers, politicians. It's the country of Lafayette and Buffon, of Descartes, Pascal, Victor Hugo.' As he elaborates, I realize that, in his mind, conquest and power, the two phases I separate in this book, blend into one. For Macron, power is a form of conquest. He seems to see himself on a campaign for the French mind, or perhaps the French soul, or at any rate the French heart, to 'awaken the spirit of conquest' and ambition.

It is impossible not to think, as he speaks, of David's oil portrait of Napoleon crossing the Alps. Here today is another precociously young French leader, mounting his steed to guide the French into battle and conquer new lands. Or of de Gaulle, that master of national myth-making, who also saw himself as a prophet and a guide. 'The mainspring of a people is ambition,' the General told a reporter a few months before he returned to power in 1958: 'France has successively had the ambition of the unity of its frontiers, the gospel of the Revolution, the domination of Europe, the restoration of Alsace-Lorraine, and finally, Liberation. Today there is no collective ambition.' France, judged de Gaulle, was a country that needed to be exhorted and inspired into greatness. Like Macron in the Puy-de-Dôme, he also ventured into its rural heartlands, folding his tall frame into the back seat of his presidential Citroën DS to head off and galvanize the people. 'France,' the General declared, 'is only true to herself when she is *en marche* towards progress.'

Does Macron, no stranger to ambition, aspire to de Gaulle-like heights? He certainly sounds as if he does. 'During the Renaissance, under François I, under Louis XIV, under Napoleon, under de Gaulle: each time there have been these moments of a new collective imagination, new mythologies, republican or anti-republican,' he tells me. 'That's the deep ambition I have, to bring this out.' If you just tell the French that they need reform 'because of some OECD ranking,' he says, 'the French won't care and they'd be right not to! It's the best way for us to say we won't do anything because we are different. If you recognize their difference, tell them that it's a transformation, a revolution, which will be different to others and better, then you can carry people with you.' And to do this, he says, they need to believe in heroes.

I want to know more about Macron's talk of heroes. It sounds at once silly, intriguing, and a personal risk for him. It is hard not to conclude, the moment he talks about heroes, that the president casts himself as one, on a glorious romantic mission – like a character in a novel he perhaps has yet to write – to rescue France from itself. Or perhaps what he really wants has more to do with the French than with him: to provide them with moments of collective exaltation, of common feeling, that bring a nation together, in awe or in sorrow. A young Tony Blair, back in the glow of his first New Labour prime ministership, understood this too. He had such a moment after the Princess of Wales's death in 1997, calling her 'the people's princess' and telling the British people that 'I feel like everyone else in this country today'. When Johnny Hallyday died on 6 December 2017, it seemed very much to be Macron's Diana moment. If you read the written words today, they do sound faintly ludicrous. 'You are here for him,' Macron began solemnly, standing in a winter overcoat on the church steps before the coffin, and addressing the crowds in a speech that was all about them. 'You had to be here for Johnny, because from the start Johnny was there for you … In his voice, through his songs, in his face, there was this indefinable humanity that would go right through you and make you feel less alone … He became an indispensable presence, a friend, a brother.' On that crisp winter day, outside the Madeleine church in Paris, however, where hundreds of thousands of people had lined the route of Hallyday's funeral cortège, the words felt not ludicrous but wholly in tune with the stunned and bereaved nation.

From the moment that the Elysée published the president's homage to Johnny at 4 a.m. on the morning that he died – and there cannot have been many people up in the palace at that time – it was obvious that Macron had grasped its significance. Johnny may have been scorned as derivative and *populaire* by the Paris *intéllos*, but for the French at large he was not just a 'French Elvis'. He was a glimpse into their soul: rebellious, nostalgic, fragile, flawed, lyrical, theatrical, passionate, proud. Astride a Harley Davidson, his arms generously tattooed, Johnny was everything that they were, or hoped to be, and his music had been the soundtrack to their lives since the 1960s. The address he gave at the church, Macron tells me, 'was not at all unintentional: I did it on purpose.' His point was 'to share a moment of popular emotion with people' and to let the French know that 'I understand your emotion as well'. 'To tell people that their passion is wonderful and very important, because it awakens something, this spirit of conquest. I totally rewrote my speech that very morning to be in phase with popular emotion.'

This comment seems important. There is something both romantic and deeply calculating about it. It reminded me of Macron's cool line about being splashed on the cover of celebrity magazines, 'because I sell. Like washing powder.' This young philosopher-king, with a sense of destiny and the part of a hero in his own unfolding drama, is also a hard-headed cynic. And perhaps that is a good thing. Perhaps we shouldn't worry that he is too flattering to Trump. He seems to mean it when he says that they have formed a bond. But he doesn't really want to be his friend. Maybe it is precisely the combination of both, the romantic and the realist, that could help Macron to create political, and diplomatic, space in the years ahead. Nothing he does is anodyne, in this search to build relationships and acquire leverage. Macron thought carefully about what he wanted to say by offering to loan the Bayeux Tapestry to Britain. 'People in the UK hear about this tapestry. They don't necessarily know what it is, but it speaks of what? Of a history,' he tells me. 'What will they talk about in their kitchens or at dinner tables? That we've had it for 1,000 years. That we fought, but we managed to reconcile. And that we are going to lend it to them when it hasn't been there for 1,000 years. It moved people. People didn't come up to me in London and say thank you for the new treaty on migration. But they did say thank you for the tapestry.'

Democratic politics needs to find a way 'to touch spirits, hearts and souls', he argues. Otherwise, the realm of the imagination is left to the nationalists, extremists and fanatics. Populists cannot be defeated only by rational arguments. Progressives need their own, rival, narrative. 'Why do we have a revival of religious and other fanaticisms?' he asks. 'Because they have a hold on the imagination, sometimes an extreme hold, which responds to an ontological need that mankind has for exaltation, for figures that count. Political leaders should never neglect the symbolic element of office. If our mission is seen only as functional, we will become mere technicians. Politics is also about emotion. If we leave emotion only to cynics or nationalists, we will be making a colossal error.' This man on a mission does not intend to lower his ambitions.

Our conversation draws to a close. The sky outside is starting to turn to dusk. As I walk back down the red-carpeted ceremonial staircase of the Elysée Palace, around the edge of the front court-yard, and out to the rue du Faubourg Saint-Honoré, it strikes me that Macron sounds less implausible in French, the language in which we had our conversation and one well suited to his exalted ambitions and glorious abstractions. When I translate his words later on, something happens. The English tongue does not really do grandeur, and seems to make his phrases sound convoluted and over-intellectual. The French like their leaders to speak this way. In English, it all risks sounding like a vanity project, dreamed up by Jupiter to justify all the palaces and parades, grand gestures and sweeping pronouncements. It strikes me that Macron really is a president for France, not for Britain or for Germany, or Texas, as his aide told me. But then the next day, on television, I see Trump calling him 'my friend, Emmanuel'. He can also connect, this scholar-president, even to a brash real-estate mogul who never reads books. There is definitely something about him. He is a leader to watch closely, and not to underestimate.

Macron is a French president who matters more than most. For his country, and for Europe. The French have put their immediate future in the hands of an untested leader, in whose hands it could yet all go horribly wrong. He may struggle to persuade Germany to move his way on Europe, and the eurozone may not have seen the last of financial crises. The continent, and France, remains vulnerable to terrorism. Europe is fringed by instability and authoritarianism, on its eastern borders, with Russia and Turkey, as well as across the Mediterranean sea. Another mass migrant influx would put the union's resilience, and Macron's liberal internationalism, sorely to the test.

At home, the odds on any leader turning around a country as proud and unruly as France are never high. There is a perfectly plausible scenario in which promise leads to disappointment. High hopes vested in young leaders often do. Revolutions are usually followed by counter-revolutions, and France is no stranger to either. Macron may not yet face any credible political opposition. But neither has he found a way to speak to those who did not vote for him, in places where his rootless internationalism and hobnobbing at Davos is an affront. If he fails to bring back jobs, investment and growth, a revived FN, under Marine Le Pen or her successor, will have learned the lessons of 2017. The party will head into 2022 having ditched its unpopular opposition to the euro. It may also have changed its name as well as its leader. Party-political boundaries remain fluid in France. A nationalist right-wing grouping could yet emerge to challenge Macron's liberal internationalism, which reaches from the Republican right wing to a newly named far right.

To fend such opposition off, Macron needs results. He may face virtually no opposition in parliament, yet those who will resist his reforms probably lurk, rather, inside the administrations and professions, which are set to lose the most. En Marche, which played its grass-roots part in Macron's conquest of France, may struggle, under Jupiter, to work out what the movement is now for, and its unity will be tested by an uncompromising approach to matters such as immigration or security. Macron is a poor delegator; yet he cannot do everything himself. At once a prince and his counsellor, he relies on his own judgement, probably to excess. His predilection for sibylline pronouncements and heroic theatre, and taste for imperial grandeur, open up his presidency to mockery in a merciless age. The Elysée Palace, behind its high wrought-iron gates, is a place of architectural isolation. Hubris could still get the better of him.

And yet you don't need to approve of everything Macron does to see this presidency as an opportunity for France. The country has entered territory that is uncharted, but promising. Its image abroad has been transformed, and the French are rather enjoying the unfamiliar glow of approbation. His popularity fell faster than any other modern president, but it has recovered somewhat. Macron was a lucky gambler, but he is also a capable, disciplined one. If he can hold his own, and tame his inner monarch, he has both the institutional power, and the political potential, to have a considerable impact, on France, Europe and even beyond.

When I turn up at the Elysée Palace in January 2018, I have understood for a while that the conquest of power the previous year was a form of bloodless political revolution such as France had not seen for over half a century. When I leave, I think I have grasped something else. Macron may not in fact believe that the French really need another revolution in order to turn their country around in the coming years. Things need fixing, for sure; but they are not critically broken. Elegant, creative, intellectual France has many deep strengths. Yet it is also a country that moves forward in spasms. It took the guillotine, Robespierre and then Napoleon for the French to shift from absolutism under Louis XVI to parliamentary monarchy in 1814. The following century, it took six weeks of turmoil in May 1968 to throw off tweed jackets and social conservatism. What Macron really means by revolution I think is not that the country needs one, but that it needs to think it is taking part in one. That to get the French moving they need to believe they are engaged in a glorious epic moment, for a grander purpose. And that this is something that they, the French, are uniquely capable of pulling off. It is a smart take, and a gamble. But if 2017 showed anything, it is that it's a mistake to bet against Emmanuel Macron.

NOTES

FOREWORD

1 Maxime Fieschi and Nathalie Schuck, 'Taxes, APL, 80 km/h . . . Quand Emmanuel Macron fait son mea culpa', *Le Parisien*, 8 December 2018.

2 Pierre Alzingre, 'Gilets jaunes: la revanche des invisibles', *Les Echos*, 3 December 2018.

3 Meeting with the Association de la Presse Présidentielle, 13 February 2018.

4 Jonathan Miller, 'Let them buy Teslas! How Macron provoked an uprising', *The Spectator*, 8 December 2018; Jacques Hubert-Rodier, 'Macron et le rêve brisé d'une France influente', *Les Echos*, 24 January 2019; Rich Lowry, 'Macron's failure', *National Review*, 12 December 2018.

5 Edward Luce, 'Macron's cautionary tale for US Democrats', *Financial Times*, 3 January 2019.

6 Isobel Thompson, 'Can Emmanuel Macron survive France's Civil War?', *Vanity Fair*, 6 December 2018.

7 Gaëtan de Capèle, 'Le prix de la lâcheté', *Le Figaro*, 21 March 2018.

8 Charles Wyplosz, 'Macron, les sondages et les réformes', *Telos*, 27 September 2018.

9 Simon Kuper, 'A victorious World Cup team made in the multi-racial Paris banlieues', *New Statesman*, 18 July 2018.

10 Ariane Chemin, '*Le Monde* identifie, sur une vidéo, un collaborateur de Macron frappant un manifestant, le 1er mai, à Paris', *Le Monde*, 18 July 2018.

11 Interview with BFM TV, 6 September 2018.

12 David Revault d'Allonnes, 'Les dix jours où Emmanuel Macron a tremblé', *Le Journal du Dimanche*, 26 January 2019.

13 Interview with the author, 5 December 2018.

14 Interview with the author, 5 December 2018.

15 Emmanuel Macron, Grand débat national, Grand Bourgtheroulde, 15 January 2019.

16 Nicolas Domenach and Maurice Szafran, *Le tueur et le poète* (Paris: Albin Michel, 2019), p. 296.

17 Emmanuel Carrère, 'Orbiting Jupiter: my week with Emmanuel Macron', *The Guardian*, 20 October 2017.

18 Interview with the author, 7 January 2019.

19 See, for example, Yascha Mounk, *The People vs. Democracy: why our freedom is in danger and how to save it* (Cambridge, MA: Harvard University Press, 2018).

20 Interview with the author, 13 November 2018.

21 Interview with the author, 19 December 2018.

22 Interview with the author, 13 November 2018.

23 Gideon Rachman, 'Donald Trump embodies the spirit of our age', *Financial Times*, 22 October 2018.

Chapter 1 The Parable of Amiens

1 Emmanuel Macron, *Révolution* (Paris: XO Editions, 2016).

2 J. Bellemère, *Amiens* (Amiens: Roger Léveillard, 1928).

3 Anne Fulda, *Emmanuel Macron: un jeune homme si parfait* (Paris: Editions Plon, 2017), p. 29.

4 Interview with the author, 5 July 2017.

5 Fulda, *Emmanuel Macron*, p. 16.

6 Ibid.

7 Manon Haussy and Claire Raynaud, 'À Bagnères, Emmanuel Macron on l'appelle "Manu"', *La Dépêche*, 14 May 2017.

8 Interview with the author, 7 June 2017.

9 Interview with the author, 20 June 2017.

10 Fulda, *Emmanuel Macron*, p. 28.

11 Ibid., p. 186.

12 Caroline Pigozzi, 'Le père Philippe Robert, professeur à la Providence, se souvient de son élève Emmanuel Macron', *Paris Match*, 13 May 2017.

13 Caroline Pigozzi, 'Brigitte et Emmanuel Macron prêts pour tous les défis', *Paris Match*, 13 April 2016.

14 Erin Doherty and Olivia de Lamberterie, 'Appelez-moi Brigitte!', *ELLE*, 18 August 2017.

15 Ibid.

16 Vanessa Schneider, 'Au lycée Henri-IV, les infortunes du jeune Macron', *Le Monde*, 3 March 2018.

17 Interview with the author, 7 March 2017.

18 Interview with the author, 19 June 2017.

19 Fulda, *Emmanuel Macron*, pp. 62–3.

20 Gaspard Gantzer, *La politique est un sport de combat* (Paris: Fayard, 2017), p. 151.

21 Doherty and De Lamberterie, 'Appelez-moi Brigitte!', 13 April 2016.

22 Caroline Derrien and Candice Nedelec, *Les Macron* (Paris: Fayard, 2017), p. 60.

23 Adam Plowright, *The French Exception* (London: Icon Books, 2017), p. 66.

24 Interview with the author, 26 June 2017.

25 Gantzer, *La politique est un sport de combat*, p. 62.

26 Interview with the author, 21 November 2017.

27 Gantzer, *La politique est un sport de combat*, pp. 22 and 151.

28 Interview with the author, 5 May 2017.

29 Interview with the author, 28 June 2017.

30 'Emmanuel Macron, 32 ans, gérant à la banque Rothschild', *Sciences Po* no. 158, April 2010.

31 Pierre Hurel, 'Emmanuel Macron, la stratégie du météore', *France 3*, 21 November 2016.

32 Stacey Meichtry and William Horobin, 'France's Hollande casts fate with ex-banker Macron', *Wall Street Journal*, 8 March 2015.

33 Anne-Sylvaine Chassany and Arash Massoudi, 'Emmanuel Macron's Rothschild years make him an easy election target', *Financial Times*, 28 March 2017.

34 Marc Endeweld, *L'ambigu Monsieur Macron* (Paris: Flammarion, 2015), pp. 131–7.

35 Yann L'Hénoret, 'Les coulisses d'une victoire', *TF1*, 8 May 2017.

Chapter 2 *Le Disrupteur*

1 Jean-Dominique Merchet, *Macron Bonaparte* (Paris: Stock, 2017).

2 Gaspard Gantzer, *La politique est un sport de combat* (Paris: Fayard, 2017), p. 73.

3 Interview with the author, 9 June 2014.

4 Gantzer, *La politique est un sport de combat*, p. 277.

5 Gérard Davet and Fabrice Lhomme, *Un président ne devrait pas dire ça* (Paris: Stock, 2016).

6 Yann L'Hénoret, 'Les coulisses d'une victoire', *TF1*, 8 May 2017.

7   Meeting with Europresse press club, Paris, 3 May 2011.

8   Interview with the author, 19 June 2017.

9   Interview with the author, 26 June 2017.

10 Interview with the author, 12 November 2013.

11 Anne Fulda, *Emmanuel Macron: un jeune homme si parfait* (Paris: Editions Plon, 2017), p. 187.

12 Interview with the author, 10 October 2017.

13 Interview with the author, 9 June 2014.

14 Interview with the author, 21 November 2017.

15 Gantzer, *La politique est un sport de combat*, p. 263.

16 Ibid., p. 264.

17 Ibid., p. 265.

18 Davet and Lhomme, *Un président ne devrait pas dire ça*, pp. 358 and 366.

19 Ibid., p. 208.

20 Ibid.

21 Ibid., p. 465.

22 David Revault d'Allonnes, 'Hollande: "Emmanuel Macron m'a trahi avec méthode",' *Le Monde*, 31 August 2016.

23 Martine Aubry, 'Ne réduisons pas l'existence à la consommation', *Le Monde*, 10 December 2014.

24 Nicolas Prissette, *Emmanuel Macron, le président inattendu* (Paris: First Document, 2017), p. 116.

25 Interview with the author, 13 November 2017.

26 Interview with the author, 29 January 2016.

27 Interview with the author, 22 June 2015.

28 Interview with the author, 21 July 2017.

29 Interview with the author, 8 July 2016.

30 Interview with the author, 5 July 2017.

31 René Rémond, *Jean Lecanuet ou la passion du centre* (Paris: Beauchesne, 2006), p. 20.

32 Interview with the author, 29 November 2013.

33 Interview with the author, 8 July 2016.

34 Interview with the author, 26 June 2017.

Chapter 3 The Roots of *Dégagisme*, 1995–2017

1   Liz Alderman, 'Uber's French Resistance', *The New York Times*, 3 June 2015.

2   'Change it – Israel: a model for French tech?', interview with *L'Atelier*, BNP Paribas, 26 November 2015.

3   François-Xavier Bourmaud, *Emmanuel Macron: Les coulisses d'une victoire* (Paris: L'Archipel, 2017), p. 200.

4   Interview on 'La marche du siècle', Antenne 2, 15 November 1995.

5   Interview with TF1, 12 December 1996.

6   Franz-Olivier Giesbert, *La tragédie du président: scènes de la vie politique 1986–2006* (Paris: Flammarion, 2006), p. 362.

7   'Référendum: en direct avec le président', TF1, 14 April 2005.

8   Nicolas Baverez, *La France qui tombe* (Paris: Perrin, 2003), p. 19.

9   Catherine Nay, *Un pouvoir nommé désir* (Paris: Grasset, 2007), p. 41.

10 Alain Duhamel, 'L'argent-diable', *Le Point*, 1 July 2010.

11 Yasmina Reza, *L'aube le soir ou la nuit* (Paris: Flammarion, 2007), p. 18.

12 Matthieu Croissandeau, Renaud Dély et Sophie Fay, 'Il faut en finir avec la gauche passéiste', *L'Obs*, 23 October 2014.

13 Emmanuel Macron, *Révolution* (Paris: XO Editions, 2016), p. 41.

14 Interview with the author, 6 June 2017.

15 Emmanuel Macron, 'Les labyrinths du politique: que peut-on attendre pour 2012 et après?', *Esprit*, March–April 2011.

16 Interview with the author, 29 September 2014.

17 Interview with the author, 9 June 2014.

18 Macron, *Révolution*, p. 59.

19 Interview with the author, 12 September 2013.

20 Interview in *L'Express*, 24 November 2011.

21 Interview with the author, 14 November 2017.

Chapter 4 En Marche to the Elysée

1   Interview with the author, 13 November 2017.

2   Interview with the author, 7 September 2017.

3   Interview with the author, 15 September 2015.

4   Interview with the author, 15 January 2018.

5   Interview with the author, 12 December 2017.

6   Interview with the author, 5 July 2017.

7   Interview with the author, 6 June 2017.

8   Antoine de Saint-Exupéry, *Vol de nuit* (Paris: Gallimard, 1972), p. 159.
9   Interview with the author, 12 October 2017.
10 Interview with the author, 11 April 2017.
11 Interview with the author, 12 October 2017.
12 Interview with the author, 5 July 2017.
13 Interview with the author, 19 June 2017.
14 Interview with the author, 8 July 2016.
15 Interview with the author, 9 April 2017.
16 Interview with the author, 7 November 2017.

Chapter 5 Jupiter Rising

1   Yann L'Hénoret, 'Les coulisses d'une victoire', *TF1*, 8 May 2017.
2   Interview with the author, 6 June 2017.
3   Interview with the author, 9 July 2017.
4   Interview with the author, 14 November 2017.
5   Interview with the author, 21 December 2017.
6   Emmanuel Carrère, 'Orbiting Jupiter: My Week with Emmanuel Macron', *The Guardian*, 20 October 2017.
7   Emmanuel Macron, speech in Paris, 17 April 2017.
8   Emmanuel Macron, speech in Reims, 17 March 2017.
9   Emmanuel Macron, speech in Dijon, 25 March 2017.
10 Emmanuel Macron, speech in Besançon, 11 April 2017.
11 'Premier tour présidentielle 2017: sociologie de l'electorat', *Ipsos*, 23 April 2017.
12 Interview with the author, 30 May 2017.
13 Nicolas Baverez, *La France qui tombe* (Paris: Perrin, 2003).
14 Franz-Olivier Giesbert, 'Le marinisation des esprits', *Le Point*, 21 September 2013.
15 Jean-Marie Rouart, *Adieu à la France qui s'en va* (Paris: Grasset, 2003).
16 Sudhir Hazareesingh, *How the French Think* (London: Allen Lane, 2015), p. 313.
17 Interview with the author, 1 June 2017.
18 L'Hénoret, 'Les coulisses d'une victoire', 8 May 2017.
19 Interview with *Der Spiegel*, 13 October 2017.
20 Philippe Besson, *Un personnage de roman* (Paris: Julliard, 2017).
21 Interview with the author, 14 November 2017.
22 'Macron, un philosophe en politique' *Le 1*, 8 July 2015.

23 Interview with *Challenges*, 16 October 2016.

24 Max Weber, *The Theory of Social and Economic Organization*, edited by Talcott Parsons (Chicago, IL: The Free Press, 1947), p. 358.

25 'Macron, confidences sacrées', *Journal du Dimanche*, 11 February 2017.

26 Soazig Quéméner and Alexandre Duyck, *L'irrésistible ascension* (Paris: Flammarion, 2017), p. 97.

27 Interview with the author, 20 June 2017.

28 Carrère, 'Orbiting Jupiter', 20 October 2017.

29 'En Marche vers l'Elysée', *Envoyé Spécial, France 2*, 11 May 2017.

30 Anne Fulda, 'Brigitte Macron, l'anti-potiche', *Le Figaro*, 25 September 2017.

31 Charlotte Chaffanjon, 'Emmanuel Macron: la fabrique d'un chef', *Le Point*, 10 May 2017.

Chapter 6 Macronism

1 Pierre-André Taguieff, *Macron, miracle ou mirage?* (Paris: L'Edition de l'Observatoire, 2017), p. 182.

2 Emmanuel Macron, 'Pourquoi nous sommes un peuple', *Le Figaro*, 16 March 2017.

3 Interview with the author, 4 May 2017.

4 Interview with the author, 26 June 2017.

5 Bernard Dauenhauer, *Paul Ricoeur: The Promise and Risks of Politics* (Lanham, MD: Rowman and Littlefield, 1998), pp. 3–4.

6 François Dosse, *Le philosophe et le président: Ricœur & Macron* (Paris: Stock, 2017), pp. 187–95.

7 Marc Endeweld, *L'ambigu Monsieur Macron* (Paris: Flammarion, 2015), p. 71.

8 'Macron, un philosophe en politique' *Le 1*, 8 July 2015.

9 Dosse, *Le philosophe et le président*.

10 'Macron, un philosophe en politique', 8 July 2015.

11 Nicolas Truong, 'Petite philosophie du macronisme', *Le Monde*, 15 May 2017.

12 'Macron, un philosophe en politique', 8 July 2015.

13 Emmanuel Macron, *Révolution* (Paris: XO Editions, 2016), pp. 20–1.

14 'Emmanuel Macron, 32 ans, gérant à la banque Rothschild', *Sciences Po* no. 158, April 2010.

15 Emmanuel Macron, 'Les labyrinths du politique: que peut-on attendre pour 2012 et après?', *Esprit*, March–April 2011.

16 Truong, 'Petite philosophie du macronisme', 15 May 2017.

17 Interview with *Der Spiegel*, 13 October 2017.

18 Macron, *Révolution*, p. 38.

19 Mathieu Laine and Jean-Philippe Feldman, *Transformer la France. En finir avec mille ans de mal français* (Paris: Plon, 2018).

20 Interview with the author, 28 June 2017.

21 Laurent Bigorgne, Alice Baudry and Olivier Duhamel, *Macron, et en même temps* (Paris: Plon, 2017) pp. 250–1.

22 Amartya Sen, *Development as Freedom* (New York: Knopf, 1999).

23 Interview with the author, 18 January 2018.

24 Ibid.

25 Lénaïg Bredoux and Joseph Confavreux, 'L'impossible définition du hollandisme', *Mediapart*, 28 October 2013.

26 Speech by President Emmanuel Macron, joint sitting of Congress, Versailles, 3 July 2017.

27 Interview with *Der Spiegel*, 13 October 2017.

28 Interview with the author, 12 December 2017.

29 Interview with the author, 21 July 2017.

30 Interview with the author, 18 January 2018.

31 Ibid.

32 Anthony Giddens, *The Third Way: The Renewal of Social Democracy* (London: Polity Press, 1998).

33 Interview with the author, 21 December 2017.

34 Emmanuel Macron, speech in Paris, 17 April 2017.

35 Zanny Minton Beddoes, 'The pendulum swings', *The World in 2018, The Economist*, 2017, p. 16.

36 'Mesure du Discours', Observatoire du discours politique français, Université Côte d'Azur http://mesure-du-discours.unice.fr/

37 Interview with *Der Spiegel*, 13 October 2017.

38 Julien Vallet, 'La culture selon Emmanuel Macron', *Classiquenews*, 4 April 2017.

39 Interview with *Der Spiegel*, 13 October 2017.

40 Ibid.

41 Brice Couturier, *Macron, un président philosophe* (Paris: Editions de l'Observatoire, 2017), p. 46.

42 Philippe Besson, *Un personnage de roman* (Paris: Julliard, 2017), p. 79.

43 Interview with the author, 14 November 2017.

44   Interview with *Der Spiegel*, 13 October 2017.
45   Macron, 'Les labyrinths du politique'.
46   Bigorgne et al., *Macron, et en même temps*, p. 251.
47   Interview with *Der Spiegel*, 13 October 2017.
48   Interview in *Le 1*, 8 July 2015.
49   Interview with *Challenges*, 16 October 2016.
50   Interview with *Der Spiegel*, 13 October 2017.
51   Interview with *Le Point*, 31 August 2017.
52   Interview with *Der Spiegel*, 13 October 2017.
53   Macron, *Révolution*, p. 34.
54   Interview with the author, 11 June 2017.
55   Interview with the author, 6 June 2017.
56   Interview with *Der Spiegel*, 13 October 2017.
57   Ibid.
58   Nicholas Vinocur, 'Emmanuel Macron's arrogance problem', *Politico*, 20 September 2017.
59   Interview with the author, 7 March 2017.
60   Interview with the author, 21 July 2017.

Chapter 7 Re-Start Nation

1   Interview with the author, 27 June 2017.
2   Luis Garicano, Claire LeLarge and John Van Reenen, 'Firm size distortions and the productivity distribution: evidence from France', *American Economic Review* 106:11, 2016, pp. 3439–79.
3   Interview with the author, 19 March 2007.
4   Interview with the author, 12 April 2012.
5   'Goodyear: la lettre de Titan à Montebourg', *Les Echos*, 19 February 2013.
6   Interview with the author, 6 November 2015.
7   Mathieu Laine and Jean-Philippe Feldman, *Transformer la France: en finir avec mille ans de mal français* (Paris: Plon, 2018).
8   René Rémond, 'La société française et l'autorité', *Ville-Ecole-Intégration* 112, March 1998.
9   Alain Peyrefitte, *Le mal français* (Paris: Plon. 1976).
10   Michel Pébereau, *Rompre avec la facilité de la dette publique* (Paris: La documentation française, 2005), p. 183.
11   OECD, 'Economic survey of France', *OECD*, 14 September 2017.

12 Emmanuel Macron, *Révolution* (Paris: XO Editions, 2016), p. 48.
13 Interview with the author, 24 September 2015.
14 Madhumita Murgia and Harriet Agnew, 'Facebook to base first business incubator in France's Station F', *Financial Times*, 17 January 2017.
15 Chris O'Brien, 'Post-Nest life in Paris, investing in deep tech, and his global search for inspiration', *VentureBeat*, 29 December 2017.
16 Interview with the author, 6 June 2017.
17 Press conference, Salzburg, Austria, 23 August 2017.
18 Interview with TF1, 15 October 2017.
19 Interview with the author, 21 July 2017.
20 Interview with the author, 19 June 2017.

CHAPTER 8 FRACTURED FRANCE

1 Interview with the author, 1 June 2017.
2 Interview with the author, 1 June 2017.
3 John Judis and Ruy Teixeira, *The Emerging Democratic Majority* (New York: Scribner, 2002), p. 8.
4 Interview with *Le Point*, 11 December 2015.
5 Interview with the author, 16 February 2012.
6 Caroline Fourest and Fiammetta Venner, *Marine Le Pen* (Paris: Grasset, 2011), p. 129.
7 Sylvain Crépon, *Enquête au coeur du nouveau Front National* (Paris: Nouveau Monde, 2012), p. 126.
8 Ibid., p. 155.
9 Ibid., p. 100.
10 Ibid.
11 Interview with the author, 8 December 2015.
12 Interview with the author, 8 December 2015.
13 Interview with the author, 17 July 2017.
14 Augustin Landier, Daniel Szomoru and David Thesmar, 'Working in the on-demand economy: an analysis of Uber driver-partners in France', working paper, 4 March 2016.
15 Interview with the author, 20 June 2017.
16 David Thomson, *Les revenants: ils étaient partis faire le jihad, ils sont de retour en France* (Paris: Le Seuil, 2016).
17 Interview with the author, 16 February 2016.

Chapter 9 The Tyranny of Normal

1 Interview with the author, 8 June 2017.
2 Interview with the author, 8 June 2017.
3 Interview with the author, 7 July 2017.
4 Pierre Mathiot, 'Un nouveau baccalauréat pour construire le lycée des possibles', Ministère de l'Education Nationale, 24 January 2018.
5 Jean-Michel Blanquer, *L'école de demain* (Paris: Odile Jacob, 2016).
6 Jean-Michel Blanquer, Ministry of Education, press release, 27 June 2017.
7 Interview with the author, 22 June 2017.
8 Interview with the author, 30 June 2017.
9 Cour des Comptes, 'L'autonomie financière des universités: une réforme à poursuivre', *Cour des Comptes*, 30 September 2015.

Chapter 10 A Certain Idea of Europe, and Beyond

1 Michaela Wiegel, *Emmanuel Macron: Ein Visionär für Europa, eine Herausforderung für Deutschland* (Berlin: Europa-Verlag, 2018).
2 Interview with the author, 21 July 2017.
3 Ibid.
4 Ibid.
5 Interview with *The Guardian*, 21 June 2017.
6 Interview with the author, 21 July 2017.
7 Jeffrey Goldberg, 'The Obama Doctrine: The U.S. president talks through his hardest decisions about America's role in the world', *The Atlantic*, April 2016.
8 Interview with the author, 9 July 2017.
9 Interview with the author, 18 January 2018.
10 Ibid.

Conclusion

1 For this and subsequent quotations in this chapter, interview with the author, 27 January 2018.
2 Interview with *Der Spiegel*, 13 October 2017.

ACKNOWLEDGEMENTS

So many people in France have helped generously with this book, some of them in ways they may not realize. Over the years that I've spent living and working in France, my understanding of the country has improved immeasurably thanks to numerous conversations, both in Paris and during my travels around the country and on the campaign trail, as well as through countless French essays, articles, books and debates.

I would like in particular to thank all those who agreed to talk to me for this book, or to arrange such conversations, including some who did so anonymously. Others are cited and, with a few exceptions, are referenced on first mention in a given chapter. I owe special thanks for their insights and time to Benoît d'Angelin, Clément Beaune, Laurent Bigorgne, Philippe Crouzet, Christian Dargnat, Renaud Dartevelle, Jacques Delpla, Ismaël Emelien, Sylvain Fort, Eric Fottorino, Etienne Gernelle, Sylvie Goulard, Benjamin Griveaux, François Heisbourg, Jean-Pierre Jouyet, Gilles Kepel, Gaspard Koenig, Mathieu Laine, Pascal Lamy, Antoine Marguet, Alain Minc, Emmanuel Miquel, Amélie de Montchalain, Jean Pisani-Ferry, Bernard Spitz, Adrien Taquet, Shahin Vallée, Hubert Védrine and François Villeroy de Galhau. In addition to those quoted in the text, I am grateful also to the many people who offered their thoughts while I was researching *The Economist*'s 2017 special report on France, on which this book draws. They include: Nicolas Baverez, Yves Bertoncini, Laurence Boone, Henri de Castries, Elie Cohen, Nicolas Colin, Christophe Gomes, Zaki Laïdi, Marie-Vorgan Le Barzic, Gilles Le Gendre, Philippe Manière, Jean-Louis Missika, Dominique Moïsi, Dominique Reynié and Ludovic Subran.

I am particularly indebted to Zanny Minton Beddoes, editor of *The Economist*, for her warm backing for this book project, as well as for permission to use material from my reporting for the paper. Thanks also go to my London colleagues Edward Carr, Emma Duncan, Robert Guest and Chris Lockwood, who have been a regular source of support and ideas, and in particular to John Peet, who made helpful suggestions on various chapters. In the Paris office, I am especially grateful to my fellow foreign correspondent Adam Roberts. He generously read through an entire first draft, and offered many candid and invaluable comments. I would also like to thank Emily Upton in Paris and Andrea Burgess in London for their tireless and meticulous fact-checking, and for giving up evenings and weekends in order to do so.

Thanks are also due to Sudhir Hazareesingh, whose deep knowledge of French thought helped refine the chapter on Macronism, as well as to other France-watchers with whom I've shared many stimulating discussions about the country. They include Hermione Gough, Charles Grant, Angus Lapsley and Gideon Rachman, along with fellow correspondents in Paris who have supplied help and advice, in particular Véronique Auger, Marie-Laetitia Bonavita, Francis Brochet, Angelique Chrisafis, Yves Clarisse, Daniel Desesquelle, Hervé Favre, Béatrice Hadjaje, Eric Le Boucher, Stéphane Leneuf, John Lichfield, Laurent Marchand, Lara Marlowe, Alberto Toscano, Marie-Christine Vallet and Michaela Wiegel.

This book would not have happened without Veronique Baxter, my enthusiastic and energetic agent, or Jamie Birkett, my editor at Bloomsbury. He first came to me with the idea of a book on France, kept faith in the project even as it evolved along with the election campaign, and made many helpful suggestions on the draft manuscript. Richard Mason brought his careful and elegant approach to the copyedit, as well as his knowledge of France. Thanks are also due to the rest of the Bloomsbury team, including Kealey Rigden, Hannah Paget and Sutchinda Thompson.

Above all, I would like to thank my family, for their patience and support throughout the researching and writing of this book. My sister, Emily Pedder, supplied advice, encouragement and her professional editing skills, which helped to fine-tune early chapters. Chloé Dedryver diligently transcribed hours of interviews in French. Luc Dedryver was on hand for regular technical (and stylistic) advice. Most of all, Bertrand Dedryver read through every chapter in detail and imposed order on the first draft with tolerance, precision, good humour and a wisely critical and constructive eye. I could not have done this without his backing. Finally, I would like to thank my late mother, Sue Pedder, who followed the twists of the French election campaign from London N1 with unflagging enthusiasm right up until the last days of her life, but did not live to see the final result.

INDEX

A NOTE ON THE AUTHOR

Sophie Pedder has been the Paris Bureau Chief of *The Economist* since 2003. As well as writing for the magazine, she has had articles published in *Prospect, Foreign Affairs, Le Monde, Paris Match* and *Le Figaro*, and appears regularly to comment on French politics on CNN, the BBC and other media. She was awarded the David Watt Prize in 2006. In 2012 JC Lattès published her (French) book *Le Déni Français*, which Reuters described as a 'media phenomenon'.

A NOTE ON THE TYPE

The text of this book is set in Linotype Sabon, a typeface named after the type founder, Jacques Sabon. It was designed by Jan Tschichold and jointly developed by Linotype, Monotype and Stempel in response to a need for a typeface to be available in identical form for mechanical hot metal composition and hand composition using foundry type.

Tschichold based his design for Sabon roman on a font engraved by Garamond, and Sabon italic on a font by Granjon. It was first used in 1966 and has proved an enduring modern classic.